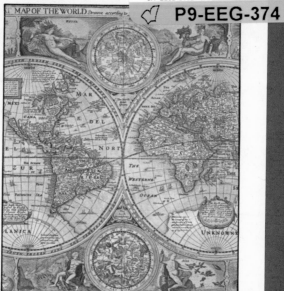

THE JOY OF LEX

GYLES BRANDRETH

THE JOY OF LEX

How to Have Fun with 860, 341,500 Words

Illustrated by George Moran

WILLIAM MORROW AND COMPANY, INC.
New York   1980

Library of Congress Catalog Card Number: 80-82360

ISBN 0-688-03709-7

Printed in the United States of America

5   6   7   8   9   10

Book Design by Betty Bins Graphics

I am grateful to the following authors, publishers and copyright owners for permission to reproduce their material. These acknowledgments are arranged alphabetically according to the name of the copyright owner.
Pages 210-211, Four Notpoems, from *Notpoems* by Adele Aldridge. Magic Circle Press, 1973. ©Adele Aldridge. / Page 230, The Sixteen Masterpieces of World Literature, from *The Lunchpack of Notre Dame* by Russell Ash with Martin Grief. The Bookseller, 1978. ©Russell Ash with Martin Grief. / Page 256, H.E. Dudeney's Alphabet, from *The World's Best Word Puzzles* by H.E. Dudeney. Daily News, 1924. ©Associated Newspapers. / Page 20, Gilbert Frankau's 1925 Crossword for the London *Daily News*. ©Associated Newspapers Group. / Page 123, Clerihews, from *Complete Clerihews* by E.C. Bentley. Laurie, 1951. ©E.C. Bentley. / Page 136, John was Gay, by Arthur Berger. ©Arthur Berger. / Pages 49-50, Anagreatest, Anabaptism, Antigrams, Anagrammatical Challenge, and, pages 186-190, Palindrome Words, Palindrome Sentences, Palindrome Stories and Semordinilaps, from *Language on Vacation* by Dmitri A. Borgmann. Charles Scribner's Son, 1965. ©Dmitri A. Borgmann. / Page 146, Croakers, from *Tom Swifties* by Roy Bongartz. Saturday Review / World, 1972. ©Roy Bongartz. / Pages 152-163, Xeme, from *Word Power* by Hunter Diack. Granada Publishing, 1975. ©Estate of Hunter Diack. / Pages 248-256, Hear Here!, You Don't Say!, Duo-Words, Meyer the Merrier and Robinson Clouseaus, from *Puzzle Quiz and Stunt Fun* by Jerome Meyer. Dover Publications, 1956. ©Dover Publications. / Page 60, Leading Lipogrammarians, page 189, Pseudodrome Poetics, page 262, Word Squares, page 281, The Briefest Poetry, from *Oddities and Curiosities of Words and Literature* by C.C. Bombaugh, annotated by Martin Gardner. Dover Publications, 1961. ©Dover Publications. / Pages 226-228, Mixed Metaphors, from *The Complete Plain Words* by Ernest Gowers, revised by Bruce Fraser. H.M. Stationery Office, 1973. ©H.M. Stationery Office. / Pages 191-193, Scrabble, from *The Scrabble Book* by Derryn Hinch. Mason Charter, 1976. ©Derryn Hinch. / Page 206, Geo-Metric Verses, from *Geometrics* by Gerald Lynton Kaufman. A. S. Barnes & Co., 1948. ©Gerald Lynton Kaufman. / Pages 128-129, Winifred's Bloomers, from *Noel Coward* by Cole Lesley. Jonathan Cape, 1976. ©Cole Lesley. / Pages 119-120, A woman asked me to rhyme a penguin, by Ira Levin. ©Ira Levin. / Pages 78-80, Superpuns, from *A Pun My Soul* by Alan F.G. Lewis. Alan F.G. Lewis, 1977. ©Alan F.G. Lewis. / Page 197, Quiz of the Century, from *Super Spider-man* by Elliot Maggin. Marvel Comics International, 1978. ©Marvel Comics International. / Page 198, Quiz of the Century, from *The Serial* by Cyra McFadden. 1977. ©Cyra McFadden. / Page 123, Tiddely Quiddely Edward M. Kennedy, by Leonard Miall. ©Leonard Miall. / Page 242, Thon, from *Words and Women* by Casey Miller and Kate Swift. Anchor Press/Doubleday, 1976. ©Casey Miller and Kate Swift. / Pages 12-13, The First Crossword, pages 13-15, The First Crossword Book, pages 16-17, Crosswords Cross the Atlantic, from *The Strange World of the Crossword* by Roger Millington. M. and J. Hobbs, 1974. © Roger Millington. / Page 121, The Bronx, by Ogden Nash. ©Ogden Nash. / Page 178, Anti-Gook, from *Shooting an Elephant and Other Essays* by George Orwell. Secker and Warburg, 1950. ©George Orwell. / Page 209, Ode to a Typeface, from *Souvenir* by Christopher Reed. The Harvard Bulletin. ©Christopher Reed. / Page 208, A Visit from Saint Nicholas, by Clement C. Moore, designed by R. Robinson Rowe. ©design, R. Robinson Rowe. / Page 13, The world's first-ever crossword puzzle, created by Arthur Wynne for the New York World in 1913. ©St. Louis Post Dispatch. / Page 259, Elizabeth Kingsley's Double-Crostic, by Elizabeth Kingsley. ©The Saturday Review, 1934. / Page 108, C.B. Monikers, from *C.B. Guide* by Edwin Schlossberg and John Brockman. Bantam Books, 1977. ©Edwin Schlossberg and John Brockman. / Pages 257-258, Nicholas Scripture's Holy Writ and Nicholas Scripture's Tetrahedron, from *Puzzles and Teasers* by Nicholas Scripture. Faber and Faber, 1970. ©Nicholas Scripture. / Page 14, The first crossword from the first book of crosswords, published by the Plaza Publishing Co. in 1924. ©Simon and Schuster. / Page 119, To find a rhyme for silver, by Stephen Sondheim. ©Stephen Sondheim. / Pages 70-72, From Acclumsid to Zuche and From Fliperous Susan, from *Poplollies and Bellibones* by Susan Kelz Sperling. Clarkson N. Potter, 1977. ©Susan Kelz Sperling. / Pages 166-168, Tom Stoppard's Game, from *Rosencrantz and Guildenstern Are Dead* by Tom Stoppard. Grove Press and Faber and Faber, 1967. ©Tom Stoppard. / Page 5, Words That Look Right, pages 178-180, The Gobbledygook Generator, from *Illusions* by Edi Lauder and Heinz Norden. Thames and Hudson, 1977. ©Thames and Hudson. / Pages 222-225, Reading between the Lines, from *English as she is Fraught* by Jonathan Thomas. Wolfe Publishing, 1976. ©Jonathan Thomas. / Page 16, The first crossword published in *The Times* of London in 1930, Max Beerbohm's 1940 *Times* crossword and the 1980 *Times* crossword. ©Times Newspapers. / Page 120, A Certified Poet from Slough, by Clifford Witting. ©Clifford Witting.

ACKNOWLEDGEMENTS

Like so many lovers of language in its lighter moments I am enormously indebted to the works of Willard Espy and in particular to his *Almanac of Words at Play,* Clarkson N. Potter, 1975, from which the following were drawn: on page 5 "Words That Look Wrong," on page 103 "Winchellese," on page 107 "Varietish," on pages 118–120 "Rhymes That Don't," on page 219 "Social Climbers," on page 258 "J. Newton Friend's 'In the Middle.'" © Willard R. Espy.

I am also indebted to Willard Espy for introducing me to the delights of A. Ross Eckler's endlessly instructive and entertaining journal *Word Ways.* In particular I acknowledge with thanks permission to reproduce "Mary Had a Lipogram" on page 61, © A. Ross Eckler, and the "Croakers" on page 146, C. James, I. Rambo and Mary J. Youngquist.

Finally I must gratefully acknowledge the inspiration and information derived from Laurence Urdang's quarterly journal *Verbatim* and in particular the following contributors for permission to reproduce their material: Professor John Algeo for "Portmanteaus, Telescopes and Jumbles" on page 81–83, Elaine Von Bruns and Josef Brand for "Threesomes" on page 113, Professor G.A. Cevasco for "Kant Spel" on page 56, Harry Cimring and Professor Roger W. Westcott for "Femglish" on page 242, Sterling Eisiminger for "Campusese" on page 103, Ormly Gumfudgin for "What Did You Say" on page 58, Philip E. Hager for "Twosomes" on page 112, John O. Herbold II for "Baseballs" on page 105, Lynne Tieslau Jewell for "Caprine & Co." on page 139, M. Jourdain and Professor L.R.N. Ashley for "Names to Conjure With" on page 134, Arthur J. Morgan for "George and Martha" on page 170, M. Panzer for "The Lunchpack of Notre Dame Recipes" on page 231, Naomi Russell for "Fifteen Danglers" on page 216–217, James D. White for "Radio Malaprop" on page 132, Judge Douglas R. Woodworth for "Good Talk/Plain Talk" on page 177. © Verbatim.

In compiling this book I have drawn on a vast range of sources and every attempt has been made to trace and acknowledge owners of copyright material. In the event of material appearing without proper acknowledgment I would be grateful for notification so that matters can be put right in subsequent editions.

Gyles Brandreth

CONTENTS

INTRODUCTION   viii

AMAZING   3

BRAVE NEW WORDS   7

CROSSWORDS   12

THE DEVIL'S DICTIONARY   26

E.G.   31

FULL MARX   33

GRAFFITI—THE GREATEST   38

HOG   46

INCOMPREHENSIBLE PROBLEM
IN CHINESE   49

JUMBO   54

KAN'T SPEL   56

LONG LIVE THE LIPOGRAM   60

MURDER!   64

NOSTALGIA ISN'T WHAT
   IT USED TO BE 69

OAT CUISINE 76

PORTMANTEAUS AND TELESCOPES 81

QUEUE IN LINE 86

REPARTEE 95

SLANGUAGE 102

TWO'S COMPANY 112

UNQUESTIONABLY! 115

VERSE AND WORSE 118

WINIFRED'S BLOOMERS 128

XERXES ZZYZZX 134

YOU COW! 138

ZAP! 141

ZZZZ 143

Y NOT? 148

XEME 152

WORDSMITHS' WORDPLAY 164

VERBARRHEA 174

UNMENTIONABLES 182

TUT-TUT 186

SCRABBLE 191

RENT-A-TONGUE 194

QUIZ OF THE CENTURY   197

POETIC PICTURES   203

OEDIPUS COMPLEX WAS A FAMOUS
    QUEEN OF EGYPT   212

NINETEEN-EIGHTY-FOUR   218

MIX ME A METAPHOR   226

THE LUNCHPACK OF NOTRE-DAME   229

KNAPSACK STRAP   233

J. Q. SCHWARTZ AND FRIENDS   237

IS GOD A WOMAN?   241

HERE LIE I   244

THE GREATS   248

FIVE BY FIVE   262

ELLIPTICAL KISS   269

DOUBLETS   274

COLLECTING COLLECTIVES   277

BE BRIEF   281

ALL'S WELL THAT ENDS WELL   283

ANSWERS   285

INTRODUCTION

I've learnt a lot writing this book. For example, I have discovered that the most frequently used words of introduction among Americans are "Hi," "Hello," "How are you?" "Good to meet you," and "How do you do?"—in that order—so: "Hi, hello, how are you, good to meet you and how do you do?"

Having greeted you, I'd better explain myself. I'm a word freak. I'm fascinated by language, the way we use it and abuse it, the way we can manipulate it and be manipulated by it, the tricks we can play with it, the marvels we can create with it, the sheer fun we can have with it. And the idea behind this A to Z and Z to A of words is to tempt you to join me on a journey along the highways and byways of our language, in my view the richest, most diverse, most exciting and most *entertaining* language in the world.

I have been speaking English for just over thirty years. Since pronouncing my very first word (it was "No" in my case—and probably in yours too, since something else I've learnt is that "No" is the first word spoken by over fifty percent of the population of the English speaking world) I have spoken a further 354,780,999 words—or so. Apparently that's about average. If you are a typical American, by the time you die you will have uttered a total of not less than 860,341,500 words.

Words are as vital to civilized life as food and drink and sex, but on the whole we don't show as much interest in language as we do in those other—more obvious—pleasures. That's a shame. And that's why I've written this book: It's a celebration of the wonder of words and what we can do.

I won't say any more at this stage, because another of the things I discovered while writing this book is the fact that eighty-seven percent of readers never look at introductions. So don't hang around here: Turn the page and join the crowd.

AMAZING!

THE SHORTEST

A is the first word in the dictionary, one of the shortest words in the language, and the fifth most common word in English literature.

In conversation *I* is the most frequently used word. In written English the ten words used most often are:

the	and	a	that	I
of	to	in	is	it

THE LONGEST

29 LETTERS

floccinaucinihilipilification

The longest word in the Oxford English Dictionary. It means "the action of estimating as worthless" and dates from 1741.

34 LETTERS

supercalifragilisticexpialidocious
A nonsense word invented for the movie *Mary Poppins* (1964). No word of more than 30 letters has ever been more widely known.

37 LETTERS

praetertranssubstantiationalistically
An adverb used in Mark McShane's novel *Untimely Ripped* (1963).

45 LETTERS

pneumonoultramicroscopicsilicovolcanoconiosis
The longest word in Webster's Third New International Dictionary. It is the name of a miners' lung disease.

100 LETTERS

bababadalgharaghtakamminarronnkonnbronntonnerronn-tuonnthunntrovarrhounawnskawntoohoohoordenenthurnuk!
From the third paragraph of James Joyce's novel *Finnegans Wake* (1939).

1,913 LETTERS

The full name of the chemical tryptophan synthetase. A protein, whose formula is $C_{1289}H_{2051}N_{343}O_{375}S_8$.

THE MOST

Nobody knows the first English word to have been spoken. Nobody can predict the last. Nobody knows how many English words there are: Webster's Third lists over 450,000, but there are over a million organic and inorganic chemical compounds, each with a name, over a million different forms of plant life, each with a name, over a million insects, each with a name.

WORDS THAT LOOK RIGHT

WORDS THAT LOOK WRONG

Bully has nothing to do with a bull: it comes from the Dutch for "lover," *boel*.

Spades in the deck of cards have nothing to do with any other spades: the word comes from the Spanish *espada*, "sword."

Humble pie has nothing to do with humility: cheap cuts of meat were once called *umbles*.

Titmice are not related to breasts or rodents: *tit* used to mean *small* and *mase* once meant a kind of bird.

Nitwits may be witless, but the word comes from the Dutch *niet wit*, "I don't know."

The big cheese comes not from cheese, but from the Hindi *chiz*, "thing."

Guinea pigs aren't pigs and don't come from Guinea.

India ink comes from China.

Turkeys come from North America, not Turkey.

Blindworms aren't blind and aren't worms; they're legless lizards that can see.

BRAVE NEW WORDS

The English language is rich because it isn't pure. It's a mongrel tongue. Emerson called it "the sea which receives tributaries from every region under heaven." It has taken almost 2,000 years to evolve. The Kelts, Jutes, Angles, Saxons, Greeks, Romans, Danes, Normans, Dutch, Germans, French, Spanish, Italians, Indians, American Indians, Africans—to name only a few—made major contributions. So did Shakespeare.

SHAKESPEARE'S WORDS

He coined 1,700 words, among them:

assassinate	*critical*	*laughable*
auspicious	*dwindle*	*leapfrog*
barefaced	*gnarled*	*lonely*
bump	*hurry*	*misplaced*
castigate	*impartial*	*monumental*
countless	*lapse*	

SCIENTIFIC WORDS

Science has contributed thousands of new words to the language:

magnetism (1616)	*atom* (1801)
telescope (1619)	*evolution* (1832)
gravity (1642)	*bacterium* (1847)
electricity (1646)	*pasteurize* (1881)
microscope (1656)	*hormone* (1904)
botany (1696)	*vitamin* (1905)
zoology (1726)	*penicillin* (1928)
oxygen (1789)	

WAR WORDS

Wars have produced scores of new words. From World War I:

binge	*cushy*	*umpteen*
camouflage	*scrounge*	*zoom*

From World War II:

blackout	*boffin*	*jeep*
blitz	*bulldozer*	*wishful thinking*

From the Korean and Vietnamese wars:

credibility gap	*kneecap, v.*	*napalm, v.*
defoliate, v.	*misspeak*	

50 YEARS OF BRAVE NEW WORDS

New words are happening all the time. Here are 50 that have come into being since 1929:

1929	*astronautics*
1930	*teenager*

1931   *microwave*
1932   *malnourishment*
1933   *doodle*
1934   *agitprop*
1935   *audition, v.*
1936   *muzak*
1937   *autobahn*
1938   *weenybopper*
1939   *loud-hailer* (bullhorn)
1940   *Mae West* (life jacket)
1941   *majorette*
1942   *astronavigation*
1943   *acronym*
1944   *aerosol*
1945   *microsleep*
1946   *microdot*
1947   *apartheid*
1948   *automation*
1949   *male menopause*
1950   *aqualung*
1951   *discotheque*
1952   *to take the mick out of* (someone)
1953   *adventure playground*
1954   *non-U*
1955   *admass*
1956   *brinkmanship*
1957   *sexploitation*
1958   *aerospace*
1959   *microbus*
1960   *biorhythm*
1961   *mini*
1962   *nonevent*
1963   *Mandrax*
1964   *monokini* (topless bikini)

1965	*metrication*
1966	*Nibmar*
1967	*monohull*
1968	*nuffieldite* (mineral)
1969	*misregister*
1970	*biofeedback*
1971	*bioethics*
1972	*precipitation factor*
1973	*streaker*
1974	*macropedia*
1975	*dis-Nixonized*
1976	*disastrophe*
1977	*skatebordello*
1978	*Travoltonic*
1979	*siliconitis*

At the time of writing it's difficult to say what words 1979 will contribute to the language. One I have hopes for is a unit of female beauty: the *millihelen,* defined as the amount of beauty required to launch one ship.

Ban the Word—18th-Century Style

New words have always met with opposition. Jonathan Swift and Samuel Johnson wanted to ban these in the 18th century:

sham	*bully*	*stingy*
banter	*clever*	*bamboozle*
mob	*fun*	

Ban the Word—20th-Century Style

Over 200 years later these are the ten vogue words I'd like to ban:

input	*output*	*feedback*

They are three examples of computerese that are now being applied to human activities.

wetware

Hardware is the computer; *software* the computer program; wetware the human brain.

ballpark figure

This is a computer's guesstimate. And five more:

chill factor (meteorologese)
increment
cholesterol
autocide (suicide in a car)
flickering blue parent (TV)

CROSSWORDS

THE FIRST CROSSWORD

Arthur Wynne was scratching his head searching for a new idea to include in his puzzle page for the magazine section of Sunday's *New York World*. For the 1913 Christmas edition he wanted something special. He had tried word squares, enigmas, hidden words, rebuses, and anagrams. Playing around with a word square, it struck him that he could break with tradition—why should the across words necessarily be the same as the down words? Wynne sketched out a diamond-shaped grid, reached for a dictionary, and a few hours later, the world's first crossword was born. It needed a name, so Wynne called it a word-cross.

The epoch-making puzzle appeared on December 21, 1913. In case you missed it, here it is again:

2-3. What bargain hunters enjoy.
4-5. A written acknowledgment.
6-7. Such and nothing more.
10-11. A bird.
14-15. Opposed to less.
18-19. What this puzzle is.
22-23. An animal of prey.
26-27. The close of a day.
28-29. To elude.
30-31. The plural of is.
8-9. To cultivate.
12-13. A bar of wood or iron.
16-17. What artists learn to do.
20-21. Fastened.
24-25. Found on the seashore.

10-18. The fibre of the gomuti palm.
6-22. What we all should be.
4-26. A day dream.
2-11. A talon.
19-28. A pigeon.
F-7. Part of your head.
23-30. A river in Russia.
I-32. To govern.
33-34. An aromatic plant.
N-8. A fist.
24-31. To agree with.
3-12. Part of a ship.
20-29. One.
5-27. Exchanging.
9-25. To sink in mud.
13-21. A boy.

(See Answers section at the end of this book.)

THE FIRST CROSSWORD BOOK

It was 11 years before the crossword puzzle made its first appearance between hard covers. Here is the first puzzle in the first-ever crossword book, published by Dick Simon and Lincoln Schuster in New York (1924):

HORIZONTAL

1. Pronoun.
3. Albumin from castor-oil bean
7. Exist.
9. Aged.
11. Negative.
12. Incite, hasten.
13. Remote.
15. Obstruction.
17. Bivalves.
21. Father.
23. Tree.
24. River in Italy.
25. Owners.
26. Printer's measure.
27. Tree.
28. Personal pronoun.
29. Legislative bodies.
31. Compact mass.
32. Moved rapidly.
34. Walk about.
35. Toss.
37. Small child.
39. Upon.
40. Small openings.
41. Act.

VERTICAL

1. Exclamation.
2. Fairy.
4. Preposition.
5. Plotter.
6. Pronoun.
7. Express generally.
8. Pronoun.
10. Obstruct.
12. Owns.
14. Disarranged.
15. Voluble talkativeness.
16. Above.
18. The bow of Vishnu.
19. Choose.

20. Assumed an attitude.
22. Limb.
24. Peer.
29. Sorrowful.
30. Rested.
31. Pale.

33. Incline the head.
34. Move.
35. Behold.
36. Exist.
38. Preposition.

(See Answers.)

The Crossword Puzzle Book was Simon and Schuster's first publishing venture. They printed 3,600 copies and were told they'd be lucky to sell half of them. Within three months they had sold 40,000. By the time their company had reached its first birthday they had produced three volumes of puzzles with total sales topping 400,000.

In 1970 Simon and Schuster published *Crossword Puzzle Book Number 100*—"a cause for cerebration and celebration." Like the preceding 99, it was edited by Margaret Petherbridge Farrar. In 1920 Margaret Petherbridge, newly graduated from Smith College, got her first job as secretary to the editor of the magazine section of the *New York World*. One of her duties was to see that the puzzles appeared without typographical errors. She was given the job for much the same reason that a cub reporter is assigned to write up the local dog show—everyone else despised the job. She became so adept at stopping errors that she became the unofficial crossword editor. In 1924, with Prosper Buranelli and Gregory Hartswick, she compiled *The Crossword Puzzle Book*.

After her marriage in 1926 Mrs. Farrar gave up newspaper work. Then in February 1942 the *New York Times* decided to start a Sunday puzzle and asked her to be editor. The *New York Times* was the last major paper in America to adopt a crossword; not until September 1950 did it print a daily puzzle. Mrs. Farrar retired in 1969, the acknowledged dean of the puzzle. During her time on the paper she regularly accepted puzzles from a high-school principal, an actress, an advertising man, three freighter captains, an army corporal, a 14-year-old schoolboy, and a good many from prison inmates. (A lifer at the Ohio State Penitentiary sold 250 puzzles to the newspapers in 1965—getting $10 apiece from daily papers and $25 from Sunday papers.)

CROSSWORDS CROSS THE ATLANTIC

In December 1924 the *London Times* decided that the crossword craze in the United States was getting out of hand. Under the headline AN ENSLAVED AMERICA The *Times* accused the crossword of being a veritable "menace because it is making devastating inroads on the working hours of every rank of society." Six years later, the *Times* surrendered and published its own first crossword:

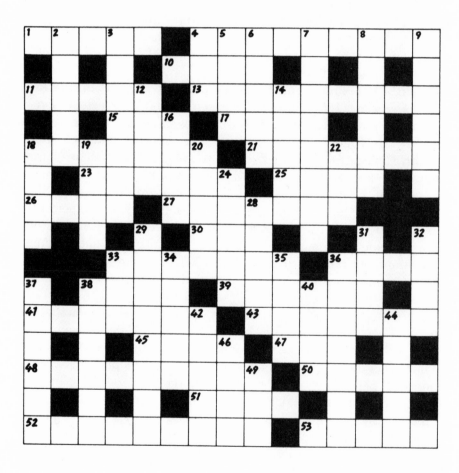

ACROSS

1. Spread unevenly.
4. Part of a Milton title.
10. A month, nothing more, in Ireland.
11. He won't settle down.
13. 22 down should be this.
15. Cotton onto, so to speak.
17. Head of a chapter.
18. Denizen of the ultimate ditch.
21. Frequently under observation.
23. What's in this stands out.
25. Flighty word.
26. If the end of this gets in the way the whole may result.
27. Retunes (anag.).
30. This means study.
33. Simply enormous.
36. There's a lot in this voice.
38. This elephant has lost his head.
39. A turn for the worse.
41. Done with a coarse file.
43. Red loam (anag.).
45. This rodent's going back.
47. Makes a plaything with its past.
48. Wants confidence.
50. A mixed welcome means getting the bird.
51. This girl seems to be eating backwards.
52. The men in the moon.
53. A pinch of sand will make it dry.

DOWN

2. Heraldic gold between mother and me.
3. Out of countenance.
4. Upset this value and get a sharp reproof.
5. Intently watched.
6. In some hands the things become trumpets.
7. A religious service.
8. This horseman has dropped an h.
9. Sounds like a curious song.
12. This ought to be square.
14. Momentary stoppage.
16. Written briefly.
18. Calverley's picturesque scholars carved their names on every one.
19. Site of 45 across.
20. Precedes advantage.
22. Parents in a negative way.
24. Used to be somewhere in France.
28. Happen afterwards.
29. Climbing instinct in man.
31. A terrestrial glider.
32. The final crack.
33. The little devil's on our money.
34. Simplest creature.
35. Time measurements.
36. Jollier than 4 across.
37. Ladies in promising mood.
38. Presents are commonly this.
40. Gets the boot.
42. Hail in Scotland may mean tears.
44. Works, but usually plays.
46. She's dead.
49. Only a contortionist could do this on a chair.

(See Answers.)

Almost half a century later, the *London Times* is still publishing a daily crossword, but the clues are no longer straightforward definitions. They are complex, cryptic and altogether more compelling. Involving anagrams, puns, literary allusions, and a very varied vocabulary, they are generally considered to be among the most challenging crosswords around. Here is the *Times* Crossword No. 14,576, a typical specimen from the late 1970s:

ACROSS

1. Stream noted for fish? (5).
4. Designer of note invested in a cert (permed) (9).
9. Repugnant to give brother an upset (9).
10. What post-mortem fears gave Hamlet (5).
11. Like Gilbert, we hear, a bit of a nut (6).
12. Old reformer gives honour to painter (8).
14. Cat charged outside, as usual (10).
16. By end of April one red-cap is drooping (4).
19. Subject of Pharaoh's dream of relations with the East (4).
20. Notice taken of many a nice song composer (10).
22. Disagreement which prevents perpetual motion (8).
23. Sweet toy (6).
26. Made no advance slowly (5).
27. Deeply influenced as the old conscripts were (9).
28. The bay for instance, in unchanging monochrome (9).
29. Elizabeth Rose (5).

DOWN

1. The Knave or another club? (9).
2. Sandwich or pie containing watery humour (5).
3. Gifts taken by a Big Steamer to the East (8).
4. His killer was a marked man (4).
5. Worthless item to sell for round coin (10).
6. Make known I am putting up the gin (6).
7. Learning issue about football code (9).
8. River detective (5).
13. Crazy incentive to make a railway engine (10).
15. One due to get goods since gone astray (9).
17. He makes a claim before getting an offer (9).
18. Reunites elements to make us hungry (8).
21. "When two —— men stand face to face" (Kipling) (6).
22. Artificial flower seen to be cut in half (5).
24. Circuit thus broken—may be joined (5).
25. Love to write manifest (4).

(See Answers)

THE WORLD'S MOST DIFFICULT CROSSWORD

My friend John Sykes, lexicographer extraordinary, editor of the *Concise Oxford Dictionary*, crossword puzzle champion, and owner of one of the world's most amazing minds, can solve a typical *London Times* crossword in ten minutes. When I showed him a crossword reprinted in *New York* magazine that claimed to be the "world's most challenging crossword," he dismissed it as "relatively easy." If I wanted to reproduce a *really* challenging crossword in my book, John suggested I try baffling you with one devised by the English novelist, Gilbert Frankau.

In 1925 the *London Daily News* ran a crossword contest with a first prize of £5,000. A hundred thousand readers entered the first round of the contest. Frankau was then called in to produce a series of four puzzles of increasing difficulty. Three hundred competitors solved the third, but no complete solution was received for the fourth, and the prize was shared by a syndicate of readers having the smallest number of errors. (I am assured that the puzzle's fiendish complexity and the fact that Frankau was three times married are in no way connected.)

ACROSS

1. Initialise a father.
202. By adding hydrogen here, help the British Dyestuffs Corporation.
303. Full of hops.

404. Curtail a formula.
5. Might describe the condition of a rustic wooer.
6. A poetess.
7. A moke.
8. The guns of Trafalgar.

9. Curtail and decapitate an enormous oven.
10. Reverse one part of a pulley block.
11. One way out of the harem.
12. Once decapitate and thrice curtail the race of a man whose skin might have been saved had he been able to exercise 11 across.
13. Decapitate and curtail something which also answers to clue 44 across.
14. Curtail and decapitate that which apparently did *not* fall.
15. Twice curtail an exiguous meadow.
16. Two code letters found on a certain brand of advertised cigarettes.
17. Reverse either three-fourths or three-fifths of a neurosis.
18. Add one and make a tragedy.
19. Curtail and decapitate a diminutive.
20. Her husband's initials were J. R.
21. Found under the table.
22. Reverse two words which might describe the influence of several specimens on the judgment of a mining engineer.
23. First reverse, then twice decapitate an idler.
24. Look for this on the end of a blowpipe.
25. Reverse one thorough paced scoundrel.
26. Reverse something made of chestnuts.
27. First reverse, then twice decapitate a city bossed by a bull.
28. Might describe hawthorn.
29. Curtail a Saracen's stronghold.
30. Curtail a word associated with mice.

31. First reverse, then invert the first two letters of a knowledge invaluable to Mr. Royce.
32. Ask your tailor about this.
33. Found under expensive cigar boxes.
34. Could also be initialised as U, Q, F, E, G, D.
35. See house agents' advertisements.
36. Start an ode.
37. Curtail one who would have been better shingled.
38. The fore-runner of the land girl.
39. Twice curtail that which put behind 72 across conveys social reform.
40. By decapitation and the alteration of one letter, make print vocal.
41. One of the lacertilia.
42. Reverse the first half of a hill.
43. A form of promotion.
44. Dished up with vegetables.
45. A female.
46. Add a couple and make a row.
47. To surround.
48. Curtail a village.
49. Set our fathers singing.
50. Curtail one who goes veiled.
51. Made men cry, 'Bring out your dead'.
52. A relative of Peeping Tom.
53. One who entered on behalf of the House.
54. Curtail a river.
55. Might have been the first two words of a historic South African cable.
56. Remove two letters from contracts.
57. ⎰ By combining these two
57a. ⎱ make a lark.
58. Decapitate a doubtful beautifier.
59. Reverse a form of communication.

60. Two-thirds of a military unit.
61. Deduct an aromatic liquid from an aromatic plant.
62. B.C. three thousand two hundred and sixty.
63. Gives knights nightmare.
64. Reverse projections.
65. The last of the fairies.
66. Curtail an inhabitant of the Gebbi.
67. Singularise and reverse a reversal.
68. First decapitate, then reverse a property vital to a play.
69. Twice beheaded a fearsome monster.
70. Nice nickname (reversed) for a brace of peeresses.
71. Once decapitate and thrice curtail a business which is also an art.
72. See 39 across.
73. A chorus.

DOWN
1. Title of a poem.
40. Seven score.
55. Reverse that which makes men distrust legality.
2. The novice oarsman's friend.
3. Halve a frisky lady.
4. Reverse a process Biblically connected with a beard.
5. An appellation of intimacy.
606. Would apply to 21 across.
7. Reverse a sign of decomposition.
38. Reverse a name.
39. A great handicap.
8. The answer the doctor made to his nagging wife.
9. Makes H. G. Wells see red.
10. Reverse an inflammation.
11. Reverse whom your curse.
12. Thrice curtail a trade-mark.
13. Reverse that which has as bad an effect as 9 down.
14. Curtail a cereal.

15. Cross.
16. Reverse a revenue payer.
202. Reverse a patient carrier.
203. A racecourse.
59. Depenultimise an African tribe.
204. The first two letters of 303 across.
205. Stops 'fans' fanning.
206. More trouble for H. G. Wells.
44. Reverse a newspaper suggestion about 46 across.
207. Half a fruit.
208. Appeal to peelers.
209. Leslie Henson does this.
210. Reverse an obsolescent individual.
211. Several Zevs.
212. What the Yorkshireman said when they offered him ginger beer.
213. Reverse, then four times decapitate a war policy.
214. The day to which no one looks forward.
215. Reverse a flapper's dream.
216. Curtail that which tallies with 40 across.
217. Initialise and reverse a preserver (?) of morality.
57a. A monopoly.
218. Reverse a headman.
303. Reverse a phrase which might be used by a Channel swimmer.
304. Halve embellished.
305. Stand a cup on its rim.
306. Halve a cake.
307. Bad in the lung, worse in the brain.
308. Deduct first an American animal, then an English interjection from a barometrical term. Then reverse your result.
309. Add a conveyance and make a spectacle.
310. One of these rarely obtains 311 down.
311. Rarely obtained by 310 down.

312. Reverse a knight.
313. Another Wells.
314. Give this to your enemies.
315. Curtail and reverse a provider of transport.
316. Reverse the last two letters of 55 across.
317. Reverse three primal liquids.
404. First deduct the opposition from, then reverse a word whose original significance is precisely the opposite of opposition.
405. Sets Chinamen gobbling.
406. The wrong way to pluralise some Orientals.
 37. The gardener's friend.
407. Not the Southern's, we hope.
408. First reverse then decapitate the forerunner of 55 down.
409. Add the beginning and the end of 65 across to the ultimate of 1 across and the penultimate of 71 across.
410. A reformer.
 51. Curtail a kicker.
411. Was used for keening.
412. Reverse a sign of utility.
 47. Initialise a story title.
413. One of the things that is his.
414. Reverse the first half of a Swinburnian town.
415. Reverse and add a couple to 317 down.
415a. Voyage, and learn this.
416. Take the last four letters of 406 down and turn them into the past.
417. Never wrote vers libre.
418. Singularise, without authority, symbols of a jolly evening.
418a. The typist's curse.
419. The largest inhabitants of a South American Republic.

(See Answers.)

   I can't begin to understand Frankau's clues, let alone begin to solve them. But if you found them easy going, this last crossword (on the next page) should present you with no problems. It was created in 1940 by the incomparable Max Beerbohm. I hope you enjoy it.

ACROSS

1. A Victorian statesman lurking in a side lair (8).
5. Milky way unseen by star-gazers (6).
9. An insect with a girl on each side (8).
10. Pugilists' wear (6).
11. Four toes are broken (8).
12. The cockney's goddess appears to have been a slimmer (6).
14. There's a little company in the meadow next month (10).
18. 'But what if memory Itself our — —s had betrayed?' (Matthew Arnold) (two words (5, 5).

22. A nudist's aunt? (6).
23. 'That day he —— the Nervii' (Shakespeare) (8).
24. Acknowledgement of debt in a vessel (6).
25. Neither animal nor mineral, and only three-fourths vegetable (8).
26. Not what the wicket-keeper tries for in Essex (6).
27. The P.R.A. is utterly confounded (8).

DOWN

1. Drum (Newbolt) (6).
2. The top of the morning, perhaps (6).
3. A Manx beverage (6).
4. Ho! Let's go in (anag.) (10).

6. Wordsworth's fan mail? (8).
7. And yet sugar *can* be refined (8).
8. They are up and doing, no doubt, in 'the sweet o' the year' (8).
13. Little Tommy thought it meant a red-faced blacksmith (10).
15. Voltaire's *prêtre enragé* (8).

16. Such buns are eaten on a good day (two words) (3, 5).
17. Caliban's seachange (8).
19. Pollarded haven (6).
20. I'm in the old Roman bath (6).
21. 'Our —— clues that do but darken counsel' (Tennyson) (6).

(See Answers.)

THE DEVIL'S DICTIONARY

According to the *Guinness Book of World Records* the world's largest dictionary is the twelve-volume *Oxford English Dictionary*, first published between 1884 and 1928. The work contains 414,825 words, 1,827,306 illustrative quotations, and 227,779,589 letters and figures.

According to yours truly the world's finest dictionary is the one-volume *Devil's Dictionary*, first published between 1881 and 1911. It is the work of one of America's greatest men of letters, Ambrose Bierce, who was born in Meigs County, Ohio, in 1842, and who vanished without trace in Mexico in 1913. The *Oxford English Dictionary* has 15,487 pages; *The Devil's Dictionary*, only 138. If you want to know why I rate Bierce's dictionary above all others, take a look at a few of his diabolical definitions:

abasement, n.   A decent and customary mental attitude in the presence of wealth or power. Peculiarly appropriate in an employee when addressing an employer.

absurdity, n.	A statement of belief manifestly inconsistent with one's own opinion.
accordion, n.	An instrument in harmony with the sentiments of an assassin.
achievement, n.	The death of endeavor and the birth of disgust.
alone, adj.	In bad company.
ambition, n.	An overmastering desire to be vilified by enemies while living and made ridiculous by friends when dead.
Bacchus, n.	A convenient deity invented by the ancients as an excuse for getting drunk.
backbite, vt.	To speak of a man as you find him when he can't find you.
barometer, n.	An ingenious instrument which indicates what kind of weather we are having.
bore, n.	A person who talks when you wish him to listen.
calamity, n.	A more than commonly plain and unmistakable reminder that the affairs of this life are not of our own ordering. Calamities are of two kinds: misfortune to ourselves, and good fortune to others.
clairvoyant, n.	A person, commonly a woman, who has the power of seeing that which is invisible to her patron—namely, that he is a blockhead.
congratulation, n.	The civility of envy.
contempt, n.	The feeling of a prudent man for an enemy who is too formidable safely to be opposed.
debt, n.	An ingenious substitute for the chain and whip of the slave driver.
déjeuner, n.	The breakfast of an American who has been in Paris. Variously pronounced.
diplomacy, n.	The patriotic art of lying for one's country.

education, n.	That which discloses to the wise and disguises from the foolish their lack of understanding.
egotist, n.	A person of low taste, more interested in himself than in me.
famous, adj.	Conspicuously miserable.
fashion, n.	A despot whom the wise ridicule and obey.
fiddle, n.	An instrument to tickle human ears by friction of a horse's tail on the entrails of a cat.
future, n.	That period of time in which our affairs prosper, our friends are true, and our happiness is assured.
habit, n.	A shackle for the free.
hand, n.	A singular instrument worn at the end of a human arm and commonly thrust into somebody's pocket.
happiness, n.	An agreeable sensation arising from contemplating the misery of another.
harbor, n.	A place where ships taking shelter from storms are exposed to the fury of the customs.
hospitality, n.	The virtue which induces us to feed and lodge certain persons who are not in need of food and lodging.
infancy, n.	The period of our lives when, according to Wordsworth, "Heaven lies about us." The world begins lying about us pretty soon afterward.
inventor, n.	A person who makes an ingenious arrangement of wheels, levers, and springs, and believes it civilization.
kilt, n.	A costume sometimes worn by Scotchmen in America and Americans in Scotland.
lawyer, n.	One skilled in circumvention of the law.

male, n.	A member of the unconsidered, or negligible sex. The male of the human race is commonly known (to the female) as Mere Man. The genus has two varieties: good providers and bad providers.
mausoleum, n.	The final and funniest folly of the rich.
Monday, n.	In Christian countries, the day after the baseball game.
noise, n.	A stench in the ear. Undomesticated music. The chief product and authenticating sign of civilization.
ocean, n.	A body of water occupying about two-thirds of a world made for man—who has no gills.
opportunity, n.	A favorable occasion for grasping a disappointment.
overwork, n.	A dangerous disorder affecting high public functionaries who want to go fishing.
peace, n.	In international affairs, a period of cheating between two periods of fighting.
poker, n.	A game said to be played with cards for some purpose to this lexicographer unknown.
politics, n.	A strife of interests masquerading as a contest of principles. The conduct of public affairs for private advantage.
positive, adj.	Mistaken at the top of one's voice.
pray, v.	To ask that the laws of the universe be annulled in behalf of a single petitioner confessedly unworthy.
price, n.	Value, plus a reasonable sum for the wear and tear of conscience in demanding it.
riot, n.	A popular entertainment given to the military by innocent bystanders.

ruin, v.	To destroy. Specifically, to destroy a maid's belief in the virtue of maids.
self-evident, adj.	Evident to one's self and to nobody else.
senate, n.	A body of elderly gentlemen charged with high duties and misdemeanors.
telephone, n.	An invention of the devil which abrogates some of the advantages of making a disagreeable person keep his distance.
truthful, adj.	Dumb and illiterate.
wit, n.	The salt with which the American humorist spoils his intellectual cookery by leaving it out.

There have been other cynical dictionaries, though none as brilliant as Bierce's. In case you might like to compile a contemporary version of *The Devil's Dictionary*, test your qualifications by dipping your pen in acid and attempting modern definitions for half-a-dozen everyday words:

1 *diplomacy*
2 *education*
3 *free press*
4 *highbrow*
5 *jazz*
6 *lowbrow*

(See Answers for suggested definitions.)

E.G.

Under the circumstances, I'd better keep this short. If you know what the letters e.g. stand for you'll find you can have a lot of fun with abbrs., e.g. by doing a quiz.

Here are 30 everyday abbreviations. What does each one mean?

1 *AC*	11 *D.G.*
2 *ad. lib.*	12 *e.g.*
3 *a.m.*	13 *GMT*
4 *AWOL*	14 *H.C.F.*
5 *B.A.*	15 *H.R.H.*
6 *BBC*	16 *i.e.*
7 *CENTO*	17 *IQ*
8 *C.O.D.*	18 *M.*
9 *cwt.*	19 *Mgr.*
10 *DDT*	20 *MS.*

21 *oz.*	26 *S.J.*
22 *p.m.*	27 *SOS*
23 *R.I.P.*	28 *SPQR*
24 *rpm*	29 *TNT*
25 *RSVP*	30 *U.S.S.R.*

(See Answers.)

GA

& if you're really into abbreviations you can play games with them, such as the '63 Game.

1963 was the year two-letter abbreviations for all states in the United States were introduced. See if you can name every state by its two-letter abbreviation: OH, AZ's asking a lot, I know, but if ME MA OR PA can do it, AL be darned if you can't. OK?

P.S.:

I'm in a 10der mood 2 day
   & feel poetic 2;
4 fun I'll just — off a line
   & send it off 2 U.

I'm sorry you've been 6 o long;
   Don't be disconsol8;
But bear your ills with 42de
   & they won't seem so gr8.

FULL MARX

MARXMANSHIP

Karl Marx died 12 years before Groucho Marx was born. Both were blessed with an unmistakable genius. It is difficult to say with certainty which one contributed more to world civilization, but I'm inclined to think it was Groucho.

THE BEST OF KARL

Die Proletarier haben nichts in ihr zu verlieren als ihre Ketten. Sie haben eine Welt zu gewinnen. Proletarier aller Lander, vereinigt euch!

THE BEST OF GROUCHO

To President Harry Truman, in a letter inviting him to visit the West Coast:

If you want to come up, I can put you up. I have a swimming
pool and a pool table. I shoot very badly and if you are any
good with the cue, you could win enough to pay your expenses.

To a man with a bushy beard:
I've heard of a five o'clock shadow, but this is ridiculous.

To a club he joined in a rash moment:
Please accept my resignation. I don't want to belong to any
club that will accept me as a member.

After handing on a restaurant bill to a woman:
Nine dollars and 40 cents. This is an outrage. If I were you, I
wouldn't pay it.

I once shot an elephant in my pajamas. How he got in there
I'll never know.

Refusing a chance to appear at the Metropolitan Opera in
New York:
They offered me $1,000 a performance. I get that much just
walking my dog round the block.

Your eyes, your eyes, they shine like the pants on my blue
serge suit. That's not a reflection on you. That's on my pants.

To a bellboy paging him in a restaurant:
Will you do me a favor and stop yelling my name all over this
restaurant. Do I go round yelling your name?

About his own name—his real name was Julius—he said:
Anything is better than Julius. I think that is why Caesar got
assassinated. I took the name of Groucho because I always
look solemn, I guess.

After taking the pulse of an unconscious man:
Either this man is dead or my watch has stopped.

To a clergyman who said that he wanted to thank him for all the enjoyment he'd given the world:

> And I want to thank you for all the enjoyment you've taken out of the world.

To Margaret Dumont, the target of many of his screen jibes:

> You'd better beat it. You can leave in a taxi. If you can't get a taxi you can leave in a huff. If that's too soon you can leave in a minute and a huff.

Of his father, a tailor:

> You could always tell his clients because their clothes didn't fit.

When Warner Brothers threatened to sue him for using the title *A Night in Casablanca* because it was too similar to their own film *Casablanca*, he replied:

> I'll sue you for using the word *Brothers*.

In a love scene:

> I could dance with you till the cows come home. On second thoughts, I'd rather dance with the cows till you come home.

In a screen proposal to Margaret Dumont:

> There are so many bonds that will hold us together. Your government bonds, your savings bonds, your Liberty bonds.

At a screenwriters' dinner:

> We in the industry know that behind every successful screenwriter stands a woman. And behind her stands his wife.

To a woman from Wales:

> Did you ever meet a fellow named Jonah? He lived in whales for a while.

WITQUIZ

In anybody's list of American wits you'd have to find the following
names:

1	Woody Allen	11	Anita Loos
2	Robert Benchley	12	Betty MacDonald
3	Ambrose Bierce	13	Dorothy Parker
4	Art Buchwald	14	S. J. Perelman
5	Ruth Draper	15	Will Rogers
6	Jules Feiffer	16	Harold Ross
7	Dick Gregory	17	Damon Runyon
8	George S. Kaufman	18	James Thurber
9	David Lardner	19	Mark Twain
10	Stephen Leacock	20	Alexander Woollcott

In anybody's Dictionary of Wit you'd have to find the following
lines. The problem is: which wit above said what below?

(a) The plot was designed in a light vein that somehow
became varicose.

(b) Even nowadays a man can't step up and kill a woman
without feeling just a bit unchivalrous.

(c) I detest life-insurance agents; they always argue that I
shall some day die, which is not so.

(d) The gambling known as business looks with austere
disfavor upon the business known as gambling.

(e) The chair . . . was upholstered in one of those flagrant
chintzes, designed, apparently, by the art editor of a seed
catalog.

(f) The buffalo isn't as dangerous as everyone makes him
out to be. Statistics prove that in the United States more
Americans are killed in automobile accidents than are killed by
buffalo.

(g) Number seven . . . What's it meant to be, dear? . . . A
study? . . . It doesn't say what of? . . . Well, that's an easy way
out for an artist.

(h) I'm never going to be famous. My name will never be writ large on the roster of Those Who Do Things. I don't do anything. Not a single thing. I used to bite my nails, but I don't even do that any more.

(i) I know she's alive. I saw her lip curl.

(j) So this gentleman said a girl with brains ought to do something else with them besides think.

(k) I was born because it was a habit in those days, people didn't know anything else . . . I was not a Child Prodigy, because a Child Prodigy is a child who knows as much when it is a child as it does when it grows up.

(l) I can feel for her because, although I have never been an Alaskan prostitute dancing on the bar in a spangled dress, I still get very bored with washing and ironing and dishwashing and cooking day after relentless day.

(m) Is Moby Dick the whale or the man?

(n) If anyone wants to trade a couple of centrally located, well-cushioned showgirls for an eroded slope 90 minutes from Broadway, I'll be on this corner tomorrow at 11 with my tongue hanging out.

(o) Whoever has lived long enough to find out what life is knows how deep a debt of gratitude we owe to Adam, the first great benefactor of our race. He brought death into the world.

(p) She developed a persistent troubled frown which gave her the expression of someone who is trying to repair a watch with his gloves on.

(q) I once knew a chap who had a system of just hanging the baby on the clothesline to dry and he was greatly admired by his fellow citizens for having discovered a wonderful innovation on changing a diaper.

(r) Isn't this the most fascinating country in the world? Where else would I have to ride on the back of the bus, have a choice of going to the worst schools, eating in the worst restaurants, living in the worst neighborhood—and average $5,000 a week just talking about it?

(s) Her figure described a set of parabolas that could cause cardiac arrest in a yak.

(t) One man's Mede is another man's Persian.

(See Answers.)

GRAFFITI—THE GREATEST

People probably chipped these things on the walls of Egyptian bathrooms 2,000 years ago. So progress is a ball-point pen.

Ever since man could write, he's written on walls. There is no form of literature so old or so universal as graffiti. It's been around since the days of the cave painters and looks like it will be with us for the rest of time.

Graffiti can be about anything, but more often than not they're about sex. You get philosophical graffiti, political graffiti, protest graffiti, racist graffiti, graffiti about graffiti, and graffiti that manage to be about graffiti *and* racist ("DOWN WITH GRAFFITI! *Yeah, down with all Italians!*"), but for every graffito that doesn't touch on any aspect of sex you'll find a dozen that do.

Just as sex and our bodily functions seem to inspire the bulk of the world's graffiti, so the toilet appears to be the place where we are most often inspired:

> There once was a fellow named Rafferty
> Who went to a gentleman's lafferty,

When he saw the sight
He said, "Newton was right,
This must be the center of grafferty!"

Graffiti can be found in the unlikeliest places—in the Reading Room of the British Museum ("It's a funny old world. Signed, Karl Marx"), on an Egyptian pyramid ("I've got pharaohs at the bottom of my garden too"), at the American embassy in London ("Remember, Yanks, if it wasn't for us British you'd all have been Spanish"), inside the Vatican ("Celibacy is not an inherited characteristic")—but the likeliest place is a public lavatory. It's not so much fun doing it on your bathroom wall at home.

We usually have time to spare in the lavatory, and more significantly, we are usually alone there. Writing on the wall is a private matter that can be indulged in with confidence because graffiti are essentially anonymous. The one important exception to this rule is Kilroy. During the Second World War, James J. Kilroy, of Halifax, Massachusetts, was employed at the Bethlehem Steel Company's Quincy shipyard, inspecting tanks and other parts of warships under construction. To satisfy his superiors that he was performing his duties, Mr. Kilroy scribbled in yellow crayon the words "KILROY WAS HERE" on everything he inspected. Soon the phrase began to appear all over the yard and Mr. Kilroy believes the 14,000 shipyard workers who entered the armed services were responsible for its subsequent worldwide use.

No doubt about it, brevity *is* the soul of wit; many of the best bits of graffiti are short, sharp slogans that pack a punch and promote a cause. Some have found their way onto buttons ("If I'm awake, try me. If I'm asleep, wake me"); some have been emblazoned on T-shirts ("People who live in glass blouses shouldn't show bones"); some have been printed on postcards ("You don't have to be crazy to work here—but it helps"); but best are scrawled on the wall.

WALLTALK—THE GREATEST

Save water—bathe with a friend.
Stamp out distemper—but don't step in it.

Support free enterprise—legalize prostitution.

Stop air pollution—quit breathing.

I am a mistake—legalize abortion.

Lower the age of puberty.

Help stamp out philately.

Support the rich.

Drive defensively—buy a tank.

Support wildlife—vote for an orgy!

Legalize necrophilia!

Legalize vandalism!

Repeal inhibition!

Help stamp in sex!

Stamp out reality!

Repeal the law of gravity!

Save our slums!

Help a nun kick the habit.

If at first you don't succeed . . . CHEAT!

Eggheads of the world unite! You have nothing to lose but your yokes.

Don't hate yourself in the morning—sleep till noon.

Earn cash in your spare time—blackmail your friends.

Hire the morally handicapped.

Start the day with a smile—and get it over with.

UP WITH MINISKIRTS!
DOWN WITH HOT PANTS!

To save face—keep lower half shut.

Visit your mother today. Maybe she hasn't had any problems lately.

Hire a freak today.

Give your child mental blocks for Christmas.

Alienation can be fun.

Asian flu for Asians only.

No arms for the Venus de Milo.

Birth-control pills are habit forming.

THINK DIRTY

Help get rid of the lunatic fringe—support your local barber.

Sibling rivalry is for kids.

Autopsy is a dying practice.

Unemployment helps stretch your coffee break.

THINK—maybe the Joneses are trying to keep up with *you!*

Take a cannibal to lunch.

Anarchists unite!

Identify your friends by their enemies.

Pray for obscene mail.

Nostalgia ain't what it used to be.

Sock it to me with apathy.

Fight poverty the American way—get a job.

Don't shoot—I don't want to be president.

I WAS BORN THIS WAY.
WHAT'S YOUR EXCUSE?

Conserve energy—make love more slowly.

Life, liberty, and the happiness of pursuit!

Be security conscious—because 80 percent of people are caused by accident.

Support your local police force—steal.

Enjoy a good laugh—go to work on a feather.

Only dirty people need to wash.

You're never alone with schizophrenia.

Clean earth smells funny.

Children—beat your mother while she is young.

WALLWISDOM—THE GREATEST

In one of the men's washrooms at the University of California at Los Angeles this message was seen:

Why do you wash these walls? Graffiti are a learning experience.

Underneath, the washroom attendant had added:

So is washing walls.

You can learn a lot from a wall and there is hardly any aspect of human endeavor that is not touched on by the graffitist's somewhat cynical philosophy:

There's more to life than meets the mind.

Why worry about tomorrow, when today is so far off?

When in doubt, worry.

Today is the first day of the rest of your life—celebrate now!

Reality is good sometimes for kicks, but don't let it get you down.

Nudists are people who wear one-button suits.

It's not the work that gets me down, it's the coffee breaks.

The difference between this company and a cactus plant is that the plant has pricks on the outside.

The best-laid plans of mice and men . . . are filed away somewhere.

We are the people our parents warned us about.

The world is going through a great big menopause.

You'll never be the man your mother was.

Earthquake predictors are faultfinders.

An elephant is a mouse drawn to government specifications.

Florists are just petal pushers.

An apple a day keeps the doctor away, but an onion a day keeps everyone away.

If you can keep your head when those about you are losing theirs, perhaps you've misunderstood the situation.

The world is your oyster, so EAT IT!

What has posterity ever done for me?

The meek shall inherit the earth—they're too weak to refuse.

Love thy neighbor—but don't get caught.

Reincarnation is a pleasant surprise.

Sudden prayers make God jump.

Old soldiers never die—just young ones.

Reality is a crutch.

Alimony is paying for something you don't get.

Even hypochondriacs can be ill.

Things are more like they used to be than they are now.

The happiest day is that day in the past that you always run back to when the present proves unbearable.

LOVE WALL

It is, of course, love that makes the world go round and the love-struck graffitist is nothing if not romantic.

Why does free love cost so much?

Put a little love into your sex life.

IF IT MOVES, FONDLE IT

Even dirty old men need love.

I love Steve.—Mary.

Tough Luck, Mary.—Steve.

Make haste! Make love!

Haste is passé and for amateurs.

Love is a many-gendered thing.

Girls, what do you do when you find your cat with another cat?

Let the cats be happy together and find a MAN.

King Kong taught me to love.

Can I have a date?

How about 1066?

This week I'm going with Bill but I like Jim.—Alice

This week I'm going with Jim but I like Bill.—Alice.

This week we are not going with Alice.—Bill and Jim.

STAR WALLS

If the true test of fame is to have a madman believe he's you, it's at least a sign of notoriety to have your name used in a piece of graffiti. If you want to be immortal, get yourself scrawled on a wall.

Lassie kills chickens.

SNOOPY HAS FLEAS

Isaac Newton counts on his fingers.

William Tell wore contact lenses.

Perry Mason bribes judges.

Batman loves Robin.

Pinocchio is a swinger.

Count Dracula, your Bloody Mary is ready.

Maria Montessori taut me to rite at age too.

SOCRATES EATS HEMLOCK

Oedipus was the first man to plug the generation gap.

Marshall McLuhan is print-orientated.

You think Oedipus had a problem—Adam was Eve's mother!

Hugh Hefner is a virgin.

Graffito was Mussolini's secretary of war.

Superman gets into Clark Kent's pants every morning.

LEDA LOVES SWANS

W. C. Fields is alive and drunk in Philadelphia.

Euclid was square.

Immanuel Kant but Kubla Khan.

Cinderella married for money.

ARCHDUKE FERDINAND FOUND ALIVE;
FIRST WORLD WAR A MISTAKE.

GROUP GRAFFITI

The best graffiti are the work of more than one mind. Someone once wrote on a wall, "I love grils." A pedant crossed out "grils" and substituted "girls." Next day another line was added: "What's wrong with us grils?"

To discover whether you have the makings of a great graffitist, here are ten lines for you to work on. Add an extra line of your own and then compare your version with the original. (See Answers.)

1 Olenka Bohachevsky lives!

2 Jesus lives!

3 Jesus saves. Moses invests.

4 It's me and you against the world.

5 Home rules for Wales.

6 Legalize mental telepathy.

7 Shakespeare eats Bacon.

8 Death is only a state of mind.

9 God isn't dead.

10 Is there intelligent life on earth?

H OG

The HOG that I've got in mind is neither a swine nor a glutton—he's a mnemonic who happens to be an acronym.

Mnemonics take their name from Mnemosyne, the goddess of memory. They are ways of helping you remember things. The first one that came into my life was SKILL. Designed to remind me of the excretory organs of the body (Skin, Kidneys, Intestines, Liver, Lungs), it is the only thing that my biology teacher taught me that I haven't forgotten. (Many things he failed to teach me I have since learned, but that's another story.)

Mnemonics don't have to be acronyms; they can be complete sentences. For the names of the zonal index fossils of part of the lower Carboniferous system (something some of us are constantly trying to bring to mind) this phrase is invaluable:

King Zog Caught Syphilis and Died

It reminds you immediately of Cleistopora, Zaphrentis, Caninia, Seminula, and Dibunophylum, which is just what you want. (I realize that Cleistopora beings with *c*, not *k*. Here, I am afraid, the geologist must make a leap of faith and when he sees *k* for the first time visualize *c* instead. In order to see *c* when he next sees *c* and not see *k* instead, he may need to make up a fresh mnemonic.)

For Ohm's law you have "Virgins Are Rare" (volts = amps × resistance), and to remember the order of nerves that pass through the superior orbital tissue in the skull (lacrimal, frontal, trochlear, lateral, nasociliary, internal, abducens) every medical student likes to remember that—

Lazy French Tarts Lie Naked In Anticipation

MEDICRONYMS

Evidently the medicos make the most use of mnemonics, and they use acronyms as well as phrases. Here are the most memorable—and alarming:

HOG	Hepatic Output of Glucose
SCUM	Secondary Carcinoma of the Upper Mediastinum
IMP	Idiopathic Myeloid Proliferation
DUMP	Diffuse Uncontrolled Monotal Peristalsis
PAL	Pyogenic Abscess of the Liver
CAD	Coronary Artery Disease
ALAS	Amino Levulose Acid Synthetase
RAPE	Right Atrial Pressure Elevation

ACROQUIZ

Everyone knows that JEEP is an acronym of sorts for General Purpose vehicle; can you supply the complete phrase that lies behind each of these familiar acronyms:

1	RADAR	6	PAKISTAN
2	LASER	7	WAVES
3	ZIP	8	TIP
4	SNAFU	9	SWAK
5	SCUBA	10	SWALBAKWS

(See Answers.)

INCOMPREHENSIBLE PROBLEM IN CHINESE?

Incomprehensible is an anagram of *problem in Chinese*. An anagram is a rearrangement of the letters in a word or phrase to form another word or phrase. It's the way in which you turn *scythe* into *chesty, roast mules* into *somersault*, and *voices rant on* into *conversation*.

ANAGREATEST

In prize-winning anagrams the ingenuity lies in changing a word into a word or phrase that is spectacularly apt. Here are ten examples where the anagram is closely related to the word:

desperation	a rope ends it
punishment	nine thumps

endearments	tender names
prosecutors	court posers
twinges	we sting
softheartedness	often sheds tears
therapeutics	apt is the cure
desegregation	Negroes get aid
degradedness	greed's sad end
panties	a step-in

The ingenuity is even greater when a whole phrase is turned into a different phrase with much the same meaning. Here are 18 of the best.

the United States of America	attaineth its cause: freedom!
a decimal point	I'm a dot in place
the countryside	no city dust here
the nudist colony	no untidy clothes
the detectives	detect thieves
a shoplifter	has to pilfer
astronomical observations	to scan a visible star or moon
one hug	enough?
the eyes	they see
the Mona Lisa	no hat, a smile
gold and silver	grand old evils
circumstantial evidence	can ruin a selected victim
medical consultations	noted miscalculations
one good turn deserves another	do rogues endorse that? no, never!
the state of North Carolina	hasten on to fair Charlotte!
Nova Scotia and Prince Edward Island	two Canadian provinces: lands I dread!
Washington crossing the Delaware	he saw his ragged continentals row
a sentence of death	faces one at the end

ANABAPTISM

The names of the great and famous sometimes make telling anagrams. *I ask me, has Will a peer?* and *we all make his praise* are two apt rearrangements of *William Shakespeare*. *Flit on, cheering angel!* was Lewis Carroll's anagram for *Florence Nightingale,* and unknown anagrammatists have concocted *truth searcher* out of *Chester Arthur, greatest born idealist* out of *Dante Gabriel Rossetti,* and the Latin *honor est a nilo* out of *Horatio Nelson.* From the names of four presidents you can create these memorable anagrams:

Grover Cleveland	govern, clever lad!
Theodore Roosevelt	hero told to oversee
President Franklin Delano Roosevelt	lo! real keen person voted first in land
Dwight D. Eisenhower	Wow! he's right indeed!

ANAQUIBBLE

We move from modern presidents to Protestant-Catholic strife of centuries ago with this remarkable—if not entirely comprehensible—example of the anagrammatist's art in which the same nine letters are served up in 14 different ways:

How much there is in a word—*monastery,* says I: why, that makes *nasty Rome;* and when I looked at it again, it was evidently *more nasty*—a very vile place *or mean sty.* Ay, *monster,* says I, you are found out. What monster? said the Pope. What monster? said I. Why, your own image there, *stone Mary.* That, he replied, is *my one star,* my Stella Maris, my treasure, my guide! No, said I, you should rather say, *my treason. Yet no arms,* said he. No, quoth I, quiet may suit best, as long as you have *no mastery,* I mean *money arts.* No, said he again, those are *Tory means;* and Dan, *my senator,* will baffle them. I don't know that, said I, but I think one might make no *mean story* out of this one word—*monastery.*

Anagrams as *ars magna,* without doubt.

ANTIGRAMS

Antigrams aren't negative weights or cables you send to your father's sister, but anagrams with a difference: the new word or words created out of the original word or words have the opposite instead of a similar meaning. Thus *real fun* is what you don't have at a *funeral* and *fluster* is far from *restful*. Here are 17 more of the best:

misfortune	it's more fun
Santa	satan
enormity	more tiny
infection	fine tonic
militarism	I limit arms
filled	ill-fed
violence	nice love
marital	martial
anarchists	arch-saints
commendation	aim to condemn
evangelists	evil's agents
discretion	is no credit
protectionism	nice to imports
a tragedy	rated gay
a picture of health	oft pale, I ache, hurt
Old Man Winter	warm, indolent
the man who laughs	he's glum, won't ha-ha

ANAGRAMMATICAL CHALLENGE

1. Devise appropriate one-word anagrams for each of these phrases:

our man earn it	made sure
sea term	unrealisms trap us
heat's throne	a stew, sir?

endless ambition	restore plush
sir, am I not pretense?	let's rush

2. Devise appropriate one-word antigrams for each of these phrases:

is it legal? no	considerate
united	real fun
restful	are advisers
flags? no, no	casual
tear no veils	care is noted

3. Can you recognize these states?

or can I fail?	work yen
lewd area	my, go win!
oil is nil	

4. And how about these musical instruments? You may not recognize them all, but they are genuine.

groan	impaint
instep	present
rubato	artist
integral	maraschino
broaden	

(See Answers.)

JUMBO

Nowadays a jumbo is a jet, but once he was an African elephant. The original Jumbo was the London Zoo's first African elephant (1865). In 1881 Phineas T. Barnum bought him (for £2,000) for his circus. Jumbo was a gigantic animal, 11½ feet in height, 6½ tons in weight, an accomplished performer and something of a star on both sides of the Atlantic. When he was struck by a train and killed on the night of September 15, 1885, the news of his death was reported around the world. His body is on view to this day—at Tufts University, Medford, Massachusetts—and his skeleton is in the Museum of Natural History in New York.

Jumbo was a legend in his own time. His name is still a household word, because he was an eponymist—one of that select band who have given their very names to the language.

Here are 30 familiar words. Each one derives from the name or nickname of a real man or woman. You'll know all the words, but how many full names of the people can you give?

amp	galvanize	pullman car
bloomer	grog	quisling
bowdlerize	guillotine	ritzy
bowie knife	hooligan	sandwich
boycott	macadam	saxophone
bunsen burner	martinet	shrapnel
chauvinist	maverick	sideburns
derrick	mesmerize	silhouette
diesel	namby-pamby	teddy bear
dunce	pasteurize	zeppelin

(See Answers.)

Kan't Spel

You're in good company if you kan't spel. Their our milions off educkated people hoo kant spel ether. If your inaccurate orthography is getting you down, cheer yourself up by reading—and attempting to interpret—the following sentences, all perpetrated by bona fide high-school or college graduates.

The Indians live very froogley.

My mother comes from Pencil vanea.

My home life is all mestup.

We live next store to the Walter Cronkites.

My admiration for you can be taken for granite.

This is the first perrigraff I have written on this subject, surprizing le enought.

The stewdress served cocktails.

He was a member of the notor republic.

I am feeling very angches about the outcome of the exam.

We don't care enough about nateral fenominum.

That's the way it supostube.

Whorship in the modern Church.

Although our societies are formed by man, he isn't able to flunksuate with it's pace.

As a catholic priest one spends most of his time teaching, praying, giving sermons, and absorbing sins given out by daily confessors.

The West's women's doubles team brought the team back from a four-game deficate.

CAN SPELL?

If you are one of those who is lucky enough to know that a *chester draws* is a piece of furniture and a *charitable* isn't (it's an adjective meaning *generous and kindly*), you may be ready for an orthographical challenge. Get a friend to dictate the following to you. If you can transcribe it faultlessly, you're a spelling wizard. Only five errors is exceptional, ten is excusable, 15 is average, 20 is below average, and 25 or more is poor.

The infectious proclivity for polysyllabic interchange of incomprehensible and occasionally irrefutable and unanswerable ratiocination, invective, and oftentimes laryngeal trivialities is a poltroonery that is permissible of the most censorious and punitive retaliation. To possess an aggrandized vocabulary is a mental endowment transcending the encyclopedical attributes of pedagogues who must investigate, peruse, and burrow for the scintillating segments of verisimilitude normally secreted from those whose knowledge is enchorial and whose verbiage is enclitic.

Exuberant and exultant propensities in phraseology continually lead to cerebral extradition for malefactors guilty of philological pyrotechnics. Perspicacious pundits scrupulously shun irreverent behaviorism and invariably take innocent refuge in the incontestable sanctuary of benign blandiloquence. Or by way of antithetical alternative, in mundane myopia.

Malicious malingerers in the realm of obsequious vacuity intermittently and agonizingly bewail the punctiliousness of those superlatively heirloomed with the gifts of psychic penetration. To their pettifogging mentalities any laboriously contrived device so minutely registering a mechanism as a micro-moto-scope would loom gargantuan by invidious comparison. To elucidate for the benefit of such individuals would parallel the espousal of eudaemonics by Italo-Ethiopian aesthetes. One unmitigated and undisputed contention is that philological parsimoniousness is particularly preferable to loquacious laxity, especially as demonstrated by evanescent nincompoops of the lower cerebral classification.

WHAT DID YOU SAY?

Taking dictation isn't always easy because sometimes what you hear isn't what you're supposed to hear. Oronyms are sentences that can be read in two ways with the same sound. To inspire you to cook up some oronyms of your own, here are a dozen of my favorites:

The stuffy nose can lead to problems.
The stuff he knows can lead to problems.

Where is the spice center?
Where is the spy center?

Are you aware of the words you have just uttered?
Are you aware of the words you have just stuttered?

That's the biggest hurdle I've ever seen!
That's the biggest turtle I've ever seen!

I'm taking a nice cold shower.
I'm taking an ice cold shower.

He would kill Hamlet for that reason.
He would kill Hamlet for that treason.

You'd be surprised to see a mint spy in your bank.
You'd be surprised to see a mince pie in your bank.

Some others I've seen . . .
Some mothers I've seen . . .

Reading in the library is sometimes allowed.
Reading in the library is sometimes aloud.

A politician's fate often hangs in a delegate balance.
A politician's fate often hangs in a delicate balance.

White shoes: the trademark of Pat Boone.
Why choose the trademark of Pat Boone?

The secretariat's sphere of competence.
The secretariat's fear of competence.

LONG LIVE THE LIPOGRAM

Any list of leading lipogrammarians has got to include Tryphiodorus, Peter de Riga, Lope de Vega, and Ernest Vincent Wright, A. Ross Eckler, and yours truly. We are famous—or not famous, depending on whether or not you happen to have heard of us—for our lipograms, which are not insulting cables but great works of literature from which we have chosen to omit certain letters of the alphabet. Call us eccentric if you like; you cannot deny our dedication.

Tryphiodorus was a poet who wrote an epic poem about the adventures of Ulysses, from each of the 24 books of which he excluded a different letter of the Greek alphabet. Peter de Riga, a canon of Rheims Cathedral in France, rewrote the entire Bible, omitting a varying letter from each chapter. Lope de Vega, Spain's first great dramatist and a tragic figure even by 16th-century standards (the death of two wives, the blindness and madness of his last mistress, the death of two sons, and the abduction of a daughter under royal protection), but he found time to write 1,800 plays—plus five novels excluding the five vowels *a, e, i, o,* and *u* in turn. Less tragic but equally lipogrammatical was Ernest Vincent Wright, whose 50,000-word novel *Gadsby* was published in 1939. Dedicated "to Youth" and intended as "a valuable aid to schoolchildren in English composition," it was written, according to the author's introduction, "with the *e* type-bar of the typewriter *tied down!*"

A. Ross Eckler is a contemporary lipogrammarian whose masterwork is the re-creation of the much-loved nursery rhyme "Mary Had a Little Lamb," minus certain letters of the alphabet. Let me remind you of the original verse:

Mary had a little lamb,
  Its fleece was white as snow,
And everywhere that Mary went
  The lamb was sure to go;
He followed her to school one day,
  That was against the rule;
It made the children laugh and play
  To see a lamb in school.

Here is Mr. Eckler's version of the verse minus the letter *s:*

Mary had a little lamb,
  With fleece a pale white hue,
And everywhere that Mary went
  The lamb kept her in view;
To academe he went with her,
  Illegal, and quite rare;
It made the children laugh and play
  To view a lamb in there.

And here is how he does it without any *a*'s:

Polly owned one little sheep,
  Its fleece shone white like snow,
Every region where Polly went
  The sheep did surely go;
He followed her to school one time,
  Which broke the rigid rule;
The children frolicked in their room
  To see the sheep in school.

Here are the first lines of the same verse minus all *h*'s, all *t*'s, and all *e*'s. See if you can complete the rhymed verses avoiding the forbidden letter in each case.

No *h*'s:

Mary owned a little lamb . . .

No *t*'s:

Mary had a pygmy lamb . . .

No *e*'s:

Mary had a tiny lamb . . .

Finally, have a go at rewriting the verse using just half the letters of the alphabet: *a, c, d, e, h, i, l, m, n, p, r, s,* and *t.* Here's the first line:

Maria had a little sheep . . .

To compare your versions with Mr. Eckler's, see the Answers. And when you feel you've exhausted the possibilities of "Mary Had a Little Lamb," you can move on to "Little Jack Horner" and "The Star-Spangled Banner."

A. Ross Eckler lipogrammatizes nursery rhymes. I do the same for Shakespeare. Just as the famous Dr. Bowdler sought to improve the works of Shakespeare by cutting out or altering all indelicacies (turning "bed" into "bridal chariot," for example), I seek to improve his plays by dropping a different letter from each one. I began with *Hamlet*, from which I scrupulously excluded the letter *i*. Here's how the most famous of all soliloquies turned out:

To be, or not to be; that's the query:
Whether you would be nobler to suffer mentally
The stones and arrows of outrageous fortune,
Or to take arms to oppose a sea of troubles,
And through combat end them? To pass on, to sleep;
No more . . .

And so it goes on for five whole acts until Hamlet expires uttering the deathless line:

The rest be hush-hush.

From *Macbeth* I dropped *a* and *e*. Here is the hero (McB'th) having one of his hallucinations:

> Is it thy tiny sword in front I'm glimpsing,
> With its blunt bit pointing to my wrist? I wish to touch it:
> I find I'm no good doing it, but I spy it still . . .

From the whole of *Twelfth Night* I excluded *l*, the twelfth letter from the beginning of the alphabet, and *o*, the twelfth letter from the end of the alphabet. In my version of the play, Orsino launches the proceedings with these lyrical lines:

> If music be desire's sustenance, make music yet;
> Give me excessive music, that, surfeiting,
> The appetite may sicken, and thus die . . .

Currently I'm working on *Othello* without the *o*'s. It isn't easy, but what is art without suffering?

Murder!

Verbicide

Back in 1858 Oliver Wendell Holmes coined the word *verbicide*. He used it to describe the "violent treatment of a word with fatal results to its legitimate meaning, which is its life."

Over a century later it seems that murdering words is even more popular than murdering people. The modern victims of verbicide tend to be everyday words that get battered to death by thoughtless or excessive use. The most obvious victims are superwords like these ten:

super	*nice*	*terrific*
great	*fabulous*	*weird*
fantastic	*stupendous*	*wonderful*
awful		

Apart from *nice*—which used to mean *precise*—the words have not changed to another category of meaning, but we use them so indiscriminately that they have lost their cutting edge. There is no feeling of awe or terror or wonder in *awful* and *terrible* and *wonderful* anymore. And it's a long time since *fantastic* and *fabulous* conjured up the magical worlds of fantasy and fable.

SUPERCIDE

Verbicide is a way of life in the entertainment industry. We've all heard failures described as "hits" and moderate successes as "smasheroos." We take it for granted that "the special guest star" is neither special nor a star. He may appear almost every week, too. When Sam Goldwyn was asked how business was, he replied as only a king of the movies could: "Colossal, but it's improving." When the remake of *King Kong* was screened in 1976 it was billed as "the most original motion picture of all time."

There are many adjectives that are uncomparable, absolute, and unmodifiable—*complete, contemporary, everlasting, indestructible, meaningless, omnipotent, perfect, supreme* are eight—but that doesn't stop people from trying to modify them, describing this cookbook as more complete than last year's, this play as more contemporary than last month's, this taste as more perfectly perfect than last minute's. Publishers, ironically, are particularly prone to verbicide—even the publishers of great books like this one.

To prove the point, here is the Bantam Blurb Generator. Take one word from each of the three colums and it should give you an apt phrase to describe any novel of your choice:

COLUMN 1	COLUMN 2	COLUMN 3
A tempestuous	magnificent	best-seller
An emotional	terrifying	best-seller
A captivating	outrageous	best-seller
An extraordinary	scorching	best-seller
A sensational	celebrated	best-seller
A phenomenal	intriguing	best-seller

A brilliant	spine-tingling	best-seller
A shattering	electrifying	best-seller
A provocative	indispensable	best-seller
A controversial	compelling	best-seller
A spellbinding	illustrious	best-seller
A riveting	towering	best-seller
A bittersweet	distinguished	best-seller
A blazing	scathing	best-seller
A breathtaking	devastating	best-seller
A shocking	explosive	best-seller
A savage	stormy	best-seller
A beloved	bizarre	best-seller
A monumental	astounding	best-seller
A beguiling	forbidden	best-seller
A defiant	bewitching	best-seller
A scintillating	blockbusting	best-seller
A mighty	inspirational	best-seller
A heart-stopping	searing	best-seller
A triumphant	stunning	best-seller

It's a joke, of course—or is it? Here are ten mind-blowing phrases taken from the covers of ten Bantam books. (I won't name the actual titles, out of fellow feeling for the authors.)

TEN TOP SUPERBLURBS

A HIGH-OCTANE INFERNO RAGING TOWARD A TERRIFYING CLIMAX ON THE CANADIAN COAST

A novel of conflicting passions and impossible love.

A sweeping novel of three recklessly passionate women and three generations spawned in the wealth, lust, and betrayals of bloomtown Texas.

A TUMULTUOUS NOVEL AFLAME WITH SCORCHING PASSIONS AND ALL-CONQUERING LOVE

A gripping, shock-wave novel of total suspense, horror—and surprise.

A sweeping, tumultuous love story, a passionate, inevitable romance.

Ablaze with romantic adventure, teeming with passion—the tempestuous novel of the woman who gambled her life on an impossible love.

AN EXPLOSION OF EXOTIC SEX, SUDDEN DEATH, AND RUTHLESS INTRIGUE

From the glittering courts of the Czar to the savage outposts of his Empire—a romance ablaze with tempestuous love.

A SCORCHING EPIC THAT WILL INTRIGUE, TERRIFY, AND GRIP YOU AS IT SOARS TOWARD ITS SHOCKING CLIMAX

SIMILICIDE

String a few victims of verbicide together and you get a cliché. So what's wrong with a cliché? Many clichés express thoughts economically and imaginatively—or rather, they did years ago, when they were new-minted. "He's at death's door," "don't beat about the bush," "the long arm of coincidence," were once fresh and telling phrases. But they have become clichés, and much as we might like to "put the clock back," it isn't possible. Instead of relying on dead-beat clichés, we could and should be devising new turns of phrase of our own. It isn't easy. I have a friend who was determined to think of a fresh way of expressing the notion contained in the cliché "the tip of the iceberg." After two days of solid head scratching, the best he could come up with was "the snout of the crocodile." Can you do any better? The tongue of the adder? The icing on the cake? The first pitch of the ballgame?

Take a look at these ten tired similes. Can you breathe new life into any of them?

bold as brass   poor as a church mouse

drunk as a lord   cool as a cucumber

obstinate as a mule   as dead as a dodo
as honest as the day is long   free as air
as right as rain   as clean as a whistle

YOU DECIDE

The -*cide* part of *verbicide, homicide,* and *suicide* comes from the Latin *caedere,* to kill. Here are ten murderous words. For how many of them can you supply a definition?

avicide   *senicide*

felicide   *uxoricide*

liberticide   *vaticide*

menticide   *matricide*

ovicide   *genocide*

(See Answers.)

NOSTALGIA ISN'T WHAT IT USED TO BE

FROM A NEW YORK CRITICAL WEEKLY

Robert Graves, the British veteran, is no longer in the poetic swim. He still resorts to traditional meters and rhyme, and to such outdated words as *tilth*; he withholds his 100 percent approbation from contemporary poems that crudely describe sexual acts.

FROM ROBERT GRAVES

Gone are the drab monosyllabic days
When "agricultural labor" still was *tilth*;
And "100 percent approbation," *praise*;
And "pornographic modernism," *filth*—
Yet still I stand by *tilth* and *filth* and *praise*.

FROM ACCLUMSID TO ZUCHE

Some of the oldest words in the language are some of the most delightful, but unless we happen to be Robert Graves we don't use them much—not because we don't want to, but simply because we're not familiar with them. Here, with definitions and a guide to pronunciation where appropriate, are 50 of my favorite lost words. Unless you're a hoddypeak you'll glop them down with adulbescence.

acclumsid	Numbed, paralyzed, clumsy. From the Old English *clumsen,* "to be stiff, numb."
acersecomic	One whose hair has never been cut. From the Greek.
adlubescence	Pleasure, delight. (Accent on *bes.*)
agathokakological	With a mingling of good and evil. (Accent on *log.*)
agruw	Horrify, cause shuddering. (Accent on *gruw.*)
ataballes	Kettledrums.
barlafumble	Call for a truce by a person who has fallen in play or wrestling; request for time out.
bawdreaing	Bawdy misbehavior.
beek	Bask in the sun or before a fire.
bellibone	Lovely maiden, pretty lass. (An anglicization of the French *belle et bonne,* "fair and good.")
bronstrops	Prostitute.
brool	Low, deep humming; a murmur.
croodle	Creep close; a faint humming, the low music of birds.
dilling	Child born when the parents are old; possibly a corruption of *darling, dilling-pig,* the weakling in a litter.
eldnyng	Jealousy, suspicion.
fadoodle	Nonsense, something foolish.

flap dragon	Sport of catching raisins in bowls of flaming brandy or drinking the brandy without getting burned as a tribute to one's mistress.
flosh	Swamp or stagnant pool overgrown with weeds.
glop	Swallow greedily; stare at in wonder or alarm.
gundygut	Glutton.
gwenders	Disagreeable tingling from the cold.
hoddypeak	Simpleton, blockhead.
killbuck	Fierce-looking fellow.
lennow	Flabby, limp.
lovedrury	Keepsake, love token.
magsman	Swindler.
malshave	Caterpillar.
nyle	Fog, mist.
okselle	Armpit.
pingle	Eat with little appetite.
poop-noddy	Fool or simpleton; the game of love.
popolly	Little darling (from the French *poupelet*); a female favorite, special loved one, or mistress.
porknell	One as fat as a pig.
quetch	Moan and twitch in pain, shake.
quop	Throb, palpitate.
ribble	Wrinkle, furrow.
ringo	Treat; a sweet made from the candied root of the sea holly, supposed to be an aphrodisiac.
spuddle	Assume airs of importance without reason; make trifles seem important.
squiddle	Waste time with idle talk.
turngiddy	Dizzy.
ug	Fear, dread.

vellication	Twitching or convulsive movement.
wallydraigle	Worthless, slovenly woman.
wheeple	Ineffectual attempt of a man to whistle loudly. An onomatopoetic term, from the low cheep of a bird.
widdershins	Unlucky, prone to misfortune.
wurp	Stone's throw; glance of the eye.
xenodochial	Hospitable to strangers.
yurky	Itchy. (Pronounced *yooky*.)
zuche	Tree stump.

FROM FLIPEROUS SUSAN

Susan Kelz Sperling not only collects lost words but uses them all the time—and it's only when you use them that you begin to realize what you've been missing. Here's her poem "Biting the Ong-Tongue":

If you hear, in a *brangling mung,*
You're the butt of a *winxing ong-tongue.*
    Lunge for her *felly,*
    Aim for mouth or for belly
Till you've an *assything* wrung.

ong-tongue	Tattle-tale.
brangling	Noisy, wrangling.
mung	A crowd of people; also chicken feed. Both definitions have to do with mixing together disparate elements.
winxing	Braying.
felly	Harshly.
assything	Compensation for an offense.

And here is one of the delicious round games that Ms. Sperling plays with her rich vocabulary of words gone-but-not-forgotten: A Round of Hum.

What is *hum*?

Hum is strong liquor made by combining ale or beer with spirits. Too much hum can make one's head *quop*.

What is *quop*?

Quop means to throb. A man's heart may quop with longing to hold his loved one's *feat*.

What is *feat*?

A feat is a dangling curl of hair. A *woup* with the feat of an elephant inside is considered lucky to wear.

What is a *woup*?

A woup is a simple metal hoop or ring not set with stones. Large woups to anchor one's feet could have been used at the base of a *gofe*.

What is a *gofe*?

A gofe is the pillory that was usually erected on the *wong,* where the greatest number of people could stroll by and see it.

What is a *wong*?

A wong is the meadowland that people used as their commons, where they would meet or take their cows to graze. Nowadays a public wong is covered with *nesh* plantings and lush trees.

What is *nesh*?

Nesh means fresh, delicate, or soft, as vegetables, foliage, or fruit should be. Braiding one's hair with nesh flowers makes a beautiful *kell*.

What is a *kell*?

A kell is a woman's headdress, be it as close set as a net or a cap or as fancy as a wig to don for a party. A lady's kell is more elaborate if she is going to a ball where *hum* is served.

ENDANGERED WORDS

Some of our oldest, finest words are gone for good. Others are with us still—but sorely neglected. Here are 25 splendid words that are in danger of disappearing.

You score a point for every word you recognize. If you score 5 that isn't bad, 10 is impressive, and if you score 15 or more you're either Susan Sperling or you cheated by looking at the Answers.

1 A *biggonet* is (a) a primitive form of bra (b) a form of female dress (c) a type of automatic rifle (d) a divorced bigamist.

2 A *cracknel* is (a) a head injury (b) a 17th-century epithet applied to a prostitute (c) a crayfish (d) a biscuit.

3 A *dziggetai* is (a) a Mongolian mule (b) an Egyptian mummy (c) an Indian spirit (d) a Greek coin.

4 *Epistaxis* is (a) a fleet of large taxis (b) a letter demanding money with menaces (c) bleeding from the nose (d) an evergreen shrub.

5 A *factotum* is (a) an unreliable piece of information (b) a pagan symbol (c) an intestinal complaint caused by excessive eating (d) a servant.

6 A *grackle* is (a) a bird (b) a rope (c) a tree (d) the noise made by feet walking on gravel.

7 A *heder* is (a) a male sheep (b) a female snail (c) an executioner (d) a kind of acid.

8 *Imparidigitate* is (a) having a disease which makes it impossible to stay still (b) suffering from the aftereffects of syphilis (c) being able to speak five or more foreign languages (d) having an odd number of fingers or toes on each limb.

9 *Jargonelle* is (a) slang used by women (b) a kind of pear (c) a primitive form of trumpet (d) a pewter drinking vessel.

10 *To kittle* is (a) to tickle (b) to burn wood (c) to tell lies (d) to make saddles.

11 A *lachrymist* is (a) someone who turns metal into gold (b) someone who collects precious stones (c) someone who weeps (d) a pearl diver.

12 *Mulierosity* is (a) being fond of women (b) being

simpleminded (c) being generous with other people's money
(d) talking very fast while remaining comprehensible.

13 A *nympholept* is (a) someone who can't resist young girls
(b) a young girl with an insatiable appetite for sex (c) a species of sea spider (d) someone who has wild and unattainable
ideals.

14 An *ogdoad* is (a) a species of frog (b) a Roman altar (c) a
series of eight of a kind (d) a poem dedicated to the ancient
gods.

15 A *pennon* is (a) a small flag (b) a writing implement (c)
a vegetable (d) a bone in the foot.

16 A *quat* is (a) a liquid measure (b) a small boil (c) a flat-
bottomed boat (d) a bat that is *not* nocturnal.

17 A *kosarian* is (a) someone who grows roses (b) a craftsman
specializing in wood carving (c) a biblical scholar (d) a
member of the Confraternity of the Rosary.

18 A *sapodilla* is (a) a South American insect (b) a large
evergreen tree (c) an intoxicating drink made from red berries
(d) the punctuation mark added to a c to make it soft.

19 A *tirrit* is (a) a small ferret (b) a fit of temper (c) a false
mustache (d) an unkind epithet for a girl of easy virtue.

20 A *uvarovite* is (a) a nomadic tribesman (b) a kind of long-
lasting glue or adhesive (c) a medieval court jester (d) an
emerald-green garnet.

21 *Venenose* refers to (a) something poisonous (b) a claret
wine in perfect condition (c) a fabric (d) a disgusting smell.

22 A *whim-wham* is (a) a tent for Red Indians (b) a trinket
or trifle (c) a drink made with eggs, milk, and brandy (d) a
spell uttered by a white witch.

23 A *xyster* is (a) a female relative by marriage (b) a plant
with leaves that sting (c) an instrument for scraping bones (d)
part of a ship's rudder.

24 A *yex* is (a) an armadillo (b) a pincushion (c)
approximately seven miles (d) a hiccup.

25 A *zopilote* is (a) a camel herdsman (b) the middle tier of
a trireme (c) the transparent cell wall of the mammalian ovum
(d) a vulture.

OAT CUISINE

Oat cuisine is what a Scotsman calls porridge—if he's an inveterate punster, as most truly civilized people are. I love puns and I'm fascinated by the paradox that lies behind them: the worse they are the better they are.

Puns come in all shapes and sizes. There are short, sharp ones—

> Puberty is a hair-raising experience.

—and long leaden ones:

> There were once three Indian squaws. One sat on a leopard skin. One sat on a doe skin. The third sat on a hippopotamus skin. The squaw on the leopard skin had one son. The squaw on the deer skin had twin sons. This, of course, proves that the squaw on the hippopotamus is equal to the sons of the squaws on the other two hides.

There are drunken puns:

> Absinthe makes the tart grow fonder.

And exceedingly drunken ones:

> Orange juice sorry you made me cry? Don't be soda pressed; them martini bruises.

There are puns that get to the heart of the matter:

> Better to have loved a short girl, than never to have loved a tall.

And puns that definitely don't:

> What a friend we have in cheeses.

There are very clever puns, like this one from Richard Hughes's 1938 novel *In Hazard*:

> Presently she told Dick she had a cat so smart that it first ate cheese and then breathed down the mouseholes—with baited breath—to entice the creatures out.

And not-so-clever ones:

> "Waiter, this coffee tastes like mud."
> "Well, it was only ground this morning."

> "And the eggs taste disgusting."
> "Don't blame me, I only laid the table."

Many literary giants of the past have been master punsters. Shakespeare reveled in puns. ("Ask for me tomorrow," says Mercutio as he is about to die, "and you shall find me a grave man.") Another playwright, Richard Brinsley Sheridan, punned his way into this compliment, addressed to the adorable Miss Payne:

> 'Tis true I am ill; but I cannot complain,
> For he never knew pleasure who never knew Payne.

Hilaire Belloc wrote his own punning epitaph:

> When I am dead, I hope it may be said:
> "His sins were scarlet, but his books were read."

And how Ernest Hemingway would have loved the headline that announced his death:

PAPA PASSES

Jesus was a punster. *Petros* is Greek for "rock," after all, so when Jesus declared that Peter was to be the rock on which the church would be built, the play on words must have been intentional.

The great create puns. They also inspire them. Here is Franklin P. Adams on Christopher Columbus:

> Oh, I should like to see Columbus's birthplace,
> And then I'd write a fine, authentic poem,
> And critics, none of whom would read it through,
> Would say, "At least we have the Genoan article."

Of all the dreadfully good and wonderfully bad puns I have come across, my favorite is the payoff in Bennett Cerf's story about the private detective hired to unearth a missing person named Rhee who used to work for *Life* magazine in New York. Eventually the detective ran his man to ground and exclaimed:

"Ah, sweet Mr. Rhee of *Life*, at last I've found you." It could hardly be better. Or worse.

SUPERPUNS

The world's greatest punster is Alan F. G. Lewis. Creating puns is his life's work—"The pun is mightier than the sword" is his family motto, *A Pun My Soul* the title of his autobiography—and of the thousands that have poured out of him here are my top 20:

> I told her no sensible man would take her dancing in her bikini, so she went with a little moron.
>
> Back-seat driving is a form of duel control.
>
> Goblin your food is bad for your elf.
>
> Bambi could never have been a mother if her hart hadn't been in the right place.
>
> I'll be with you—
> in two sex, said the hermaphrodite
> in half a tick, said the vivisectionist

in two shakes, said the freemason
in half a mho, said the electrician
in a trice, said the Third Man
in necks to no time, said the executioner
in a flash, said the magician
in an instant, said the marketing man
in a twinkling, eye said.

When a liar gets pharyngitis he loses his vice.

A white lie is aversion of the truth.

Is a group of trainee secret service agents aspiring?

When the witch said Abradacabra, nothing happened. She's a
hopeless speller.

Baldness is a kind of failure. Wish I'd made the grayed.

If a man asks a woman to help him with a crowbar, it's because
he can't lever alone.

Soupçon is French for a small amount, only morceau.

Chalet or shanty? It's a decision he should dwell on.

He's a theater buff with a tendency to fawn.

If his new secretary isn't sweet in the daytime and a little tart
at night, he'll saccharin the morning.

Schnapps and hock are my favorite Teutonics.

A true adman writes the prose and cons.

She told me he was just a traveling companion, but I sensed
arrival.

Why piccolo profession like music that's full of viol practices,
confirmed lyres, old fiddles, and bass desires?
For the lute, of course.

The Moses film project was abandoned after they'd seen the rushes.

PICK A PUN

The pun's missing from each of these sentences. Can you supply it? (If you can't, see Answers.)

1 In a church, it's an accepted custom never to talk above a _____.

2 A married man who wants to conceal his drunken infidelities can easily wake up in the morning wondering who he's _____ next to.

3 Two cheerleaders ended up at the altar. They met by _____.

4 You can see by her light touch that she has a _____ for the piano.

5 "Shall we have salad?"
   "Yes, _____."

6 Some thought Edgar Allan Poe was a _____ lunatic.

7 Bad news about the two lighthouse keepers—their marriage is on the _____.

8 When the fencing team tried to wrap up the tournament, they kept getting _____.

9 In Chicago, every prospect _____.

10 There once was a _____ about a girl named Pearl who was so _____-headed, she didn't have anything to _____.

Eye fink that's snuff, don't ewe?

PORTMANTEAUS AND TELESCOPES

Portmanteaus and telescopes, as well as being suitcases and optical instruments, are useful ways of creating new words.

PORTMANTEAUS DE LUXE

Lewis Carroll adapted the word *portmanteau* to describe a word created by packing two other words together. *Galumph* was one of his most famous portmanteaus: he got it by combining gallop and triumph.

Of more modern portmanteaus, these are my prizners.* The first ten are well established; the second ten are newcomers.

> *anecdotard*   *anecdote + dotard*, a dotard given to telling anecdotes (1894).

*Prize + winners, a portmanteau designed to capture your attention.

botel	*boat + hotel*
brunch	*breakfast + lunch* (1896)
cheeseburger	*cheese + hamburger* (1938)
citrange	*citrus + orange,* a hybrid fruit
liger	*lion + tiger,* the offspring of a lion and a tigress
macon	*mutton + bacon,* mutton salted and smoked like bacon (Second World War)
mocamp	*motor + camp,* an area providing parking and camping facilities
moondoggle	*moon + boondoggle,* a trivial undertaking, wasteful expenditure
motel	*motor + hotel* (1925)
beautility	*beauty + utility*
dat	*dog + cat,* a crossbreed hoax
Demopublican	*Democrat + Republican,* another crossbreed, though no hoax
diplonomics	*diplomacy + economics,* use of economic power for diplomatic ends
frarority	*fraternity + sorority,* a college social organization that admits both sexes
gasid indigestion	*gas + acid indigestion,* a minor medical complaint which, if television advertisements are to be believed, afflicts most of the population
glommentary	*glossary + commentary,* such as the present remarks
ninny	*nickel + penny,* a proposed 2½-cent coin
pickel	*penny + nickel,* the same; according to Mr. Bert Casper of White Bear Lake, Minnesota, who proposed the terms, the second commemorates the present economic situation, and the first those who are responsible for it
slumpflation	*slump + inflation,* the economic situation itself

TELESCOPES

Some people don't call portmanteaus "portmanteaus" they call them "telescopes" instead. To keep them happy, here are ten telescopes that have gained currency and at least one admirer (me) in the past ten years:

adflation	*advertising inflation,* the high cost of ads
administrivia	*administrative trivia,* what most administrators do most of the time
bitini	*bitsy bikini*
ecotecture	*ecological architecture,* as practiced by those who build their own houses
feminar	*feminine seminar,* a meeting for women
femsymp	*feminine movement sympathizer,* by analogy with *comsymp*
flextime	*flexible time,* an arrangement that permits workers to set their own schedules
medevac	*medical evacuation,* as from a battlefield or a rock concert
vodkatini	*vodka martini*

JUMBLES

Jumbles are the portmanteaus and telescopes devised by people who don't like calling them portmanteaus and telescopes. Here are 15 of the best:

bibulography	Biography of a bibulous person.
Californication	Unplanned and uncontrolled development of a region, like the way California has been fornicated up.
hashaholic	One addicted to hashish as an alcoholic is to alcohol.
hymnenanny	Religiously oriented hootennanny.

imagineer	Engineer who receives an award for imaginative ideas.
McGovernment	Governmental politics advocated by George McGovern.
Nixnik	Member of the White House staff under Richard Nixon.
Nova Scotiable	Sociable, in a manner characteristic of Nova Scotia.
plotboiler	Literary work with a trite, improbable plot.
pornicator	Producer, performer, or purveyor of vicarious libidinous stimulation.
rumortism	Chronic inflammation of the body politic.
sextrovert	One in no need of the services of a pornicator.
tripewriter	Typewriter used exclusively for political speeches.
watergaffe	Bungled effort to cover up.
wordsical	Theatrical performance that blends music with the recitation of Ogden Nash's verse.

CARRY YOUR OWN PORTMANTEAU

Devising your own portmanteaus, telescopes and jumbles calls for skill and ingenuity. To get into training, take these 50 words, jumble them, telescope them and turn them into 25 recognizable portmanteaus.

Take one group of words at a time and try to combine the words on the left with the words on the right. Gluck!

Group 1:	free	accident
	gawky	artistic
	grand	awkward
	happen	dandy
	heart	ride

Group 2:	identify	flimsy
	jumble	indicate
	limp	mix
	number	numeral
	oblivion	obliteration
Group 3:	preview	aristocratic
	prompt	crumble
	prance	musical
	ritzy	flounce
	squeeze	punctual
Group 4:	squash	amateur
	sham	blizzard
	sizzle	crush
	screachy	slippery
	slick	creaky
Group 5:	slice	crunch
	squeeze	privation
	starvation	replace
	stuffy	slash
	supercede	suffocation

(To see one way of combining the words, see Answers.)

QUEUE IN LINE

"The English have really everything in common with the Americans, except, of course, language," said Oscar Wilde when he heard that audiences in New York weren't *queuing* to see his plays: they were *standing in line* at the box office.

There are scores of English words about which the British and the Americans don't seem to agree. Here are 30 which may make perfect sense to you, but which only a transatlantic Londoner would understand.

What would a Britisher call each of these words?

1 *apartment*	7 *closet*
2 *backup lights*	8 *cream of wheat*
3 *band-aid*	9 *elevator*
4 *bathrobe*	10 *faucet*
5 *bill*	11 *flashlight*
6 *checkers*	12 *hamburger meat*

13 *lima bean*	20 *sidewalk*
14 *molasses*	21 *spool*
15 *nightstick*	22 *thumbtack*
16 *odometer*	23 *tick-tack-toe*
17 *panty hose*	24 *vest*
18 *private school*	25 *zucchini*
19 *raisin*	(See Answers.)

BRITISH SPOKEN HERE

Being very British and fairly friendly—or fairly British and very friendly, depending on the mood you catch me in—when we meet I want you to understand me. That's why I'm offering you this concise Anglo-American Dictionary. With the 25 pairs above, it includes all the everyday British words an American might misunderstand, and when you come to spend a *fortnight's holiday* with us in the *autumn* I *trust* you'll find it useful—if you know what I mean.

Bon voyage!

BRITISH	AMERICAN
alsatian	*German shepherd/police dog*
anorak	*parka*
articulated lorry	*trailer truck*
bank holiday	*legal holiday*
bap	*hamburger bun*
bat (ping-pong)	*paddle*
bath, n.	*bathtub*
bath, v.	*bathe*
bespoke (made to measure)	*custom-made*
big dipper	*roller coaster*
bill (restaurant)	*check*

BRITISH	AMERICAN
billion = million million	*billion* = thousand million
biscuit (sweet)	*cookie*
biscuit (unsweetened)	*cracker*
black or white? (milk/cream in coffee)	*with or without?*
blackleg	*scab*
block of flats	*apartment house/building*
bomb (success)	*bomb* (disaster)
bonnet (car)	*hood*
book, v.	*make reservation*
boot (car)	*trunk/rear deck*
bootlace	*shoelace*
bottom drawer	*hope chest*
bowler/hard hat	*derby*
box room	*lumber room*
braces	*suspenders*
break (school)	*recess*
bridge roll	*hotdog roll*
candy floss	*cotton candy*
caravan	*trailer*
caretaker/porter	*janitor*
catapult	*slingshot*
cattle grid	*Texas gate*
centre (city/business)	*downtown*
centre reservation	*median strip/divider*
chemist's shop	*drugstore*
chickory	*endive*
chips	*french fries*
cinema	*movie house/theater*
class/form (school)	*grade*
cloakroom	*checkroom*
clothes peg	*clothespin*
collar stiffener	*collar stay*

BRITISH	AMERICAN
collar stud	collar button
conscription	draft
convoy	caravan
cooker	stove
corn flour	cornstarch
cot	crib
cotton	thread
cotton wool	absorbent cotton
cow gum	rubber cement
cream cracker	soda cracker
crisps	potato chips
cul-de-sac	dead end
diamanté	rhinestone
directory enquiries	information/directory assistance
district	precinct
diversion	detour
drain (indoors)	sewer pipe/soil pipe
draper	dry-goods store
draught excluder	weather stripping
dual carriageway	divided highway
dummy	pacifier
dungarees	overalls
dynamo	generator
earth wire/earth	ground wire
eiderdown	comforter
endive	chicory
estate agent	real estate agent
estate car	station wagon
face flannel	washcloth
fair (fun)	carnival
first floor	second floor
fish slice	spatula/turner

BRITISH	AMERICAN
fitted (carpet)	*wall-to-wall*
flex	*electric cord*
fly-over	*overpass*
football	*soccer*
fortnight	*two weeks*
foyer	*lobby*
full stop	*period*
gallery (theater)	*balcony*
gangway	*aisle*
gaol	*jail*
garden	*yard*
gear lever	*gearshift*
geyser (gas)	*water heater*
goods truck (railway)	*freight car*
green fingers	*green thumb*
guard (railway)	*conductor*
haberdashery	*notions*
hair grip/kirby grip	*bobby pin*
hair slide	*barrette*
hardware	*housewares*
hire purchase	*time payment/installment plan*
holiday	*vacation*
homely = pleasant	*homely* = ugly
hoover, n.	*vacuum cleaner*
hoover, v.	*vacuum*
ice/sorbet	*sherbet*
iced lolly	*popsicle*
icing sugar	*confectioners' sugar*
identification parade	*lineup*
immersion heater (electric)	*water heater*
interval	*intermission*
ironmonger	*hardware store*
jab (injection)	*shot*

BRITISH	AMERICAN
joint (meat)	*roast*
jug	*pitcher*
jumper	*sweater*
kiosk (telephone)	*booth*
knock up (from sleep)	*call*
knock up (tennis)	*warm up*
label	*tag*
larder	*pantry*
lavatory/WC	*john/bathroom*
lay-by	*pull-off*
leader (in newspaper)	*editorial*
leader (first violin in orchestra)	*concertmaster*
left luggage office	*baggage room*
let	*lease/rent*
level crossing (railway)	*grade crossing*
limited (company)	*incorporated*
liver sausage	*liverwurst*
lorry	*truck*
lost property	*lost and found*
lounge suit	*business suit*
mackintosh	*raincoat*
marrow	*squash*
methylated spirits	*denatured alcohol*
mincer	*meat grinder*
motorway	*freeway/thruway*
nappy	*diaper*
neat (drink)	*straight*
net curtains	*sheers/underdrapes*
newsagent	*news dealer*
nought	*zero*
number plate	*license plate*
off licence	*liquor store*
oven cloth	*pot holder*

BRITISH	AMERICAN
overtake (vehicle)	*pass*
packed lunch	*sack lunch*
pantechnicon	*moving van*
pants (underwear)	*shorts*
paraffin	*kerosene*
pelmet	*valance*
personal call	*person-to-person*
petrol	*gas*
pillar box	*mailbox*
plus-fours	*knickers*
point/power point	*outlet/socket*
post	*mail*
postal code	*zip code*
postponement	*rain check*
press studs	*snaps*
public convenience	*restroom*
pudding	*dessert*
pushchair	*stroller*
put down/entered (goods bought)	*charged*
put through (telephone)	*connect*
quay	*wharf/pier*
queue, n.	*line*
queue, v.	*stand in line/line up*
rasher (bacon)	*slice*
reception (hotel)	*front desk*
receptionist	*desk clerk*
return ticket	*round-trip ticket*
reverse charges	*call collect*
ring up	*call/phone*
robin (small red-breasted bird, symbol of Christmas)	*robin* (large red-breasted bird, first sign of spring)
roof/hood (car)	*top*

BRITISH	AMERICAN
roundabout (road)	*traffic circle*
saloon (car)	*sedan*
scribbling pad/block	*scratch pad*
sellotape	*scotch tape*
service flats	*apartment hotel*
settee	*love seat*
shop assistant	*salesclerk*
shop walker	*floorwalker*
sideboards (hair)	*sideburns*
silencer (car)	*muffler*
single ticket	*one-way ticket*
skipping rope	*jump rope*
skirting board	*baseboard*
smalls (washing)	*underwear*
solicitor	*lawyer/attorney*
sorbet	*sherbet*
spanner	*monkey wrench*
spirits	*liquor*
staff (academic)	*faculty*
stalls (theatre)	*orchestra seats*
stand (for public office)	*run*
standard lamp	*floor lamp*
state school	*public school*
sticking plaster	*adhesive tape*
stone (fruit)	*pit*
sump (car)	*oil pan*
surgery (doctor's/dentist's)	*office*
surgical spirit	*rubbing alcohol*
suspender belt	*garter belt*
suspenders	*garters*
swede	*turnip/rutabaga*
sweet shop/confectioner	*candy store*
sweets	*candy*

BRITISH	AMERICAN
Swiss roll	*jelly roll*
teat (baby's bottle)	*nipple*
tin	*can*
tip n., v.	*dump*
trunk call	*long distance*
tube/underground	*subway*
turn-ups	*cuffs*
undergraduates:	
1st year	*freshman*
2nd year	*sophomore*
3rd year	*junior*
4th year	*senior*
unit trust	*mutual fund*
upper circle	*first balcony*
valve (radio)	*tube*
vest	*undershirt*
wardrobe	*closet*
wash up	*do the dishes*
wash your hands	*wash up*
Welsh dresser	*hutch*
windcheater	*windbreaker*
windscreen	*windshield*
wing/mudguard	*fender*
zed	Z

REPARTEE

"You can stroke people with words," said F. Scott Fitzgerald, and when it came to stroking people, he knew a thing or two.

You can choke people with words as well, and there must be a cruel streak in me somewhere because I think I admire the choking words rather more than the stroking ones.

Watching a razor-sharp wit at work is always exhilarating— provided the witty wounding words are not aimed in your direction—and over the years I've built up quite a collection of classic epeegrams. The ones that follow are my favorites—but who knows whether the individuals to whom I have attributed them actually originated them? You'll recall the famous story of how Oscar Wilde admired one of the witticisms of James McNeill Whistler.

"I wish I'd said that," said Wilde.

"You will, Oscar, you will," said Whistler.

Many of the best jests attributed to Oscar Wilde in Britain are attributed to Mark Twain in the United States (and vice versa) and some of the most memorable of the celebrated Algonquips were going the rounds in Britain and America when Kaufman, Benchley, Parker, and the rest were still in short pants. Who actually said what, where, and when hardly matters. What counts is the quality of the quips themselves.

Hotel receptionist (on telephone): "I beg your pardon, Miss Ferber, but is there a gentleman in your room?"

Edna Ferber: "I don't know. Wait a minute and I'll ask him."

A Hollywood star returned to Britain to make a movie after an absence of ten years. She particularly asked to be photographed by the same cameraman as before.

When she saw the rushes, she was disappointed and exclaimed to the cameraman:

"These are not nearly so good as the ones you last took of me."

"I know, my dear," replied the cameraman, "but you must remember that I am ten years older."

During the Civil War a lady exclaimed effusively to Lincoln:

"Oh, Mr. President, I feel so sure that God is on our side, don't you?"

"Ma'am," replied the president, "I am more concerned that we should be on God's side."

A young composer had written two pieces of music and asked the great Rossini to hear them both and say which he preferred. He duly played one piece, whereupon Rossini intervened.

"You need not play any more," he said. "I prefer the other one."

The dancer Isadora Duncan suggested to Bernard Shaw that they should have a child together.

"Imagine," she said, "a child with my body and your brain!"

"Yes," replied Shaw, "but suppose it had my body and your brain."

"What do you think of marriage as an institution?"

"I think it's fine for people who like living in institutions."

A reporter once asked the great Italian composer Giuseppe Verdi for his full address.

"I think," said Verdi, "that Italy will be sufficient."

Khrushchev, when he was still master of Russia, was discoursing before a large audience on the iniquities perpetrated by Stalin, when a voice at the back of the hall cried out:

"You were one of his colleagues, why didn't you stop him?"

In the terrible silence which followed not a man in the audience moved a muscle. Raking the assembly with his eyes, Khrushchev thundered:

"Who said that?"

But still not a man moved and the tension was becoming unbearable, when Khrushchev said quietly:

"Now you know why."

At an ambassadorial banquet, after everyone was seated, one of the lady guests complained a little too loudly that, according to the official order of precedence, she ought to be seated next to the ambassador. She was found to be right and several of the guests had to get up and move down to make room for her.

Feeling somewhat conscience-stricken at the fuss she had made, the lady said to the ambassador:

"You and your wife must find these questions of precedence extremely troublesome."

"Not really," was the reply. "We have found by experience that the people who matter don't mind and the people who mind don't matter."

Whistler had been commissioned to paint the portrait of an exceptionally ugly man and the two of them were contemplating the finished work.

"Well," exclaimed the subject of the portrait, "you can't call that a great work of art."

"Perhaps not," replied Whistler, "but then you can hardly call yourself a great work of nature."

An infatuated young man was sending his girlfriend a telegram which read:

"Ozzy loves his Woozy Woozy Woozy Woozy Woozy Woozy."

"You can have another 'Woozy' without it costing any more," said the post-office clerk.

"No, thanks," replied the young man. "I think that would sound rather silly."

A reporter asked Marilyn Monroe: "Did you really have nothing on when you posed for those pictures?"

"Oh, no," said Marilyn, smiling, "I had the radio on."

A young man sitting next to a very attractive woman at dinner found himself at a loss for conversation and said, merely for the sake of saying something:

"I hate that man sitting opposite us."

"You mean the man with the mustache?" asked the young woman. "That's my brother."

"No, no," stammered the young man hastily. "I mean the one without the mustache."

"That's my husband."

"I know," replied the young man, "that's why I hate him."

Dorothy. Parker was discussing with another woman a man whom they both knew.

"You must admit," said the friend, "that he is always courteous to his inferiors."

"Where does he find them?" asked Miss Parker.

A young man championing the works of an ultramodern writer and seeking to convince a friend of their excellence said that they would be read when Homer and Shakespeare were forgotten.

"And not until," replied his friend.

Dorothy Parker and a young actress were both about to pass through the same doorway when the actress drew back with the words, "Age before beauty."

"Yes, my dear," replied Miss Parker, "and pearls before swine."

Dorothy Parker, on being told that Calvin Coolidge was dead, asked, "How can they tell?"

Two men were discussing a third.
"He thinks he's a wit," said one of them.
"Yes," replied the other, "but he's only half right."

When Spencer Tracy first met Katharine Hepburn, she remarked: "I'm afraid I'm a little tall for you, Mr. Tracy."
"Never mind, Miss Hepburn," replied Tracy. "I'll soon cut you down to my size."

Zsa Zsa Gabor, when asked how many husbands she had had, replied: "You mean apart from my own?"

In reply to a lady who asked whether genius was hereditary, Whistler said:
"I cannot tell you, madam. Heaven has granted me no off-spring."

"All these people sleeping together before they're married! I didn't sleep with my wife before we were married. Did you?"
"I don't know. What was her maiden name?"

Mahatma Gandhi was asked what he thought about Western civilization.
"I think," he said, "that it would be a very good idea."

A conceited young man attending a dinner party in company with Dr. Johnson was so unmannerly as to taunt the old gentle-man.
"Tell me, doctor," he said, "what would you give to be as young and sprightly as I am?"
"Why sir," said Johnson, "I should almost be content to be as foolish and conceited."

A lady in an advanced stage of pregnancy was approached by the village gossip who said: "Excuse me, but are you going to have a baby?"

"Oh no," replied the other dryly, "I'm just carrying this around for a friend."

PREPARTEE

The essence of repartee is that it should be spontaneous. Most of us, however, don't think of a deft and devastating retort until after the time for using it has passed. The French have a neat phrase to describe these "wish words": *l'esprit d'escalier,* that is, the witty remarks you think of while going down the stairs from a party. It's all too easy to be after-witted and come up with a post-riposte, but repartee that's actually departee is useless.

Here's a simple test that should help you become a master of genuine repartee. Look at each of the next ten lines and see if you can come up with a riposte to each one that matches or rivals the original. (See Answers.)

    1 *Friend:* "Isn't your dress a little too young for you, dear?"
    Dorothy Parker:

    2 *Barber:* "How would you like your hair cut, sir?"
    George S. Kaufman:

    3 *Reporter:* "Can you play the violin?"
    George Burns:

    4 *Irate female heckler:* "If you were my husband, I'd poison your coffee."
    Winston Churchill:

    5 *Reporter:* "Can I ask you what you wear at night, Miss Monroe?"
    Marilyn Monroe:

    6 *Reporter:* "Do you know what an extravaganza is?"
    Groucho Marx:

    7 *Lewis Morris:* "There's a conspiracy of silence against me. What should I do, Oscar?"
    Oscar Wilde:

8 *Notorious bore:* "I passed your house yesterday."
   Oscar Wilde:

9 *George S. Kaufman:* "Is life worth living?"
   Harold Ross:

10 *Fellow actor:* "Well, we live and learn."
   John Barrymore:

If you feel you simply haven't been blessed with a rapierlike wit, don't worry. As G. K. Chesterton said, "Silence is the unbearable repartee."

S LANGUAGE

skidoo	*hit the trail*	*shag out*
vamoose	*take a powder*	*cut out*
beat it	*drag out*	*split*
scram		

For the benefit of those born yesterday, that's *get lost* in ten slanguages.

Almost everyone has a slanguage of their own—the Mafia, the middle class, sportswriters, disk jockeys, teachers, blacks, cowboys, gays, even undertakers (they call coffins *cans* and corpses *heavies*)—and with time and custom slanguages develop and grow. When old ones die, new ones are born. Since there's probably no group of people—certainly no minority group—that doesn't have its own slanguage, I've only got space to touch on my favorites: remarkable slanguages, some now dead, some very much alive, all adding a special richness to the language. As Carl Sandburg said, "Slang is the language that rolls up its sleeves, spits on its hands, and goes to work."

CAMPUSESE

If you're currently at college, you should ace on this test. It's a suckin' wind for you if you're not. (If you bomb, see answers.)

Give a meaning for each of these words and phrases:

1 *ace,* v.

2 *bean up,* v.

3 *bitch building*

4 *bomb,* v.

5 *Bugs Zoo*

6 *dude ranch*

7 *Flick Lit.*

8 *get jacked*

9 *goob*

10 *gorp*

11 *Grit Lit.*

12 *grub,* v.

13 *hunk*

14 *lavaliered,* adj.

15 *library*

16 *lunch lip*

17 *munchies*

18 *mystery meat*

19 *nerd*

20 *Pimple Lit.*

21 *Po*

22 *pork it*

23 *query,* n.

24 *rack,* n.

25 *rack monster*

26 *scope,* v.

27 *shoot some hoops*

28 *spaced*

29 *suckin' wind*

WINCHELLESE

Walter Winchell—dean of columnists in the heady heyday of gossip 40 years ago—had a way with words. He was born in 1897, and his unique slanguage deserves to live forever. Only Winchell could report on the lives and loves of his "celebs" as he did.

Here, they are falling in love:

Dorothy Parker is riding the skies again with Alan Campbell.

Drew Eberson and Betty Boyd have that droopy look in their orbs.

Eileen Wenzel and Nicholas Blair are plenty Voom Voom.

Here, they are getting married:

Jayne Shattuck and Jack Kirkland blend on Friday.
Charles Chaplin is about to announce his Secret Merger.
Jack Pickford and Mary Mulhern will probably middle-aisle
it.

Here, they are getting unmarried:

The Robert Carses are unraveling.
Lord and Lady Cavendish will have it melted soon.
Marion Batista and Tom Hamilton have phfftt.

And here, they are going to have a baby:

The Jack Dempseys will be a trio in later July.
The Al Trahans are threeing.
The John LaGattas are infanticipating.

Hip rap

Man, it's cool—

electric	*outasight*
far out	*together*
freaky	*too much*
groovy	*totally*
heavy	*way out*

—it's hip talk.
If you dig it too, it'll be no hassle to work out the meaning of
these hip words and phrases:

1 *blow your cool*	7 *crash*, v.
2 *bread*	8 *dig*
3 *bum*, v.	9 *don't freeze me*
4 *burn*, v.	10 *flip*
5 *buzz*, n.	11 *freak out*
6 *cage*, n.	12 *hacked off*

13 *laid back*

14 *on the road*

15 *out front*

16 *psyched out*

17 *rap*

18 *scene*

19 *score*, v.

20 *slide*, v.

21 *split*, v.

22 *suss out*

23 *turn off*, n.

24 *turn-on*, n.

25 *walking soft*

26 *wheels*

27 *where is it with you?*

28 *wired*

(See Answers.)

BASEBALLESE

Legend has it that in the early days of the 20th century a college professor exclaimed: "To understand America, you must first understand baseball." And he was probably right; except for the horse ("you can lead a horse to water ..." "horse of a different color," "cart before the horse," etc.), no other subject has contributed as many terms as has the "horsehide" sport.

Even Americans who have rarely seen a baseball game sprinkle some of the following terms into their daily conversation:

He was born with two strikes against him.

He couldn't get to first base with that girl.

He sure threw me a curve that time.

I'll take a rain check on it.

He went to bat for me.

I liked him right off the bat.

He was way out in left field on that one.

He's a foul ball.

I think you're way off base on that.

It was a smash hit.

Let's take a seventh-inning stretch.

I hope to touch all the bases on this report.

Could you pinch-hit for me?

He doesn't even know who's on first.

I just call 'em as I see 'em.

He's only a bush leaguer.

Major league all the way.

We'll hit 'em where they ain't.

He was safe by a mile.

He has a lot on the ball.

He really dropped the ball that time.

We'll rally in the ninth.

No game's over until the last man's out.

And is there any term in our language more indicative of failure than "to strike out"?

Had President Nixon stayed in office a while longer, it's possible that football might have begun to approach baseball in the number of terms used (*game plan, kickoff,* etc.); but the Nixon *team* got its *signals crossed,* so then it was *a whole new ball game.*

Baseball, like other occupations, has its own terminology and nomenclature, understood only by the esoteric few. For example, your grandfather would speak of Christy Mathewson's *fadeaway,* of Walter Johnson's *inshoot,* or of three-fingered Brown throwing an *outdrop.* Your father spoke of Bob Feller *throwing heat,* while Tommy Bridges had a good *deuce, jug, hook,* or *Uncle Charlie*—all synonyms for the curveball. Jim Tobin threw a *butterfly* pitch because he *pulled the string on it,* making it come in slow.

Today the pitches are pretty much the same, but the terminology has altered some, largely because of the influx of black players. The fast ball becomes *the express;* the hard curve is a *slider;* and the off-speed pitch is a *change-up.* And whether you call a high, hard one thrown at the batter's head a *purpose pitch,* a *knockdown pitch,* or a *beanball,* the message remains the same: *Metala en su oreja*—stick it in his ear!

JAIL TALK

The Hardy Boys are here to introduce you to some of the more respectable slang of the criminal fraternity of yesteryear. In *The*

Mystery of the Spiral Bridge, Joe and Frank heard some jailhouse language from convicts. Write in what you think each term means.

1 *pair of bins*	7 *bice*	12 *arkitnay*
2 *oiler*	8 *baron*	13 *bit note*
3 *half stamp,* n.	9 *torch man*	14 *bindlestiff*
4 *clobby joint*	10 *cheeser*	15 *in the bing*
5 *long nit*	11 *layabout*	16 *finger man*
6 *bathe in the canal*		17 *equalizer*

(See Answers.)

VARIETISH

Variety, the weekly show business bible, has its own slanguage that was virtually created by one man, the editor for 40 years, Abel Green, whose everyday vocabulary included such ingenious coinages as *yocks, yix, pix, crix, nix, plushery,* and *fests,* who would say "Gimme an Ameche" when he wanted you to telephone him (because Don Ameche had played Alexander Graham Bell in the "biopic") and whose description of the closing of a show business restaurant began with the immortal line, "The raison d'être for el foldo . . ."

Imagine that you were going to work for Mr. Green (an impossibility, alas, since he died in 1973) and that on your first day you had to find bright Green headlines to cover the nitty-gritty of these four stories:

1 One of the TV networks decided to drop a well-known female master of ceremonies.

2 Leading movie producers vigorously criticize the newspaper critics.

3 The box-office figures for movies about farmers are a disappointment in the rural areas.

4 *Deep Throat,* with Linda Lovelace, opens in New York.

For the headlines in pure Varietish, see Answers.

CB Talk

Breaker one-nine, this is Mean Machine looking for a southbounder on I-eighty with ears on. How 'bout it? C'mon.

Breaker one-nine for that southbounder, I got you wall to wall, Mean Machine. This is Caterpillar. You got a picture taker in a plain brown wrapper at two-oh-one marker. What's your ten-twenty, good buddy?

Breaker one-nine for Caterpillar. I'm at one ninety-eight marker. Thanks for the Smokey report. Put your hammer down and I'll shut your back door tight.

Breaker one-nine for Mean Machine. Ten-four, good buddy, I'll keep an eyeball on your front door. Keep your shiny side up and your greasy side down and Caterpillar'll catch ya on the flip-flop. Ten-ten. Grinnin' and spinnin' we go!

According to the latest official *CB Guide*—the bible of citizens band radio operators—that conversation took place on Interstate Route 80. Two long-haul truckers, with CB handles (CB nicknames) of Mean Machine and Caterpillar, broke the silence ("breaker") of the night, the loneliness of the road, and began to communicate with each other.

Since CB radio began in 1947, the truckers have brought it from a small and fragmented radio service to a booming network of 10 million operators.

CB is a two-way radio network that anyone can join. All you need is a CB set and a license. Knowing the CB slanguage is useful too. How many of these do you understand?

1	*ace*	8	*bubblegummer*
2	*anchor clanker*	9	*cactus juice*
3	*astronaut*	10	*cookies*
4	*backyard*	11	*double L*
5	*barley pop*	12	*gate jaw*
6	*bearded buddy*	13	*good numbers*
7	*blinkin' winkin'*, n.	14	*Harvey Wallbanger*
15	*hot pants*	24	*wall-to-wall bears*

16 *jawjacking*

17 *lettuce*

18 *mud*

19 *panic in the streets*

20 *picture taker*

21 *posts*

22 *seven-three*

23 *Smokey*

25 *XL*

26 *XY*

27 *XYD*

28 *XYL*

29 *XYM*

30 *YL*

31 *yo*

(See Answers.)

BLACK SLANG

A complete glossary of black slang—from *a* meaning *yes, correct, right* through *zap* meaning *to move quickly*—would take up a whole book. (Indeed it's already taken up several books, the best being Clarence Major's *Dictionary of Afro-American Talk*.) To find out if you need such a book, try this simple intelligence test. It's different from most standard English tests. It is not biased to favor a white, middle-class experience. It is deliberately biased to favor a black, nonmiddle-class experience, and was developed by former Watts manpower specialist Adrian Dove.

If you score less than 14 (67 percent) on the test, you are virtually failing and can conclude that you have a low ghetto IQ. As white, middle-class educators would put it, you are "culturally deprived."

1 T-Bone Walker got famous for playing (a) trombone (b) piano (c) "t-flute" (d) guitar (e) hambone.

2 Stagger Lee (in the famous blues legend) killed (a) his mother (b) Frankie (c) Johnny (d) his girlfriend (e) Billy.

3 If a man is called a blood, he is a (a) fighter (b) warlock (c) black man (d) hungry hemophile (e) redman or Indian.

4 If you throw the dice and seven shows on top, what is facing down? (a) seven (b) snake eyes (c) boxcars (d) little Joes (e) eleven.

5 In C. C. Rider, C. C. stands for (a) Civil Service (b) Church Council (c) County Circuit preacher or old-time rambler (d) Country Club (e) "Cheatin' Charlie" (the Boxcar Gunsel).

6 Cheap chitlings (not the kind you purchase at a frozen-food counter) taste rubbery unless they are cooked long enough. You can quit cooking them after (a) 15 minutes (b) 2 hours (c) 24 hours (d) 1 week (on a low flame) (e) 1 hour.

7 A hype is a person who (a) always says he feels sickly (b) has water on the brain (c) uses heroin (d) Is always ripping and running (e) is always sick.

8 Hully Gully came from (a) East Oakland (b) Fillmore (c) Watts (d) Harlem (e) Motor City.

9 Willie Mae's last name is (a) Schwartz (b) Matauda (c) Gomez (d) Turner (e) O'Flaherty.

10 The opposite of *square* is (a) *round* (b) *up* (c) *down* (d) *hip* (e) *lame.*

11 If I was playing the dozens I'd be talking mostly about (a) water bread (b) your mama (c) the digit man (d) wrinkles.

12 A handkerchief head is (a) a cool cat (b) a porter (c) an Uncle Tom (d) a hoddi (e) a preacher.

13 The Dixie Hummingbirds are (a) part of the KKK (b) a swamp disease (c) a modern gospel group (d) the Mississippi Black Liberation Army (e) deacons.

14 Jet is (a) an East Oakland motorcycle club (b) one of the gangs in *West Side Story* (c) a news and gossip magazine (d) a way of life for the very rich.

15 And Jesus said, "Walk together children . . ." (a) ". . . don't get weary. There's a great camp meeting in the promised land" (b) ". . . for we shall overcome" (c) ". . . for the family that walks together talks together" (d) ". . . by your patience you will win your souls" (Luke 21:19) (e) ". . . find the things that are above, not the things that are on Earth" (Col. 3:3).

16 "Money don't get everything, it's true . . ." (a) ". . . but I don't have none and I'm so blue" (b) ". . . but what it don't get I can't use" (c) ". . . so make do with what you've got" (d) ". . . but I don't know that and neither do you."

17 "You've got to get up early in the morning if you want to . . ." (a) ". . . catch the worms" (b) ". . . be healthy, wealthy, and

wise" (c) ". . . try to fool me" (d) ". . . fare well" (e) ". . . be the first one on the street."

18 Bo Diddley is a (a) camp for children (b) cheap wine (c) singer (d) new dance (e) mojo call.

19 The word that is out of place here is (a) splib (b) blood (c) gray (d) spook (e) black

20 Many people say that "Juneteenth" (June 19) should be made a legal holiday because this was the day when (a) the slaves were freed in the USA (b) the slaves were freed in Texas (c) the slaves were freed in Jamaica (d) the slaves were freed in California (e) Martin Luther King, Jr., was born (f) Booker T. Washington died

21 If a dude is up tight with a woman who gets state aid, when he talks about "Mother's Day" he means (a) the second Sunday in May (b) the third Sunday in June (c) the first of every month (d) the first and fifteenth of every month (e) none of these.

(See Answers.)

TWO'S
COMPANY

TWOSOMES

Some words go together like a horse and carriage:

aches and pains   law and order

bag and baggage   mix and match

body and soul   nice and cozy

cut and thrust   pride and joy

high and mighty   time and tide

And most of the twosomes would look unnatural if you reversed their order:

call and beck   furious and fast

fall and decline   dandy and fine

tongs and hammer
caboodle and kit
cranny and nook

tumble and rough
nonsense and stuff
vigor and vim

THREESOMES

Twosomes are part and parcel of the language. There are hundreds of them at our beck and call, but because we can pick and choose them with so little stress and strain, we tend to take them for granted.

That's a pity because their linguistic potential is immense—as you'll discover if you introduce a familiar twosome to an unlikely friend. Introduce a legal word couple to a third word and you may set into language a newly meaningful relationship, turning an innocent twosome into an illicit threesome.

Sometimes the single will cling to one partner of the couple, sometimes to the other. And sometimes, when built like one of the partners, only bigger, the single will break up the couple and claim the other partner. Occasionally, the interplay will change the appearance and even the character of the partners. Watch.

INNOCENT TWOSOMES	ILLICIT THREESOMES
ball and chain	ball and chainSTORE (shopping mart for sadomasochists)
comb and brush	comb and brush-OFF (a new way of parting)
Thanksgiving turkey	Thanksgiving turkey TROT (Pilgrim frolic)
tar and feather	tar and featherBED ("You've made your bed, now lie in it," said the patriot to the tar)
draw and quarter	draw and quarterBACK ("occupations of an artistic athlete")
scotch on the rocks	HOPscotch on the rocks (game for the inebriated)
running nose	running noseDIVE (hangout for snifflers)

dinner pail	dinner paleFACE (nervous guest)
threadbare	threadbearHUG (lukewarm welcome)
stop and go	stop and go-GO (traffic signals from a lissome police-woman)
black and blue	black and blue LAWS (the punishing edict of never on Sunday)
milk and honey	milk and honeyMOONERS (Prohibition era newlyweds)
bow and arrow	bowTIE and arrow (Robin Hood goes formal)
fish and chips	fish and chips OFF THE OLD BLOCK (back-home lunch)
bird in the hand	bird in the hand-ME-DOWN (impoverished girl)
cloak and dagger	cloak and daguerreOTYPE (old photo of Zorro)
barbershop pole	barbershop polTERGEIST (spirit in the hair tonic)
bottleneck	bottlenecCROPHILIA (unmentionable interaction with nonre-turnables)
sock hop	CASsock hop (fun for clergymen)
skin and bones	skin and bonsAI (Japanese strip show)
cash and carry	cash and carriON (profits from grave robbing)

U
NQUESTIONABLY!

"Unquestionably!" is the answer to give when someone asks you for an English word that contains all five vowels and the letter Y. What answers should you give to the next 20 questions?

1 There are two English words that contain the vowels *a-e-i-o-u* once and once only in their alphabetical order. Can you think of them?

2 Name three English words that contain the vowels *a-e-i-o-u* once and once only in their reverse alphabetical order (*u-o-i-e-a*).

3 There are two 17-letter words that contain the same 17 letters.
What are they?

4 Find a nine-letter English word that contains only one vowel.

5 Find a 15-letter word containing all the vowels in which no letter is used more than once.

6 Which one of these seven groups of letters is the odd one out, and why?

hi	*ctav*	*ratori*
sl	*pti*	*tt*
rland		

7 Find a seven-letter word which does not include any of the five vowels.

8 Find a common English word that has 15 letters in it. Five of these letters are the same vowel and the word contains no other vowels.

9 There is a 16-letter everyday English word in which only one vowel is used (repeatedly). What is the word?

10 Name two words that contain the first six letters of the alphabet, yet are only eight letters long.

11 A toddler could make good use of a word with the letters *shch* grouped together in the middle of it. What is the word?

12 What is a word which contains three sets of twin letters, each pair coming directly after the one before?

13 What is the longest word you can play using the eight notes in an octave (*c, d, e, f, g, a, b, c*), given that hyphenated words aren't allowed? (Letters may be repeated.)

14 Take the letters *ergro*, add three letters to the front and the same three letters in the same order to the rear and you have what everyday English word?

15 In what English word does the letter *i* appear seven times? The word contains no other vowel.

16 Here are nine words with something important in common:

brandy	*grangers*	*stores*
chastens	*pirated*	*swingers*
craters	*scampi*	*tramps*

What is it?

17 There is a word which indicates a good deal of anxiety which runs to 15 letters and which can be printed without any letters sticking up (e.g., *d*) or sticking down (e.g., *q*). Can you think of it?

18 There is a word that takes on airs of being true: it contains 15 letters and its vowels and consonants alternate. What is it?

19 What incomprehensible English word makes sense and contains eight syllables?

20 What revolutionary English word contains all five vowels and the letter *y*.

(See Answers.)

V

ERSE AND WORSE

Rhymes That Don't

"You can't," says Tom to lisping Bill,
　"Find any rhyme for *month*."
"A great mistake," was Bill's reply;
　"I'll find a rhyme at *onth!*"

There are some words that would defeat all but the most ingenious rhymesters. *Month* is one.

Christina Rossetti (who shed rhymes like confetti) almost managed it, with the aid of a well-placed apostrophe:

How many weeks in a month?
Four, as the swift moon runn'th.

118

Oranges and lemons are almost as impossible:

I gave my darling child a lemon,
That lately grew its fragrant stem on;
And next, to give her pleasure *more* range
I offered her a juicy orange.

In a competition at school I was challenged to find rhymes for *carpet* and *velocity*. I failed; so did the rest of the class. Our teacher then lorded it over us with these two verses, the first of which he claimed as his own composition (it wasn't) and the second as the work of Richard Barham (it was). The carpet rhyme:

Sweet maid of the inn,
    'Tis surely no sin
To toast such a beautiful bar pet;
    Believe me, my dear,
    Your feet would appear
At home on a nobleman's carpet.

The velocity couplet, from the dextrous pen of the clerical poet best known for "The Jackdaw of Rheims":

Having once gained the summit, and managed to cross it, he
Rolls down the side with uncommon velocity.

Silver has always been regarded as unrhymeable. Stephen Sondheim rose to the challenge:

To find a rhyme for silver
Or any "rhymeless" rhyme
Requires only will, ver-
bosity and time

Ira Levin went one better than Sondheim by finding rhymes for *silver* and *penguin*, another notoriously unrhymeable word:

A woman asked me to rhyme a penguin.
I said, "Does the erstwhile Emperor Eng win?
If not, I'll send a brand-new tractor
To "Big Boy" Williams, cinemactor;
On the card attached, a smiling penguin

Will say, "You're truly a man among men, Guinn."
"All right," she said, "so now rhyme silver,"
But I left because I'd had my filver.

When next you're lying awake with a dismal headache (and repose is taboo'd by anxiety) you might attempt to induce a drowsy numbness by finding rhymes for *Niagara, Timbuctoo,* and *Massachusetts.* It can be done—just:

Take instead of rope, pistol, or dagger, a
Desperate dash down the falls of Niagara.

If I were a cassowary
  On the plains of Timbuctoo,
I would eat a missionary,
  Cassock, band, and hymnbook too.

Of tennis I played one or two sets
On a court at Richmond, Massachusetts.

Finding words that rhyme to the eye but don't rhyme to the ear is almost as difficult as finding perfect rhymes for unlikely place-names. Clifford Witting managed it in this artful limerick— for the full appreciation of which you must understand that *Slough* (an English city) really rhymes with *cow:*

A certified poet from Slough,
Whose methods of rhyming were rough,
    Retorted, "I see
    That the letters agree
And if that's not sufficient I'm through."

RHYMES THAT DO

Some poets are such determined rhymesters that they'll sacrifice anything to get their rhyme, including reason and orthography. This verse by Joe Ecclesine is called "Van Gogh, Van Gogh, Van Gogh":

It seems rather rough
On Vincent Van Guff

When those in the know
Call him Vincent Van Go

For unless I'm way off
He was Vincent Van Gogh.

And here is one of Ogden Nash's many mini-masterpieces:

The Bronx?
No, thonx.

This verse so offended some of his readers that Nash later offered them an apology:

I wrote those lines, "The Bronx? No, thonx";
I shudder to confess them.
But now, a sadder, wiser man,
I say, "The Bronx? God bless them!"

It is not generally recognized that some of America's finest poetry comes from the Bronx. I offer these two anonymous verses as evidence:

THIRTY PURPLE BIRDS

Toity poiple boids
Sitt'n on der coib
A' choipin' and a' boipin
An' eat'n doity woims.

THE BUDDING BRONX

Der spring is sprung
Der grass is riz
I wonder where dem boidies is?

Der little boids is on der wing,
Ain't dat absoid?
Der little wings is on der boid!

LIMERICKS

Monsignor Ronald Knox once inserted this advertisement in a newspaper:

Evangelical vicar in want of a portable secondhand font, would
dispose of the same for a portrait (in frame) of the Bishop-
Elect of Vermont.

It may not look like much of a limerick to you, but read it out
loud and you'll find that's what it is. One doesn't normally
associate the clergy with limericks because, as everyone knows:

The limerick is furtive and mean;
You must keep her in close quarantine,
    Or she sneaks to the slums
    And promptly becomes
Disorderly, drunk, and obscene.

Of the handful of respectable limericks I know, this is my
favorite:

A silly young fellow named Hyde
In a funeral procession was spied;
    When asked, "Who is dead?"
    He giggled and said,
"I don't know; I just came for the ride."

HAIKUS

Haikus, by contrast, are nothing if not respectable. They are
verses with three lines and 17 syllables, five in the first and third,
seven in the second. Composing them isn't easy. Nor is understanding them, as you can see from this English haiku translation
of a famous Japanese haiku:

Utter stillness! Through
The rainy dark of midnight
The sound of a bell.

The appeal of the haiku is to the highbrow. As Willard Espy
put it:

Haikus show IQ's.
High IQ's like haikus. Low
IQ's—no haikus.

CLERIHEWS

No intellectual prowess is required for the appreciation of cleri-hews: four-line versified biographies named after the inventor of the form, Edmund Clerihew Bentley (1875–1956).

Here are three by the master:

The digestion of Milton
Was unequal to Stilton.
He was only feeling so-so
When he wrote *Il Penseroso*.

Geoffrey Chaucer
Took a bath (in a saucer)
In consequence of certain hints
Dropped by the Black Prince.

"Susaddah!" exclaimed Ibsen,
"By dose is turdig cribson!
I'd better dot kiss you.
Atishoo! Atishoo!"

This one is by Robert Longden:

The Emperor Caligula
's habits were somewhat irrigula.
When he sat down to lunch
He got drunk at onch.

HIGGLEDY-PIGGLEDIES

Higgledy-piggledies are more sophisticated than clerihews: they comprise double dactyls and rhymes and aren't always biographi-cal. This one is by Leonard Miall:

Tiddely Quiddely
Edward M. Kennedy
Quite unaccountably
Drove in a stream.
Pleas of amnesia
Incomprehensible
Possibly shattered
Political dream.

RUTHLESS RHYMES

Poets can be cruel—and cynical. Harry Graham was both, and delightfully so. Here are two of his most ruthless rhymes:

Late last night I slew my wife,
Stretched her on the parquet flooring;
I was loath to take her life,
But I *had* to stop her snoring!

"There's been an accident!" they said,
"Your servant's cut in half; he's dead!"
"Indeed!" said Mr. Jones, "and please
Send me the half that's got my keys."

POETIC INJUSTICE

The terse verse I like best expresses a clear opinion. You don't have to agree with the poet, but at least you can see what he's getting at. Here are five very different examples of terse verse at its very best:

MARRIAGE

The glances over cocktails
    That seemed to be so sweet
Don't seem quite so amorous
    Over the Shredded Wheat.

A 1931 GRACE

Heavenly Father bless us,
And keep us all alive;
There's ten of us for dinner
And not enough for five.

ADDENDUM TO THE TEN COMMANDMENTS

Thou shalt not covet thy neighbor's wife,
Nor the ox her husband bought her;

But thank the Lord you're not forbidden
To covet your neighbor's daughter.

MODERN MANNERS

I eat my peas with honey,
I've done it all my life;
It makes the peas taste funny,
But it keeps 'em on the knife!

PAMPHLET FROM THE
RIGHT TO LIFE FOUNDATION

To abort little Willy
Is silly.
That's what war
Is for.

ODES AND ENDS

If you don't like what a particular poet happens to be saying, you
don't need to let him have the last word.
    Sir Walter Scott once wrote:

O what a tangled web we weave,
When first we practise to deceive!

To which Phyllis McGinley replied:

Which leads me to suppose the fact is
We really ought to get more practice.

J. R. Pope added:

But when we've practiced quite a while
How vastly we improve our style!

And Willard Espy concluded:

Forget, dear friends, that practice angle!
You'll only tangle up the tangle.

Here are six poems to conclude. When you have supplied your own last lines, you can compare them with the official versions in the Answers.

Mary had a little lamb,
　　She ate it with mint sauce,
And everywhere that Mary went
　　The . . .

Mary had a little lamb,
　　But her sister came to grief—
She lived in 1931
　　And . . .

Mary had a little bear
　　To which she was so kind
And everywhere that Mary went
　　You . . .

Mary had a little car,
　　She drove in manner deft,
But every time she signaled right
　　The . . .

Mary had a little lamb,
　　Its fleece was white as snow,
She took the lamb to Pittsburgh
　　And . . .

Mary had a little lamb,
　　The . . .

If you enjoy Mary's adventures as much as I do, you'll have no difficulty in recognizing and understanding this favorite nursery rhyme (see Answers):

Scintillate, scintillate, globule orific,
Fain would I fathom thy nature's specific.
Loftily poised in ether capacious,
Strongly resembling a gem carbonaceous.

When torrid Phoebus refuses his presence
And ceases to lamp with fierce incandescence,
Then you illumine the regions supernal,
Scintillate, scintillate, semper nocturnal.

Then the victim of hospiceless peregrination
Gratefully hails your minute coruscation.
He could not determine his journey's direction
But for your bright scintillating protection.

W
INIFRED'S
BLOOMERS

In the matter of verbal bloopers, the Reverend Spooner and Mrs. Malaprop are famous for their malapropisms and spoonerisms, but nobody seems to know much about Winifred and her bloomers. Well, I'm going to reveal all—about Mrs. M., the Reverend S., *and* Winifred.

WINIFRED'S BLOOMERS

Who was Winifred and what were her bloomers?

Winifred was a novelist and playwright better known as Clemence Dane. Her bloomers were her matchless verbal slips.

Miss Dane was known as Winifred to her friends, the closest of whom included Noël Coward, Joyce Cary, and Gladys Calthrop. They reveled in her facility for uttering innocently outrageous *doubles ententes*. In his biography of Coward, Cole Lesley records a few of the choicest of Winifred's bloomers:

> The first I can remember was when poor Gladys was made by Noël to explain to Winifred that she simply could not say in her latest novel, "He stretched out and grasped the other's gnarled, stumpy tool." The bloomers poured innocently from her like an ever-rolling stream: "Olwen's got crabs!" she cried as you arrived for dinner, or, "We're having roast cock tonight!" At the Old Vic, in the crowded foyer, she argued in ringing tones, "But Joyce, it's well *known* that Shakespeare sucked Bacon dry." It was Joyce too who anxiously inquired after some goldfish last seen in a pool in the blazing sun and was reassured, "Oh, they're all right now! They've got a vast erection covered with everlasting pea!" "Oh, the pleasure of waking up to see a row of tits outside your window," she said to Binkie during a weekend at Knott's Fosse. Schoolgirl slang sometimes came into it, for she was in fact the original from whom Noël created Madame Arcati: "Do you remember the night we all had Dick on toast?" she inquired in front of the Governor of Jamaica and Lady Foot. Then there was her ghost story: "Night after night for weeks she tried to make him come . . ."

Ambiguous statements even more innocuous than Clemence Dane's can be just as engaging:

> "If the baby does not thrive on raw milk, boil it."

> "Will you lend me your rifle so I can shoot myself?"

> "It was here that the emperor liked to put on his grand alfresco spectacles."

> "Nothing is less likely to appeal to a young woman than the opinions of old men on the pill."

SPOONERISMS

A spoonerism is the accidental transposition of the initial letters of the words in a phrase so as to change the phrase's meaning or make nonsense of it:

"You have tasted a whole worm."

"You have hissed all my mystery lectures."

"You were fighting a liar in the quadrangle."

"You will leave by the town drain."

"I have just received a blushing crow."

"Is the bean dizzy?"

"Let us toast the queer old dean!"

These classic spoonerisms have been attributed to the Reverend William Spooner, Warden of New College, Oxford, from 1903 to 1924. He is supposed to have created the original spoonerism by getting up in college chapel and announcing the next hymn as "Kinquering kongs their titles take." He did no such thing. Nor was he responsible for the other classic spoonerisms attributed to him. He was certainly an absent-minded professor ("In the sermon I have just preached, wherever I said Aristotle I meant St. Paul"), a shortsighted albino with a knack for getting things muddled ("I remember your name. I just can't think of your face"), but apart from once admitting to looking in "a dark, glassly" he was not a perpetrator of spoonerisms. "Give me a well-boiled icycle," "It's roaring pain outside," "May I sew you to another sheet?" are spine foonerisms by any standard, but they are probably making the good warden gurn in his trave.

MALAPROPISMS

If there was any justice in the world of words, malapropisms would have been named after Shakespeare's Constable Dogberry rather than Sheridan's Mrs. Malaprop. Malapropisms are ludicrous misuses of words, especially by confusion with similar words, and Dogberry, in *Much Ado About Nothing*, indulges in them with abandon. Here he is instructing the Watch:

> DOGBERRY: You are thought here to be the most senseless and fit man for the constable of the watch, therefore bear you the lantern. This is your charge: you shall comprehend all vagrom men: you are to bid any man stand, in the prince's name.

WATCH: How, if a' will not stand?

DOGBERRY: Why, then, take no note of him, but let him go: and presently call the rest of the watch together, and thank God you are rid of a knave . . . You shall also make no noise in the streets; for, for the watch to babble and to talk is most tolerable and not to be endured.

As Dogberry sensibly observes, "comparisons are odorous," so that any "caparison," as Mrs. Malaprop has it, of the level of malapropisms used by these two great comic creations can only be of academic interest (and so can be safely left to the academics). It is just over 200 years since Mrs. Malaprop first walked the stage in Richard Brinsley Sheridan's comedy *The Rivals*, but the passage of time has not dulled the sparkle of the great lady's malapropisms:

"She's as headstrong as an allegory on the banks of the Nile."

"Illiterate him, I say, quite from your memory."

"I own the soft impeachment."

"An aspersion upon my parts of speech! Was ever such a brute! Sure, if I reprehend anything in this world, it is the use of my oracular tongue, and a nice derangement of epitaphs!"

SUPERMALAPROP

Of the modern malapropisms I've seen or heard, here are my top ten:

"I was so surprised you could have knocked me over with a fender."

"He works in an incinerator where they burn the refuge."

"He had to use biceps to deliver the baby."

"He communicates to work."

"My husband is a marvelous lover. He knows all my erroneous zones."

"My sister uses massacre on her eyes."

"He's a wealthy typhoon."

"My father is retarded on a pension."

"No phonographic pictures allowed."

"The English language is going through a resolution."

RADIO MALAPROP

If you're a serious collector of bloomers, bloopers, and malaprops you should listen to the radio—especially late at night when the insomniacs in search of company give the talk-show jockey a call:

"Too many people have been sold down the drain."

"If the circumstances were on the other foot."

"I don't pull any bones about it."

"You're talking around the bush."

"You are out of your rocker."

One jockey, perhaps deliberately, boggled a caller with this reproof: "You have just used two words that set my hair on edge." No hint of whether his teeth were on end, and the listener gave no indication of finding anything unusual about the broadcaster's phrase.

On another occasion a listener flabbergasted his talk-show guru by declaring: "I think we need to get down to the brass roots of the problem." Silence, with the man at the mike presumably sorting out brass roots from grass tacks.

Those are specimens from fast-moving exchanges, but people with more time to think also contribute.

"The nutshell of it is . . ." explained a locally famous trial lawyer.

"I believe they are cut out of the same mold," said a San Francisco mayoral candidate of two rivals.

And a radio commentator gave this reply during a law-and-order panel discussion: ". . . if he had actually broken a crime or could be accused of breaking a crime . . ."

The newscasts contain occasional gems—the traffic accident report which described a victim as "killed fatally," for example.

The advertising copywriter contributes now and then, as in a public service announcement which asserted that "fatigue is a major cause of automobile safety." Or the finance company plug with an announcer intoning: "It's Christmas, and you're socked under with bills . . ." Or another finance company barker who urged the listener to "discuss this in the confidence of your home."

MILHOUS MALAPROP

To err is human and lest one be deluded into thinking that the mighty, if fallen, are immune, out of the past comes Richard M. Nixon's comment, long before the distractions of Watergate, on the death of Adlai Stevenson:

> In eloquence of expression, he had no peers and very few equals.

XERXES ZZYZZX

X

ERXES ZZYZZX

NAMES TO CONJURE WITH

The telephone company owes a debt of gratitude to Hero Zzyzzx of Madison, Wisconsin, son of Xerxes Zzyzzx.

Zzyzzx (pronounced Ziz Icks) gets lots of telephone calls—profitable for the telephone company but both a problem and a blessing to Mr. Zzyzzx.

His name is the last name in the directory and for people who amuse themselves by reading telephone books, Hero Zzyzzx is a name hard to ignore. He gets calls at all hours from drunks, children, insomniacs, and jokers.

But once in a while Zzyzzx, 31 and single, gets one from "an interested young lady." And that's why he does not have his number unlisted.

Zzyzzx is his real name, he swears. It's an amalgam of Finnish, Lithuanian, Russian, French, German, and Central European family backgrounds.

134

Mr. Zzyzzx is not alone in having a name to conjure with. The world is full of ordinary people with extraordinary names—none more so than these 20—each one quite genuine, I promise you.

A. Moron (Virgin Islands education officer)

Cardinal Sin (archbishop of Manila)

Madame Fouqueau de Pussy (author)

Mrs. Friendly Ley (lived in Mission Hills, California)

Groaner Digger (Texas undertaker)

Justin Tune (chorister, class of 1947, Westminster Choir, Princeton)

T. Hee (works in a restaurant in New York City)

Mr. Vroom (South African motorcycle dealer)

Dr. Zoltan Ovary (New York gynaecologist)

Safety First (lives in Leisure World, Sea Beach, California. "Every time I get a traffic ticket, I get a column in the newspaper . . . I've been in Ripley's 'Believe It or Not' three times. My sister June has been in only once")

Jean Sippy (recently divorced but still calls herself Mrs. Sippy)

Paul Butcher (veterinarian in Orange County)

Howard Bonebrake (dentist)

Dr. Skinner (surgeon)

Dr. Lantz (general practitioner)

Judge Law and Judge Judge (dispensers of justice in Santa Ana, California)

Lieut. Lynch (Long Beach police officer)

Fire Chief Sam Sparks (settles burning issues in Garden Grove)

Ima Hogg (Houston social and cultural leader)

NAME GAMES

Name games are games you play with names. Can Alastair Cooke? Did Ezra Pound? Does Saul Bellow? Was Clare Boothe Luce?

John
Was Gay
But Gerard Hopkins
Was Manley

Dame May
Was Whitty
But John Greenleaf
Was Whittier

Oscar
Was Wilde
But Thornton
Was Wilder

WEDDING BELLS

In the Wedding Name Game you make up marriages. If dancer Ginger Rogers had married novelist Thomas Mann she'd have been a Ginger Mann. If Mitzi Green had married Orson Bean she'd have been Mitzi Green Bean. If Bella Abzug had married Red Buttons she'd have been Bella Buttons. If Tuesday Weld had married Fredric March II, she'd have been Tuesday March 2nd.

CALL ME ADAM

In the Stage Name Game you discover that Red Buttons's real name is Aaron Schwatt. You also get to know that Douglas Fairbanks, Jack Benny, Cary Grant, Peter Lorre, Mike Nichols, Marlene Dietrich, El Greco, and King Edward VII started life as plain Nicholas Bronstein, Benjamin Kubelski, Archie Leach, Laszlo Loewenstein, Michael Igor Peschkowsky, Maria Magdalena von Losch, Domenico Teotocopulo and Albert of Saxe-Coburg. What's more, you can invent stage names for the stars of tomorrow (or for yesterday's stars who deserve to make a comeback under a new name): Ida Hope, Annie Seedball, Astrid de Stars, Bella de Ball, Ken John Peel, May Morning, Ella Vagirl, Luke Warm, Rachel Prejudice, Sibyl Rights . . .

HOLD THE FRONT PAGE

In the Newsman's Name Game you just say who you are: "I'm Trumpett from the *Herald,* I'm Sign of the *Times,* I'm Tied from the *Post,* I'm Brown from the *Sun,* I'm Justice from the *Tribune,* I'm Shakespeare of the *Globe,* I'm Sick of the *News* . . ."

HELLO OLLIE

In the What's in a Name Game you look up your own name in a dictionary and see if it means what you think it sounds as if it ought to mean. (A brandreth is a wooden stack for a cask. Very boring.) If the dictionary doesn't give a definition for your name (say, Denver or Polawsky), devise a definition of your own. And if you don't like the name you've got, change it. You can give yourself a unique name (like Zero Zzyzz and Vladimir Zzzyd, the last two names in the Miami telephone directory) or a name shared by 2,382,509 other Americans at the last count (Smith). If you want the commonest name on earth, you'll have to change to Chang, the surname of at least 75 million people.

YOU COW!

"You cow!" is not something a gentleman should call his wife unless he's a pig—in which case his armory of matrimonial abuse is sure to include some if not all of these hurtful adjectives:

batty	*dogged*	*ratty*
bitchy	*fishy*	*sheepish*
bovine	*foxy*	*sluggish*
catty	*lousy*	*swinish*
cocky	*mousy*	*waspish*
crabby	*mulish*	

Every one of the adjectives derives from the name of a bird or beast. Not content with killing animals for food and fun and clothes and cosmetics, we involve them in the vocabulary of abuse as well. The irony is that the man who calls his wife a bitch and the wife who calls her husband a dog are as often as not animal lovers who adore the dogs and bitches they keep as pets.

One or two animal adjectives can be taken as complimentary, but on close examination they are not so generous as all that. Some girls are happy to be called *kittenish*, but the word carries an undertone of feline minxishness that is not altogether flattering. *Owlish* suggests scholarship, but it hints at bovine and dogged qualities as well.

Few of us relish being called a pig or a cow or a stoat or a shrew or a cur, let alone a goose or a peacock or a popinjay. And while we never describe people as dog-fresh or clean dogs or as healthy as a dog, we don't hesitate to describe them as dog-tired or dirty dogs or as sick as a dog. If you dog people you're a nuisance, if you bitch at them you're unkind, and even if you are just monkeying about they want you to stop.

What, I ask myself a little sheepishly, have the animals done to deserve such swinish treatment?

CAPRINE & CO.

And what, I ask you, does *caprine* mean? If you're as nimble-witted as the animal the adjective relates to is nimble-footed, you'll know the answer.

If you don't know (because you're as dumb as a sheep) you can look it up in the Answers along with these other animal adjectives:

1	*accipitrine*	11	*equine*
2	*anguine*	12	*feline*
3	*anserine*	13	*herpestine*
4	*aquiline*	14	*hircine*
5	*asinine*	15	*lacertine* or *lacertilian*
6	*bovine*	16	*lemurine*
7	*canine*	17	*leonine*
8	*cervine*	18	*lupine*
9	*colubrine*	19	*lutrine*
10	*elephantine*	20	*murine*

21 *oscine*

22 *ovine*

23 *passerine*

24 *pavonine*

25 *piscine*

26 *porcine*

27 *ranine*

28 *serpentine*

29 *suilline*

30 *suine*

31 *taurine*

32 *ursine*

33 *viperine*

34 *vulpine*

ZAP

Professor Abel T. Jackson, head of the English department at Western Community College in Indiana, has concluded an unusual piece of research, on the use of onomatopoeic exclamations in 20th-century comic books. He and his students have carefully examined several hundred thousand strips—from Krazy Kat, Batman, and Popeye right the way through to the Incredible Hulk, Star Wars, and Shreeeeek!—and have listed each and every exclamation. Says the professor: "We deliberately excluded from the scope of the survey everyday exclamations like 'Oh!' and 'Ah!' and 'Hi!' and 'Hey!' What interested us were the exclamations used as stage directions within the strips—the dramatic sounds that gave life and meaning to the action."

Here are the top 50 of the 20th century's most popular onomatopoeic exclamations:

Zap!	*Wow!*	*Aw!*
Pow!	*Ooo!*	*Yuk!*

142 JOY OF LEX

Bang!	*Gulp!*	*Splosh!*
Ugh!	*Smash!*	*Boof!*
Bonk!	*Thwack!*	*Slurp!*
Splat!	*Woweeee!*	*Oik!*
Fut!	*Zing!*	*Clang!*
Eee!	*Oi!*	*Splot!*
Whizz!	*Scrunch!*	*Clatter!*
Jeepers!	*Koing!*	*Ulp!*
Cripes!	*Ping!*	*Kersplat!*
Klunk!	*Kerr-unch!*	*Yikes!*
Aaagh!	*Weee!*	*Vroomvroom!*
Crack!	*Jipes!*	*Kerplop!*
Klonk!	*Crumbs!*	*Klink!*
Crash!	*Krunk!*	*Yarooo!*
Bong!	*Och!*	

Compiling the list—which includes over a thousand words—has taken Professor Jackson and his team three years. Was it all worthwhile? "Definitely," says the professor. "This has been no dry semantic exercise. Comic strips and comic books are an integral part of American culture. These extraordinary exclamations have given a new richness to our language. They add a vital dimension to the 20th-century experience."

Ouch!

Z
ZZZ

Insomnia isn't good for you. Complete lack of sleep will kill you more quickly than complete lack of food.

Elephants and dolphins can survive happily with 2 hours sleep out of every 24 and the Emperor Napoleon, who loved his bed ("I would not exchange it for all the thrones in the world"), rarely took more than 5 hours a night, but the average night's sleep among normal human beings (that's us) is now reckoned to be 7 hours 36 minutes.

People in their fifties tend to sleep less than those in their twenties, but people in their sixties get more sleep than at any time since childhood. Men sleep 10 minutes more than women, and the difference rises to 20 minutes more in the fifties and 50 minutes more in the seventies. Extroverts of both sexes, not to mention those with low IQ's, sleep a little longer than the average.

If you suffer from insomnia, whatever the cause (hypertension, indigestion, a lousy marriage, inability to reconcile yourself to spending 20 to 30 years of your precious life asleep), you need a zzzz game.

Zzzz games played in your head in your bed with the lights out and your eyes closed will make you doze off in no time. And if they don't, it doesn't matter: they're such great games you'll find you don't mind staying awake.

Here are the five best zzzz games of all time.

SLIPPERS

Starting at *a* and traveling through to *z*, think of all the words you can that begin *and end* with the same letter:

area, aria, alpha
bomb, bulb, boob
chronic, clinic, cardiac
divided, dread, dunderhead
elope, evade, emanate
fluff, fief
gong, going, gag
hunch, hush, health
knock, kink, kick
level, lull, liberal
minimum, maximum, mechanism
noon, nun, nation
overdo, olio, oratorio
peep, plump, pip
revolver, rear, rooster
slippers, stress, sexless
tint, tournament, trumpet
wallow, willow, window
yearly, yesterday, yeomanry

If you are very tired you may include proper names (like *Ifni* and *Xerox*), foreign words (like *uhuru*), exclamations (like *wow!*), acronyms (like INRI), and colloquialisms (like *zzzz*). If you get through the alphabet and are still awake, you can start again at *a* or move on to Nightcap.

NIGHTCAP

In the traditional version—known in old England as I Love My Love and in New England as Jump Rope—several players take turns declaring that they love their love because she is "adorable Alice from Alabahma," "beautiful Beatrice from the Bronx," "classy Clarisse from Colorado," and so on until "zappy Zoe from Zanesville, Ohio." In the insomniac version that you play alone, you don't name your love, you don't locate her, and you are unlikely to get beyond *a*. Not until you have exhausted the possibilities of one letter with several hundred adjectives can you move on to the next.

"I love my love with an *a* because she is abandoned, abbatial, abbreviated, abdominal, abducted, Aberdonian, aberrant, abhorrent, abiding, able . . ." After only ten adjectives (which need not be in alphabetical order) you've got yourself a stunted Scottish nun with bad habits, loose morals, and a huge stomach, who is capable and ready to stick around despite being kidnapped. It's not exactly erotic, but it proves the game has potential.

ALWIN'S AMIABLE AARDVARK

"Wacky Walter Wiesman was Warsaw's wittiest waltzing waiter. When Walter wooed women, wow! . . ."

Tell yourself a bedtime story in which every word begins with a chosen letter of the alphabet. Way before Wacky Walter's wenches are worn out and world-weary, you'll be snoozing gently. (And silently too, I trust. As the man said, laugh and the world laughs with you; snore and you sleep alone.)

TOM SWIFTIE

Tom Swiftie is a man to take to bed. He is a wit and raconteur with a pun in his every adverb, as you can tell from samples of his

small talk recorded for us by his close friend and associate Edward
J. O'Brien:

"Zero," said Tom naughtily.

"Brothers," said Tom grimly.

"Gold leaf," said Tom guiltily.

"Maid's night off," said Tom helplessly.

"Pass the cards," said Tom ideally.

"I bequeath," said Tom willingly.

"*Drei . . . fünf,*" said Tom fearlessly.

"And lose a few," said Tom winsomely.

"X's and," said Tom wisely.

"*Newsweek,*" said Tom timelessly.

"Coda," said Tom finally.

To play the game, curl up in bed and devise your own Tom
Swifties.

CROAKERS

Tom Swiftie has a cousin called Croaker. With him the pun is
purely verbal:

"I'm dying," he croaked.

Roy Bongartz is the man responsible for the Croaker craze. Here
are a half dozen of his gems:

"My experiment was a success," the chemist retorted.

"You can't really train a beagle," he dogmatized.

"That's no beagle, it's a mongrel," she muttered.

"The fire is going out," he bellowed.

"Bad marksmanship," the hunter groused.

"You ought to see a psychiatrist," he reminded me.

James I. Rambo and Mary J. Youngquist have novel names
and an equally novel collection of Croakers. Here are the best, in
ascending order of punning complexity:

"You snake!" she rattled.

"Someone's at the door," she chimed.

"Company's coming," she guessed.

"Dawn came too soon," she mourned.

"I think I'll end it all," Sue sighed.

"I ordered chocolate, not vanilla," I screamed.

"Your embroidery is sloppy," she needled cruelly.

"Where did you get this meat?" he bridled hoarsely.

Do as Bongartz, Rambo, and Youngquist do. Ease yourself to sleep creating Croakers in the dark.

Y NOT?

Y not relax with a rebus? You don't know what a rebus is? Well, U R never 2 old or YY 2 learn something new. My dictionary definition of a rebus is "an enigmatic representation of a name or a word or a phrase by pictures or letters or numbers or other words or phrases."

Wood
John
Mass.

is the rebus way of addressing an envelope to be sent to:

John Underwood

Andover, Mass.

And "If the B mt put:" is the rebus way of saying: "If the grate be empty put coal on."

Now try to unravel the following rebuses.

1. Usually you would find meat on this word. What is it:

B

E

2. What's this?

    ONE ANOTHER
    ONE ANOTHER
    ONE ANOTHER
    ONE ANOTHER
    ONE ANOTHER
    ONE ANOTHER

3. Popeye would have loved this. What is it:

    C   SP   H

4. What is the name of this young lady?

    MARY
    2,000 pounds

5. This is a rebus fit for a court of law. What does it mean?

    STAND   OATH
    U   UR

6. Have you been to this play?

            ADO
    ADO   ADO
    ADO   0   ADO
    ADO   ADO
            ADO

7. There are six letters here, all pointing to a cold climate. What are they?

    WETHER

8. What word is this?

    C
    T

9. What does this mean?

    STAND   TAKE   TO   TAKING
    I   YOU   THROW   MY

10. Here is a well-known phrase. Can you spot it?

    ONALLE

11. This is the alcoholic's lament to his bottle. Can you translate it into sober English?

OICURMT

12. You should have one of these every day. Do you know what it is?

M E
A L

13. This should be quickly put to rights. Can you do it?

FRIEND   STAND   FRIEND
m

14. Are you able to recite this famous quatrain?

YYURYYUBICURYY4ME

15. And do you recognize this well-known maxim?

16. What's this?

E
M
A
R
F

17. Here's a question that calls for lateral thinking. How are these five words to be read?

OZⵑOZ ZO ИOO ZOOZ ИⵑOZ

18. Can you follow this sound advice?

19. If JOANB means "an inside job" (reading it as *an* inside *job*), what are these meant to mean?

HODRME	CHE
OIT	AⱮL
THE	Sπ
CHE	AGE

20. And here is a rebus to end a prayer or a series of puzzles. What does it say?

WORLAMEN

(See Answers.)

X EME

Xeme is a bird or a bucket or a bison or a butterfly. Which is it? You're quite right: it's a bird, a fork-tailed gull. Your vocabulary is obviously impressive—but is it good enough? How many words do you know?

The tests that follow—scientifically devised by experienced educationalists and philologists and developed and refined over a period of years—will tell you accurately the size of your vocabulary. Ten independent tests follow. In each test, every word you know stands for 600 words in your general vocabulary. If you get 30 words right out of 60, your vocabulary is about 30 × 600 words = 18,000 words.

Average your results for as many of the ten tests as you care to take. The more tests you complete the more accurate the average will be.

What do your score and size of vocabulary signify?

LEVEL 1: 0–6,000 WORDS

Most of those who score from 0 through 10 out of 60 are children aged 6 through 9. Others include older backward children and adult illiterates. The latter may have a speaking vocabulary of more than 6,000 words, but score 0 because they cannot read.

LEVEL 2: 6,600–12,000 WORDS

A score of 11 through 20 out of 60 is usually attained at age 10 or later. Those who reach it at age 10 are likely to score 40 or more out of 60 as adults. About 25 percent of adults have vocabularies no greater than 12,000 words.

LEVEL 3: 12,600–18,000 WORDS

Among adults, this score of 21 through 30 out of 60 is the most common range. In the range 12,600–15,000 are most of the adults who left school as soon as the law would let them; they have done hardly any reading since. In the range 15,600–18,000 are many adults who left school early but continued with some reading or are in jobs that involve language skills, such as secretarial work.

An 18-year-old who intends to get further education should have reached the top of this range.

LEVEL 4: 18,600–24,000 WORDS

Adults with little or no college education may get 31 through 40 out of 60 right if they have maintained a keen interest in what is going on in the world, plus a wide range of reading. Most college graduates are in this range, and so are the members of most of the professions.

LEVEL 5: 24,600–30,000 WORDS

Men and women in this range (41 through 50 out of 60 right) are well educated and do a lot of reading. They are in the top echelons of their professions or heading in that direction.

LEVEL 6: 30,600–36,000 words

The few who fall into this category (51 through 60 out of 60 right) do not necessarily achieve more in their professions than those at level 5. At this level, the tests become more an intellectual game than an important scientific measurement.

If you are in doubt whether one of your answers is correct, consult a dictionary—at level 6, an unabridged dictionary. The tests can be used to build vocabulary as well as to measure it.

TEST NO. 1

LEVEL 1	LEVEL 2	LEVEL 3
1 *abroad*	11 *abandon*	21 *abridge*
2 *binoculars*	12 *ballot*	22 *aggregate*
3 *daily*	13 *chaos*	23 *bivouac*
4 *expedition*	14 *contraband*	24 *chronology*
5 *horizon*	15 *excavate*	25 *credulous*
6 *jangle*	16 *fatigue*	26 *hireling*
7 *limit*	17 *laboratory*	27 *indolent*
8 *pattern*	18 *manual*	28 *meager*
9 *rate*	19 *purchase*	29 *nomadic*
10 *stroke*	20 *shuttle*	30 *occidental*

LEVEL 4	LEVEL 5	LEVEL 6
31 *abhorrent*	41 *abscissa*	51 *abulia*
32 *amorphous*	42 *badinage*	52 *bicuspid*
33 *crustacean*	43 *cartel*	53 *caracole*
34 *declivity*	44 *daemon*	54 *chalybeate*
35 *emaciated*	45 *dendrite*	55 *croton*
36 *fabrication*	46 *exordium*	56 *dysphoria*
37 *galaxy*	47 *inchoate*	57 *gazebo*
38 *heretical*	48 *moraine*	58 *kymograph*
39 *igneous*	49 *rubric*	59 *ortolan*
40 *nomenclature*	50 *soutane*	60 *quadrat*

TEST NO. 2

LEVEL 1	LEVEL 2	LEVEL 3
1 *alter*	11 *beverage*	21 *biography*
2 *barometer*	12 *cardinal*	22 *decarbonize*
3 *distinct*	13 *demolish*	23 *domicile*
4 *festival*	14 *graph*	24 *facet*
5 *hardship*	15 *humdrum*	25 *impunity*
6 *harpoon*	16 *impulsive*	26 *lore*
7 *matinee*	17 *memorial*	27 *mercenary*
8 *reign*	18 *parallel*	28 *phantasm*
9 *report*	19 *terminate*	29 *restive*
10 *waste*	20 *vivacious*	30 *taboo*

LEVEL 4	LEVEL 5	LEVEL 6
31 *actuate*	41 *antinomy*	51 *antonomasia*
32 *bravura*	42 *carronade*	52 *cartouche*
33 *comber*	43 *dithyrambic*	53 *dorter*
34 *gouache*	44 *hebdomadal*	54 *elvan*
35 *hieroglyphic*	45 *infusoria*	55 *filemot*
36 *hybrid*	46 *linage*	56 *isomer*
37 *iconoclast*	47 *medusa*	57 *lasher*
38 *maelstrom*	48 *myrmidon*	58 *noumenon*
39 *muezzin*	49 *paradigm*	59 *pulvinate*
40 *resurgent*	50 *topology*	60 *velleity*

TEST NO. 3

LEVEL 1	LEVEL 2	LEVEL 3
1 *explosion*	11 *fledgling*	21 *cosmopolitan*
2 *impatient*	12 *hatchet*	22 *diverge*
3 *kangaroo*	13 *impact*	23 *interpose*
4 *pirate*	14 *javelin*	24 *lateral*
5 *prowl*	15 *landlubber*	25 *niche*
6 *referee*	16 *novelist*	26 *porous*
7 *slant*	17 *primitive*	27 *rampant*
8 *solo*	18 *renown*	28 *territory*
9 *unique*	19 *tradition*	29 *voodoo*
10 *waste*	20 *urban*	30 *yeoman*

LEVEL 4	LEVEL 5	LEVEL 6
31 *ecology*	41 *asymptotic*	51 *bisque*
32 *laconic*	42 *burlap*	52 *colporteur*
33 *linden*	43 *echidna*	53 *decuman*
34 *maxilla*	44 *henry*	54 *grallatorial*
35 *paragon*	45 *interfacial*	55 *isomorphous*
36 *prolixity*	46 *jeton*	56 *orc*
37 *redolent*	47 *paregoric*	57 *parataxis*
38 *stertorous*	48 *rachitic*	58 *rivière*
39 *timbre*	49 *tanager*	59 *tanagra*
40 *vellum*	50 *syncretism*	60 *urticant*

TEST NO. 4

LEVEL 1	LEVEL 2	LEVEL 3
1 *ballad*	11 *abyss*	21 *adaptable*
2 *canoe*	12 *bale*	22 *capsule*
3 *external*	13 *canyon*	23 *daub*
4 *icicle*	14 *exterminate*	24 *embargo*
5 *lame*	15 *instrument*	25 *gargoyle*
6 *magazine*	16 *lizard*	26 *justify*
7 *martyr*	17 *obvious*	27 *liberate*
8 *mass*	18 *password*	28 *memento*
9 *patriot*	19 *rhythm*	29 *naturalize*
10 *patrol*	20 *stoppage*	30 *oblivion*

LEVEL 4	LEVEL 5	LEVEL 6
31 *calculus*	41 *aclinic*	51 *Babbittry*
32 *debouch*	42 *banshee*	52 *calumet*
33 *gargantuan*	43 *illation*	53 *dehiscent*
34 *ibid.*	44 *keelson*	54 *gault*
35 *laissez-faire*	45 *lachrymal*	55 *hypocaust*
36 *literati*	46 *martingale*	56 *kenosis*
37 *neurology*	47 *newton*	57 *knap*
38 *obloquy*	48 *occipital*	58 *limnology*
39 *patois*	49 *petrology*	59 *mithridatism*
40 *rabid*	50 *ratline*	60 *unau*

TEST NO. 5

LEVEL 1	LEVEL 2	LEVEL 3
1 *belfry*	11 *besiege*	21 *aquiline*
2 *bulge*	12 *bronze*	22 *botanist*
3 *outlaw*	13 *gorge*	23 *captious*
4 *package*	14 *import*	24 *furtive*
5 *pillar*	15 *judo*	25 *initiate*
6 *rental*	16 *ledger*	26 *jaded*
7 *riddle*	17 *limpet*	27 *kaleidoscopic*
8 *shellfish*	18 *penetrate*	28 *limerick*
9 *vanish*	19 *resort*	29 *mutual*
10 *varnish*	20 *warbler*	30 *stratagem*

LEVEL 4	LEVEL 5	LEVEL 6
31 *aurochs*	41 *bergamot*	51 *ablegate*
32 *beriberi*	42 *brevier*	52 *algorism*
33 *cornice*	43 *deemster*	53 *baltimore*
34 *denary*	44 *homologous*	54 *bezel*
35 *gratuitous*	45 *lamina*	55 *leat*
36 *hertz*	46 *largo*	56 *mittimus*
37 *hiatus*	47 *pantheon*	57 *myosotis*
38 *medial*	48 *refulgence*	58 *peneplain*
39 *teredo*	49 *savory*	59 *prunella*
40 *valetudinarian*	50 *triolet*	60 *windlestraw*

TEST NO. 6

LEVEL 1	LEVEL 2	LEVEL 3
1 *anthill*	11 *absurd*	21 *acoustics*
2 *climate*	12 *collapse*	22 *bicker*
3 *container*	13 *entire*	23 *bison*
4 *endeavor*	14 *generation*	24 *centripetal*
5 *immediately*	15 *immigrate*	25 *emancipation*
6 *jingle*	16 *jealous*	26 *garbled*
7 *outcast*	17 *mature*	27 *lichen*
8 *rhyme*	18 *raid*	28 *mattock*
9 *signal*	19 *satellite*	29 *outshine*
10 *tank*	20 *slipshod*	30 *perimeter*

LEVEL 4	LEVEL 5	LEVEL 6
31 *botulism*	41 *chamfer*	51 *champlevé*
32 *cutaneous*	42 *eschatology*	52 *deadlight*
33 *datum*	43 *giaour*	53 *enchiridion*
34 *distrait*	44 *imprest*	54 *geodic*
35 *encyclical*	45 *lapidate*	55 *jokul*
36 *gamma*	46 *nadir*	56 *laches*
37 *lacerate*	47 *oblate*	57 *maud*
38 *mandate*	48 *samphire*	58 *pedicular*
39 *martinet*	49 *satrap*	59 *spandrel*
40 *nacelle*	50 *ukase*	60 *vavasor*

TEST NO. 7

LEVEL 1	LEVEL 2	LEVEL 3
1 *humbug*	11 *autobiography*	21 *alloy*
2 *ivy*	12 *corrugated*	22 *brevity*
3 *legend*	13 *extinct*	23 *deportation*
4 *magnet*	14 *gladiator*	24 *hinterland*
5 *nickname*	15 *deputy*	25 *inscrutable*
6 *probably*	16 *hooligan*	26 *lineage*
7 *ripple*	17 *lanky*	27 *mucilage*
8 *situation*	18 *magistrate*	28 *omen*
9 *tattoo*	19 *nozzle*	29 *persecute*
10 *theater*	20 *offend*	30 *repertoire*

LEVEL 4	LEVEL 5	LEVEL 6
31 *agoraphobia*	41 *animism*	51 *acarpous*
32 *barograph*	42 *boulevardier*	52 *chanterelle*
33 *concatenation*	43 *canticle*	53 *demersal*
34 *demography*	44 *homophone*	54 *eclampsia*
35 *hierarchy*	45 *lammergeier*	55 *gonfalon*
36 *iceblink*	46 *mangonal*	56 *jeofail*
37 *megrim*	47 *natterjack*	57 *orris*
38 *olfactory*	48 *Paleozoic*	58 *pyx*
39 *radian*	49 *peignoir*	59 *ret*
40 *risotto*	50 *reticle*	60 *sachem*

TEST NO. 8

LEVEL 1	LEVEL 2	LEVEL 3
1 *badger*	11 *brewer*	21 *breaker*
2 *capture*	12 *charity*	22 *cumbersome*
3 *fresh*	13 *generosity*	23 *detention*
4 *hiss*	14 *idol*	24 *fumigate*
5 *ironmonger*	15 *lathe*	25 *humane*
6 *ladle*	16 *orderly*	26 *juggernaut*
7 *mermaid*	17 *orient*	27 *kayak*
8 *parade*	18 *quest*	28 *lineal*
9 *rear*	19 *rowlock*	29 *objective*
10 *swindle*	20 *summit*	30 *sorcery*

LEVEL 4	LEVEL 5	LEVEL 6
31 *chicanery*	41 *ablaut*	51 *chibouk*
32 *gravamen*	42 *belvedere*	52 *disembogue*
33 *holocaust*	43 *dimity*	53 *gemmule*
34 *lethargic*	44 *gelation*	54 *idolum*
35 *monograph*	45 *homeopathy*	55 *lasque*
36 *pinnace*	46 *morpheme*	56 *oroide*
37 *ramify*	47 *pis aller*	57 *quintan*
38 *scrutineer*	48 *psephology*	58 *rampion*
39 *tangential*	49 *regulus*	59 *scammony*
40 *unction*	50 *sawder*	60 *sullage*

TEST NO. 9

LEVEL 1	LEVEL 2	LEVEL 3
1 *batter*	11 *barbed*	21 *dabble*
2 *chest*	12 *chemistry*	22 *exhaustive*
3 *engineer*	13 *exception*	23 *filtrate*
4 *funnel*	14 *fascinating*	24 *garnish*
5 *horn*	15 *gibberish*	25 *indifferent*
6 *mean*	16 *hydrogen*	26 *kaiser*
7 *outrun*	17 *Latin*	27 *metronome*
8 *pickax*	18 *microscope*	28 *naive*
9 *remove*	19 *shield*	29 *patronize*
10 *search*	20 *suburb*	30 *reinforce*

LEVEL 4	LEVEL 5	LEVEL 6
31 *bêtise*	41 *aperçu*	51 *crucian*
32 *clamant*	42 *bleb*	52 *deuteragonist*
33 *dirigible*	43 *decorticate*	53 *encaustic*
34 *epitome*	44 *gauss*	54 *hoveler*
35 *histrionic*	45 *involute*	55 *immortelle*
36 *logarithm*	46 *lambent*	56 *limpkin*
37 *panegyric*	47 *peculation*	57 *mort*
38 *rowel*	48 *recidivist*	58 *peen*
39 *simoom*	49 *semiotics*	59 *regelate*
40 *stricture*	50 *speculum*	60 *sandever*

TEST NO. 10

LEVEL 1

1 *battery*
2 *carnation*
3 *drowsy*
4 *forecast*
5 *guilty*
6 *jellyfish*
7 *mention*
8 *pathless*
9 *result*
10 *screen*

LEVEL 2

11 *crag*
12 *dwindling*
13 *easterly*
14 *hilt*
15 *impetuous*
16 *instinct*
17 *pike*
18 *regulation*
19 *verge*
20 *warehouse*

LEVEL 3

21 *bristling*
22 *devious*
23 *entangle*
24 *mere*
25 *precipitous*
26 *scurvy*
27 *summons*
28 *territorial*
29 *unkempt*
30 *vindicate*

LEVEL 4

31 *burnous*
32 *cadenza*
33 *debenture*
34 *flense*
35 *franklin*
36 *habergeon*
37 *ignis fatuus*
38 *jocund*
39 *mutability*
40 *napoleon*

LEVEL 5

41 *catchpole*
42 *Greek calends*
43 *Heaviside layer*
44 *ichor*
45 *jussive*
46 *limen*
47 *nescience*
48 *obi*
49 *panhandle*, n.
50 *ramose*

LEVEL 6

51 *calamary*
52 *eparch*
53 *fleury*
54 *grangerize*
55 *jacobus*
56 *levigate*
57 *marshalsea*
58 *narthex*
59 *obol*
60 *tetterwort*

Wordsmiths' Wordplay

All writers play with words, some more obviously than others. Here are five of the world's best word games. Each game happens to be or have been a favorite of one of the world's most distinguished wordsmiths.

Walt whitman's game

FORBIDDEN VOWELS

The aim is to write the longest possible sentence without using a certain vowel. In the first round *a* is forbidden, in the second *e*, and so on.

The players are given paper and pencil and five minutes in which to concoct their sentences. When the time is up, the players read out their efforts, which must make some sort of sense, and count the number of words they have used. Any player who has let the forbidden vowel slip into his sentence is disqualified. The player with the longest sentence wins.

A more difficult version can be played without paper and pencil. The players take turns asking each other questions—to which one-word answers are not allowed. Any player uttering a word that contains the forbidden vowel is out of the game. The last player left talking is the winner. This is the version that Whitman played. Sadly, no written record exists to show how good—or bad—he was at it.

TOM STOPPARD'S GAME

QUESTIONS!

In Questions! the first player begins with a question, his opponent must reply with another question, the first player puts a third question, the opponent responds with a fourth, until one of the players falters and fails to ask a question. Repeating questions is not allowed.

Here is a brief bout between Adam and Eve:

ADAM: What time is it?

EVE: Why do you want to know?

ADAM: Why do you ask that?

EVE: Why can't you answer a civil question?

ADAM: Why can't you look at your watch?

EVE: When are you going to get yourself a watch?

ADAM: What's that got to do with it?

EVE: Who do you think you are talking to me like that?

ADAM: Where can I find someone who will tell me the time?

EVE: Where can I find a husband who can afford a watch of his own?

ADAM: When do you stop nagging?

EVE: Why don't you stop going on like this?

ADAM: Do you know something?

EVE: What?

ADAM: Do you know who you remind me of?

EVE: Who?

ADAM: Your mother!

In Tom Stoppard's version of the game the rules are tighter. The player tries to make the opponent respond with a statement or repeat a previous question, *or* ask the equivalent of an earlier question, *or* ask a question that has no connection with the previous question, *or* indulge in bombastic rhetoric.

In his play *Rosencrantz and Guildenstern Are Dead* Stoppard has the title characters play the game, in a verbal tennis match that Jimmy Connors and Björn Borg would be hard put to equal at Wimbledon:

ROS.: We could play at questions.

GUIL.: What good would that do?

ROS.: Practice!

GUIL.: Statement! One-love.

ROS.: Cheating!

GUIL.: How?

ROS.: I hadn't started yet.

GUIL.: Statement. Two-love.

ROS.: Are you counting that?

GUIL.: What?

ROS.: Are you counting that?

GUIL.: Foul! No repetitions. Three-love. First game to . . .

ROS.: I'm not going to play if you're going to be like that.

GUIL.: Whose serve?

ROS.: Hah?

GUIL.: Foul! No grunts, Love-one.

ROS.: Whose go?

GUIL.: Why?

ROS.: Why not?

GUIL.: What for?

ROS.: Foul! No synonyms! One-all.

GUIL.: What in God's name is going on?

ROS.: Foul! No rhetoric. Two-one.

GUIL.: What does it all add up to?

ROS.: Can't you guess?

GUIL.: Were you addressing me?

ROS.: Is there anyone else?

GUIL.: Who?

ROS.: How would I know?

GUIL.: Why do you ask?

ROS.: Are you serious?

GUIL.: Was that rhetoric?

ROS.: No.

GUIL.: Statement! Two-all. Game point.

ROS.: What's the matter with you today?

GUIL.: When?

ROS.: What?

GUIL.: Are you deaf?

ROS.: Am I dead?

GUIL.: Yes or no?

ROS.: Is there a choice?

GUIL.: Is there a God?

ROS.: Foul! No non sequiturs, three-two, one game all.

GUIL. (*seriously*): What's your name?

ROS.: What's yours?

GUIL: I asked you first.

ROS.: Statement. One-love.

GUIL.: What's your name when you're at home?

ROS.: What's yours?

GUIL.: When I'm at home?

ROS.: Is it different at home?

GUIL.: What home?

ROS.: Haven't you got one?

GUIL.: Why do you ask?

ROS.: What are you driving at?

GUIL. (*with emphasis*): What's your name?

ROS.: Repetition. Two-love. Match point to me.

GUIL. (*seizing him violently*): WHO DO YOU THINK YOU ARE?

ROS.: Rhetoric! Game and match!

FRANCES HODGSON BURNETT'S GAME

PECULIAR LEADER

Despite its name, this game has nothing to do with politics. It is a parlor game in which you as leader get up and tell the other players what you do and don't like. When one of the players feels he understands the rationale of why you like this but you don't like that, he raises up his hand and gives an example of what he thinks you do and don't like. (He does not explain how he thinks you choose your likes and dislikes.) If he is right, congratulate him. The last player to give a correct example is the loser, and has to do the washing up after the party.

See how long it takes you to get the message from this list:

I like coffee, but I don't like tea.

I like trees, but I don't like flowers.

I like yellow, but I don't like blue.

I like balloons, but I don't like party hats.

I like butterflies, but I don't like moths.

I like bees, but I don't like wasps.

I like slippers, but I don't like shoes.

I like spoons, but I don't like forks.

I like doors, but I don't like windows.

I like glasses, but I don't like monocles.

I like Kennedy, but I don't like Carter.

I like swimmers, but I don't like divers.

I like football, but I don't like boxing.

I like tennis, but I don't like golf.

I like noon, but I don't like night.

I like mushrooms, but I don't like tomatoes.

I like cabbage, but I don't like cauliflower.

I like winners, but I don't like losers.

I like *Little Lord Fauntleroy,* but I don't like *The Secret Garden.*

Did you guess that the items "I like" include a pair of vowels or consonants side by side, but the items "I don't like" don't include such a pair?

Here is a second, perhaps more difficult set of likes and dislikes:

I like wasps, but I don't like bees.

I like the stupid, but I don't like the wise.

I like what I am, but I don't like what you are.

I like snap beans, but I don't like peas.

I like noses, but I don't like eyes.

I like sheep, but I don't like ewes.

I like a box of chocolates that's full, but I don't like one that's empty.

I like hard work, but I don't like ease.

I like lakes, but I don't like the sea.

I like the blackbird, but I don't like the jay.

I like coffee, but I don't like tea.

I like me, but I don't like you.

The things "I don't like" sound like letters of the alphabet: b's, y's, ur, p's, i's, u's, mt, e's, c, j, t, u.

With three or more players, the loser of one round should be the leader of the next.

JAMES THURBER'S GAMES

GHOST

Few games can sort out the impressive vocabularies from the little ones as well as the game of Ghost. In this game each player tries to add one more letter to an incomplete word without actually finishing a word.

The first player calls out a letter, and the second player adds another, making sure that the two-letter combination begins at least one real word. The third player adds a third letter; he too is thinking of a real word—not necessarily the same one. Two- and three-letter words don't lose, so the fourth player (or the player who adds the fourth letter if there are less than four players) is the first one to risk a losing word. When a player is forced to finish a word he becomes a *g*, and on further losses an *h*, an *o*, an *s*, and finally a *t*, which spells *ghost* and loses the game.

To check that a player has a real word in mind, the next player can challenge. If the first player cannot name an acceptable word, he loses the round. But if he does name a word, the challenger loses the round.

Here is an example:

TOM: *A*. (He is thinking of *axis*.)

DICK: *A-r*. (He is thinking of *arena*.)

HARRY: *A-r-c*. (Although *arc* is a word, three-letter words don't count. Harry is thinking of *arch*.)

TOM: *A-r-c-a*. (He is thinking of *arcadia*.)

DICK: *A-r-c-a-n*. (He is thinking of *arcane*.)

HARRY: (He cannot think of a letter to follow *a-r-c-a-n*, so he challenges Dick. When Dick meets the challenge with *arcane* and the dictionary confirms that *arcane* means *mysterious*, Harry loses the round.)

Again:

GEORGE: *G*. (He is thinking of *gate*.)

MARTHA: *G-r*. (She is thinking of *grain*.)

GEORGE: *G-r-a*. (He is thinking of *gravid*.)

MARTHA: *G-r-a-n.* (She is thinking of *grand.*)

GEORGE: *G-r-a-n-u.* (He is thinking of *granular.*)

MARTHA: *G-r-a-n-u-l.* (She is thinking of *granule.*)

GEORGE: *G-r-a-n-u-l-a.* (But he is still thinking of *granular,* which would win.)

MARTHA: *G-r-a-n-u-l-a-t.* (She has saved herself by suddenly thinking of *granulate.*)

GEORGE: *G-r-a-n-u-l-a-t-e.* (George loses the round. But he wouldn't have if he knew the word *granulator.*)

SUPERGHOST

Superghost is Ghost for masterminds. The added attraction is that in Superghost you can add a letter to either end of the group of letters as it is being built up:

ADAM: *R.* (He is thinking of *rice.*)

EVE: *R-o.* (She is thinking of *robot.*)

ADAM: *T-r-o.* (He is thinking of *trombone.*)

EVE: *N-t-r-o.* (She is thinking of *introduce.*)

ADAM: *O-n-t-r-o.* (He is thinking of *controvert.*)

EVE: *C-o-n-t-r-o.* (She is thinking of *control.*)

ADAM: *N-c-o-n-t-r-o.* (He is thinking of *uncontrolled.*)

EVE: *N-c-o-n-t-r-o-v.* (She is thinking of *uncontroversial.*)

ADAM: *N-c-o-n-t-r-o-v-e.* (He is thinking of *uncontroversial* too.)

EVE: *N-c-o-n-t-r-o-v-e-r.* (The same.)

ADAM: *I-n-c-o-n-t-r-o-v-e-r.* (He has just realized that if they continue with *uncontroversial* he will lose the game, so he has changed to *incontrovertible.*)

EVE: *I-n-c-o-n-t-r-o-v-e-r-t.* (She has realized that she too must change to *incontrovertible* and that she must lose.)

ADAM: *I-n-c-o-n-t-r-o-v-e-r-t-i.*

EVE: *I-n-c-o-n-t-r-o-v-e-r-t-i-b.*

ADAM: *I-n-c-o-n-t-r-o-v-e-r-t-i-b-l.*

EVE: *I-n-c-o-n-t-r-o-v-e-r-t-i-b-l-e.*

In his story "Do You Want to Make Something Out of It" Thurber described the typical Superghost enthusiast:

> The Superghost aficionado is a moody fellow, given to spelling to himself at table, not listening to his wife, and staring dully at his frightened children, wondering why he didn't detect, in yesterday's game, that "cklu" is the guts of "lackluster," and priding himself on having stumped everybody with "nehe" the middle of "swineherd." In this last case, "bonehead" would have done, since we allow slang if it is in the dictionary, but "Stonehenge" is out, because we don't allow proper nouns.

GEORGE S. KAUFMAN'S GAME

STINKETY PINKETY

In Stinkety Pinkety the first player offers a definition—one as long as he likes—and the other must translate it into a noun modified by a rhyming adjective.

The elementary examples are called Stink Pinks: the nouns and adjectives are monosyllabic.

Definition: An obese piece of headgear.

Answer: A fat hat.

Definition: A very unmelodious group of singers.

Answer: A dire choir.

Try to find answers to these three, attributed to Kaufman himself:

1. *Definition:* A canine quadruped from a muddy backwater.
   Answer:
2. *Definition:* A young man who has lost his wits.
   Answer:
3. *Definition:* A particularly stupid donkey.
   Answer:

Stinky Pinkies call for nouns and adjectives of two syllables which both rhyme:

Definition: A rather too revealing item of night attire.
Answer: A flighty nightie.
Definition: A foolish fellow called William.
Answer: A silly Billy.

Now try finding answers for these three:

4. *Definition:* An enthusiastic and devoted slave.
   Answer:

5. *Definition:* The uppermost part of the house that won't move even in an earthquake.

   Answer:

6. *Definition:* A Trojan horse.
   Answer:

The really difficult ones, calling for trisyllabic nouns and adjectives, with the last two syllables rhyming, are Stinkety Pinketies:

Definition: A man both arty and austere.
Answer: An aesthetic ascetic.
Definition: A washing-up powder that takes over the world.
Answer: An insurgent detergent.

Now it's your turn:

7. *Definition:* A cactus in a bad mood.
   Answer:

8. *Definition:* A male member of the audience who   s made out a will; a female ditto.

   Answer:

9. *Definition:* A dull work of art produced by joining together minute pieces of glass and stone.

   Answer:

10. *Definition:* A southern German baby delivered by means of surgery.

    Answer:

(See Answers.)

V ERBARRHEA

Compare this—

> To everything there is a season, and a time to every purpose
> under the heaven: A time to be born, and a time to die; a time to
> plant, and a time to pluck up that which is planted.

—with this:

> Over the past ten years the school has evolved a child-centered
> individual-learning situation with a degree of integrated day
> organization and close cooperation between each year's mixed-
> ability classes. Basic-work morning programs are carefully struc-
> tured but allow for integration . . .

Both passages are examplars of their times. The first comes
from the King James Version of the Bible (1611). The second is
from an ad for a junior-high-school teacher (1978).

What happened to the language between 1611 and 1978?
The answer, in a word, is gobbledygook.

People from all walks of life, from the lowest to the highest—especially perhaps the lower who feel that they really belong to the ranks of the higher—seem unable to resist the temptation to use two or three, or better still, four words where one will do. The simple is eschewed in favor of the complex, the monosyllabic in favor of the polysyllabic, the easily comprehensible in favor of the almost incomprehensible. Man has always been prolix, but in the last quarter of the 20th century his verbosity has reached new heights.

Witness these two winners of the Verbarrhea of the Year Award:

> The cognitive continuum is concerned with objectives related to knowledge and the intellectual abilities and skills, rising from comprehension to evaluation. The effective continuum covers the range of behavioral responses, from passive acceptance of stimuli to the organization of taught values into a complex system which constitutes the whole characterization of an individual.

> In the second place there are grounds for thinking that the availability of analytical assessments of jobs would facilitate the preparation of grade-descriptions for a new structure in a situation in which the allocation of jobs to grades at the stages of implementing and maintaining that structure would be undertaken by whole-job procedures.

It's not just because the words are long that they're lousy. It would be a mistake to become indignant every time we read a passage that contains long words which didn't make much sense to us; if we heard that—

> Reaction kinetics and gas absorption, as well as catalysis and granulation, are technical fields in which the division is particularly interested.

—we could do little but admit that nowadays there is more to fertilizer than following a horse with a shovel. It's only when the words are long but don't need to be that a protest is called for.

And not only protest, but translation. Have a go at translating these eight gems of gobbledygook. The first six are for real, the last two just for fun.

Translation please

1 There is a degree of precipitation in the atmosphere. (Three-word translation, please.)

2 There is an obligation to work with unusually distant time horizons. (Four words.)

3 Basically, we are endeavoring to review the validity of the schedules. (Seven words.)

4 On initial arrival relevant information was laid before us indicative of the conversion now being of limited duration equipmentwise. (Thirteen words.)

5 A set of arrangements for producing and rearing children the viability of which is not predicated on the consistent presence in the household of an adult male acting in the role of husband and father. (Four words.)

6 Experiments are described which demonstrate that in normal individuals the lowest concentration in which sucrose can be detected by means of gustation differs from the lowest concentration in which sucrose (in the amount employed) has to be ingested in order to produce a demonstrable decrease in olfactory acuity and a noteworthy conversion of sensations interpreted as a desire for food into sensations interpreted as a satiety associated with ingestion of food. (Twenty-eight words.)

7 A slight inclination of the cranium is as adequate as a spasmodic movement of one optic to an equine quadruped utterly devoid of any visionary capacity. (Eleven words.)

8 Such are the vicissitudes of this our sublunary experience. (Three words.)

(See Answers.)

Gobbledygook

Plain talk has become so rare that there is money to be made out of it. Alan Siegel, a Miami-based communications and design consultant, has made hundreds of thousands of dollars translating the incomprehensible English of government departments, banks, and insurance companies into English that ordinary people can understand. And President Carter—a Plains speaker by birth, of course—has insisted that every government department engage "a simple-writing expert." As the White House lawyer said when Carter protested about an incomprehensible piece of legalese, "I see your point, Mr. President. I had better laymanize the whole thing."

If you're as determined as the White House lawyer, here are the 20 top gobbledygook words to avoid:

GOBBLEDYGOOK	PLAIN TALK
subsequent to	after
prior to, antecedent to	before
rationale	reason
conjecture, speculate	guess
converse	talk
interrogate	question
hypothesize	suppose, let's say
in the vicinity of	near
approximately	about, around
audible	aloud, out loud
perceptible, visible	in sight, noticeable
negligent	careless
preponderance	greater weight
acquiesce, concur	agree
emphasize	stress
substantially contemporaneous	at about the same time
equitable	fair
aggregate of, totality of	all
totality of circumstances	whole picture
earned compensation	pay
supersede	replace

ANTIGOBBLE

For a set of rules for plain talk, it would be difficult to better the six offered by George Orwell in 1946:

1 Never use a metaphor, simile, or other figure of speech which you are used to seeing in print.

2 Never use a long word where a short one will do.

3 If it is possible to cut a word out, always cut it out.

4 Never use the passive where you can use the active.

5 Never use a foreign phrase, a scientific word, or a jargon word if you can think of an everyday English equivalent.

6 Break any of these rules sooner than say anything outright barbarous.

Follow the rules and your writing may not be as good as Orwell's, but it will be to the point. What's more, as Orwell noted, "When you make a stupid remark its stupidity will be obvious, even to yourself."

GOBBLEDYGOOK GENERATOR

If, on the other hand, you do not wish to have the stupidity of your remarks made obvious, our Gobbledygook Generator is your kind of toy. To invest your every utterance with a modern-as-tomorrow ring of decisive, knowledgeable authority, pick a word from each of the three columns and string the words together. You will never be short of something to say because the Generator can provide you with 140,608 three-word combinations, from *inherent coincidental interference* to *distributive exponential feasibility.*

inherent	*coincidental*	*interference*
emancipative	*exemplificatory*	*efficiency*
substantial	*preventive*	*interdependence*
ambivalent	*expansive*	*projection*
reversible	*participatory*	*motivation*
permanent	*degenerative*	*eventuality*
gradual	*aggregating*	*diffusion*

partial

societal

adequate

global

responsive

traditional

dialectical

fictitious

defunctionalized

existential

positivistic

elitist

predicative

ultimative

temporal

intransigent

obsolete

antiauthoritarian

flanking

multilateral

bilateral

representative

quantitative

concentrated

ameliorating

divergent

indicative

immanent

synchronous

contradictory

differentiated

systematized

inductive

universal

falsificatory

evolutionary

appropriative

prior

illusory

concordant

allocated

frustrated

restrictive

accidental

fluctuating

simulated

digital

convergent

totemic

elongating

innovative

homogeneous

identifying

transfigurative

discrepant

culminating

diversifying

alliterative

usurpative

erupting

deteriorative

obstructive

decentralized

imitative

cooperative

conglomerate

mobility

vacancy

flexibility

finality

phase

transparency

adaptation

factionalism

extension

periodicity

denudation

affinity

transcendence

specification

psychosis

competence

structure

disparity

escalation

synthesis

consistency

motivation

mobility

cancellation

sufficiency

equivalence

turbulence

discontinuity

potency

expectancy

accumulation

plasticity

stagflation

structural	progressive	permanence
integrated	recessive	epigenesis
determinative	programmed	solidification
coincidental	eliminative	application
nonfragmenting	differential	implication
interfractional	complementary	deterioration
descriptive	dynamic	constructivism
coherent	substantive	polarity
fortuitous	contributory	classification
proliferative	component	deformation
compatible	uniform	extrapolation
distributive	exponential	feasibility

For practice, fill the gaps in the following speech with three-word phrases from the Gobbledygook Generator.

Ladies and Gentlemen, I speak to you in the name of the Preparatory Commission, appointed in January '84 by the Conference for _____. The Commission was given the mission of clarifying the question of _____. I shall dispense with the preliminaries, since you all know the background, and come immediately to the point.

From the moment that press and television postulated the _____, the insistent call for _____ has never ceased, rightly or wrongly. The fact is that no one disputes the need for _____. It is further true that neither _____ nor _____ has changed the situation in any way.

Your Preparatory Commission therefore immediately tackled the idea of _____ raised before, and subjected it to careful analysis. We concluded that the only new approach would be _____, although we realized at the same time that one obstacle would be _____, which might indeed result in _____. Fortunately, this unwelcome eventuality could be forestalled by means of _____. Let the gentlemen who believe in _____ take note of this!

We should bear in mind that _____ and _____ are likely to favor our plan, and in the existing situation, we have no choice but to agree to _____.

Ladies and gentlemen! the alarming increase in _____ challenges us to take farsighted measures that are not without risk. There are, of course, possible alternatives, such as _____ and _____, to say nothing of _____, which should not be underestimated. We shall not know the chances of success, until, with the help of _____ and the deliberate use of _____, we launch a pilot project. _____ might possibly bring an adverse reaction, but we must take that chance, for to resort to _____ would be to invite _____, confusing the public. Only time will tell whether we may then proceed to realize _____ and _____, but much water will flow under the bridge before then.

This much is certain even today, ladies and gentlemen: in the long run, _____ and _____ will not meet the needs of this generation. Whether these needs lie in the direction of _____ cannot be foreseen today. We are confident, however, that _____ and _____ will help us on our way.

I trust I have not presumed on your _____, ladies and gentlemen, and I thank you for having given me your attention.

U NMENTIONABLES

Can you guess the nature of the garment that a century ago could have been described as:

irrepressibles, *indispensables,*

indescribables, *innominables,*

ineffables, *inexplicables,*

inexpressibles, *unwhisperables,*

unutterables, *unmentionables?*

Well, you're wrong. These weren't originally euphemisms for underpants. They were euphemisms for ordinary trousers! What went into those "unmentionables" (which were trousers to the early Victorians but more daringly underpants to the late Victorians) were *benders, understandings, underpinners, extremities,* or even—wait for it—*crural appendages.* The Victorian piano didn't have legs: it was supported on *limbs.*

Euphemism ("the substitution of a mild or vague expression for a harsh or blunt one") is an instinct as old as language itself. The Greek historian Plutarch, writing in the first century A.D. about life in the sixth century B.C., recorded that "the ancient Athenians used to cover up the ugliness of things with auspicious and kindly terms, giving them polite and endearing names. Thus they called harlots *companions*, taxes *contributions*, and prison a *chamber*."

To the genteel of only a generation or two ago a bitch was always *a lady dog* and a bull a *he-cow* or a *gentleman-cow* or a *male beast* or a *critter* or a *sire* or a *brute* or *the big animal* or anything but a bull. And I admit that until recently I always referred to going to the lavatory by means of euphemism. I was cured of the habit when a not-very-close acquaintance came to dinner. On arrival I asked him if he'd like to go upstairs to "wash his hands." "No, thanks," he replied, "I washed them in the bushes on the way here."

A lavatory, after all, is a lavatory: it is not *the throne room, the holy of holies, the Chamber of Commerce, the little boys' room,* or *the little girls' room;* and when you want to go there you want to go there, you do not want to *powder your nose* or *discover the geography of the house,* let alone *make a telephone call* or *spend a penny.* A lavatory may well be *the smallest room in the house,* but it could never be described accurately as a *toilet* (which is where one attends to one's toilet) or a *cloakroom* (which is where one leaves one's cloak) or a *restroom* (which is where, presumably, one rests), let alone a *comfort station* (which is where one—what *does* one do in a comfort station?). To call the lavatory *the john* is sexist and unkind to people called John, and the same goes for *ruth. WC* at least stands for *water closet,* which is what it is, and *crapper* was at least the name of the Victorian plumber who pioneered the design of the modern lavatory. I suppose *thunderbox* and *biffy* have onomatopoeia on their side, but the English *loo* and the American *can* have nothing but their brevity to commend them.

Public lavatories are indeed *public conveniences* and when labeled frankly, are simply marked *Men* and *Women.* At Disneyland they may be *Princes* and *Princesses,* at English holiday camps *Lads* and *Lasses,* at pony clubs *Colts* and *Fillies,* at the seaside honeymoon hotel *Buoys* and *Gulls*, at a pub in Stratford-upon-Avon *Romeos* and *Juliets*, at the Four Seasons restaurant in New York *Gentlemen* and *Ladies*, and at the Hou e of Lords in London *Peers* and *Peeresses*. When words fail the sign writers, they draw pictures instead—of a man and a woman (which could confuse a Scot for a moment should he be sporting his kilt) or a king and a queen or a cock and a hen or a bull and a cow or two dogs: a pointer for the men and a setter for the women.

When we use a euphemism it's usually because we feel it's more discreet. Sometimes, however, discretion is forced upon us. In 1973 New York automobiles began to display their new golden license plates with three numbers and three letters in blue. The Department of Motor Vehicles was proud that the new plates, designed to replace the old blue plates with yellow numbers, "offer an almost infinite number of combinations," but was nervous about where some of those combinations might lead. The department was "determined to avoid sequences of letters that are obscene, suggestive, or insulting," and so put a ban on WET and DRY, on PIG and RAT, on FAG and DYK, on FEM and GYP, on ODD and POT, as well, of course, as the more obvious SEX and SIN.

The department's attitude, however laudable, is surprising in an age when, in linguistic terms, anything goes and the taboos themselves have become taboo. There was a time when you never saw obscenities in print: they may have been there implicitly, but all you got were euphemisms and well-placed asterisks:

> An author owned an asterisk
> And kept it in his den
> Where he wrote tales which had large sales
> Of erring maids and men,
> And always, when he reached the point
> Where carping censors lurk,
> He called upon the asterisk
> To do his dirty work!

It was about the time that D. H. Lawrence's notorious *Lady Chatterley's Lover* made its first unexpurgated appearance in the United States in 1959 (31 years after Lawrence intended it should be published) that attitudes began to change and the unmentionables became mentionable even in the politest society.

There are those who still do their best to restrict the use of written or spoken obscenities, but the problem is that you can't force people to *think* clean. When I visited Kansas State University I was interested to discover that there is a legal stricture on the use of obscenity by faculty members on university property, but I'm sure the men and women I met there are as filthy-minded as the people you meet on any other college campus.

The corollary of not being able to force people to think clean is that you can't force them to think dirty either. And if you want evidence of that, here is a 1959 review of *Lady Chatterley's Lover* from the magazine *Field and Stream:*

> Although written many years ago, *Lady Chatterley's Lover* has just been reissued by the Grove Press, and this pictorial account of the day-by-day life of an English gamekeeper is full of considerable interest to outdoor-minded readers as it contains many passages on pheasant-raising, the apprehending of poachers, ways to control vermin, and other chores and duties of the professional gamekeeper.
>
> Unfortunately one is obliged to wade through many pages of extraneous material in order to discover and savor these sidelights on the management of a Midland shooting estate, and in this reviewer's opinion the book cannot take the place of J. Miller's *Practical Gamekeeping.*

T UT-TUT

TUT-TUT

Tut-tut is one of the oldest and most international palindromes. If they spoke English in the Garden of Eden, then "Madam, I'm Adam" was the first palindrome. If they didn't, then probably the Greek poet Sotades devised the first palindrome.

A palindrome is a word, like *deed* or *level* or *repaper* or *noon* or *redder* or *civic* or *tenet* or *kayak* or *nun*, or a phrase or a sentence, like "Madam, I'm Adam," that reads the same backward as forward.

PALINDROME WORDS

The longest known palindromic word is *saippuakauppias*. It is a 15-letter Finnish word that means "soap seller."

The longest palindromic word in everyday English is *redivider*, with nine letters.

Malayalam, the language of the Malayali people in Kerala, southern India, also has nine letters. *Rotavator* is a nine-letter registered trademark that has found its way into the dictionary; and *detartrated*, with 11 letters, is a contrived chemical term still hoping to find its way there.

American Indian dictionaries already feature the 12-letter *Kinnikkinnik*, a dried leaf and bark mixture smoked by Cree Indians.

PALINDROME SENTENCES

John Taylor is credited with having created the first English palindromic sentence at the beginning of the 17th century:

Lewd did I live & evil I did dwel.

Spelling habits have changed; today a more acceptable version would read:

Evil I did dwell; lewd did I live.

Many recent palindromes involve people's names, some of them quite famous:

Was it Eliot's toilet I saw?

No mists reign at Tangier, St. Simon!

Sums are not set as a test on Erasmus.

Some palindromes are supposed to have been spoken by the famous. The composer Henry Purcell is said to have remarked:

Egad, a base tone denotes a bad age!

And it is well known that the Emperor Napoleon was wont to moan during his exile:

Able was I ere I saw Elba.

For a modern palindrome that succinctly tells a story, it would be hard to beat this one by Leigh Mercer:

A man, a plan, a canal—Panama.

And here are the runners-up on my scoresheet of top palindromic sentences. Each one makes sense—of a sort.

Now, Ned, I am a maiden won.

Was it a car or a cat I saw?

Pull up if I pull up.

Ten animals I slam in a net.

In a regal age ran I.

Yawn a more Roman way.

Some men interpret nine memos.

PALINDROME STORIES

Thurber enjoyed palindromes—"He goddam mad dog, eh?" was his best effort—but few other great writers have attempted them. The problem is that once they stretch beyond about 50 letters they cease to make sense. A 51-letter palindrome by Penelope Gilliatt is an exception:

Doc, note I dissent. A fast never prevents fatness. I diet on cod.

The longest recorded palindromic composition runs to 2,769 letters but it's mostly gobbledygook. The story begins, "Spot stops to hoot at a mad sung aria . . ." And you can guess how it ends: ". . . Agnu's damn, at a too hot spot, stops." Not so much a story, more a palindrone.

However, there is still hope for palindromic fiction. The American wit and versifier Willard Espy recently reported an entertaining interview in the *Harvard Bulletin* between "Professor R. Osseforp, holder of the Emor D. Nilap Chair in Palindromology at Harvard, and Solomon W. Golomb (Ph.D., '57)" in which the reply to every question was a neat palindrome:

"And what about your new novel, could you tell me the title?"
"Dennis Sinned."
"Intriguing. What is the plot?"
"Dennis and Edna sinned."
"I see. Is there more to it than that?"
"Dennis Krats and Edna Stark sinned."
"Now it all becomes clear," I agreed. "Tell me, with all this concern about the ecology, what kind of car are you driving nowadays?"

"A Toyota."

"Naturally, and how about your colleague, Professor Nustad?"

"Nustad? A Datsun."

PSEUDODROMES

Pseudodromes take several forms. The most common are palindromes where words, rather than individual letters, read the same forward or backward. Pseudodromes may not be genuine palindromes, but they can be quite as entertaining:

So patient a doctor to doctor a patient so.

You can cage a swallow, can't you, but you can't swallow a cage, can you?

Women understand men; few men understand women.

God knows man. What is doubtful is what man knows God.

Does milk machinery milk does?

Bores are people that say that people are bores.

Girl, bathing on Bikini, eyeing boy, finds boy eyeing bikini on bathing girl.

PSEUDODROME POETICS

Here's another kind of a pseudodrome: a poem that tells the same story in reverse order when you read it backward:

Dies slowly fading day, winds mournfully sigh,
   Brightly stars are waking;
Flies owlet hooting, holding revel high,
   Nightly silence breaking.

In a third approach, each line of a poem is the unit. The poem can then be read forward or backward—or you might say, upward and downward:

As I was passing near the jail
I met a man, but hurried by.
His face was ghastly, grimly pale.
He had a gun. I wondered why

He had. A gun? A wondered . . . why?
His face was ghastly! Grimly pale.
I met a man, but hurried by,
As I was passing near the jail.

The author of the verse, J. A. Lindon, also concocted the only conventional palindrome to include an 18-letter word. To understand it (and excuse it) you need to know that Beryl has a hippie husband who is something of a sun worshiper and runs around his backyard in the nude. His friend Ned asks him if he does this to annoy poor Beryl and this is the palindromic reply:

Named undenominationally rebel, I rile Beryl? La, no! I tan. I'm, O Ned, nude, man!

Semordnilaps

Most people wouldn't know a semordnilap if they fell over one. Here are 15 for you to fall over:

bard	dog	rail	stop
deliver	golf	redrawer	strap
desserts	maps	reknits	straw
devil	mood	repaid	

If you don't see what the words have in common, take a closer look at the word *semordnilap*. Yes, you've got it! It's *palindromes* spelled backward, and, in the same way that a palindromic word reads the same backward as forward, a semordnilapic word becomes a new word when spelled backward.

Curiously, semordnilapic sentences, which make sense and are composed entirely of semiordnilapic words, are rare.

Here's one: "Dog a devil!"

Here's another: "Was no diaper on Dennis?"

As a distraction from the toothache you might try to devise some more.

Palindrome for Premier!

Finally, can you think of three internationally known 20th-century government leaders whose names are palindromes?

(See Answers.)

S CRABBLE

If you open *Funk & Wagnalls Standard College Dictionary* and turn to page 813, halfway down the second column you'll find:

> Scrabble (skrab'el) *v.* -bled, -bling, *v.i.* 1. To scratch, scrape or paw, as with the hands. 2. To make irregular or meaningless marks; scribble. 3. To struggle or strive—*v.t.* 4. To make meaningless marks on; scribble on. 5. To gather hurriedly; scrape together. —*n.* 1. The act of scrabbling or scrambling. 2. A scrawling character mark, etc.; scribble. 3. A sparse growth, as of underbrush. 4. The game of Scrabble.

Jimmy Carter plays Scrabble with Amy. During one of his many estrangements from Elizabeth Taylor, Richard Burton played Scrabble with Sophia Loren. Pope John Paul I played Scrabble in the Vatican. Queen Elizabeth II plays Scrabble at Buckingham Palace. James Bond played Scrabble. So did Mickey Spillane. So does Richard Nixon. It is played the world over—in more than 30 languages—and is without question the most popular word game in history.

191

It's largely to anagrams that we owe the invention of Scrabble. Not just to anagrams, of course: the depression and Alfred Mosher Butts made share some of the credit. Butts invented the game and he claims that "if there hadn't been any depression in the thirties there wouldn't have been any Scrabble." In 1931 he was an out-of-work architect in Jackson Heights, New York; to help make his enforced idleness tolerable he set about devising a game based on the anagram games he loved as a child. The game was called It at first; then it became Criss-Crosswords; eventually it emerged as Scrabble and swept the world. Butts tells the story of how, in the early days, he was introduced to a woman as the inventor of Scrabble and she gushed, "Oh, is that so? My husband just loves it. I wish you'd tell me how to cook it." Over 50 million Scrabble sets have been sold since then, and the game is no longer confused with the Pennsylvania dish of fried pork scraps called scrapple.

In 1971 I launched the British Scrabble Championships and quickly discovered how fanatical Scrabble enthusiasts can be. During the run-up to the finals I was phoned by an anxious player at 4:00 a.m. He asked: "Is the word *yex* allowed?" (Yes: it's a kind of hiccup.) After the contest was over, I was invited to hold a Scrabble seminar at Oxford University.

Here are the five sets of words I gave my Scrabble students, allowing them a mere 60 seconds for each set, five minutes in all. All but one managed with ease. See how you fare.

Turn each word into one other word:

1 *ache*	11 *hewn*	21 *quote*
2 *arid*	12 *hinge*	22 *sheet*
3 *aside*	13 *jaunt*	23 *stripes*
4 *cartel*	14 *kale*	24 *unite*
5 *cause*	15 *laces*	25 *use*
6 *cited*	16 *lilts*	26 *vase*
7 *daze*	17 *meteor*	27 *veal*
8 *denied*	18 *night*	28 *went*
9 *finger*	19 *ought*	29 *wider*
10 *girth*	20 *quiet*	30 *wont*

Turn each word into two other words:

1 *aids*	5 *below*	9 *dealer*
2 *ales*	6 *bleats*	10 *detail*
3 *angel*	7 *chaste*	11 *earth*
4 *beard*	8 *dare*	12 *ether*

13 *fares*	17 *paws*	20 *saint*
14 *filed*	18 *pest*	21 *tires*
15 *itself*	19 *pines*	22 *wards*
16 *lame*		

Turn each word into three other words:

1 *amen*	5 *emit*	9 *mate*
2 *coins*	6 *glare*	10 *parts*
3 *dale*	7 *hares*	11 *paste*
4 *diet*	8 *inks*	

Turn each word into four other words:

1 *abets*	3 *drapes*	5 *pares*
2 *aster*	4 *notes*	6 *skate*

Turn *scrape* into five other words.

(See Answers.)

If you think Scrabble seminars and tests like these are gamesman's garbage, don't worry: I agree. Faced with an over-earnest Scrabbler who is as determined to take the fun out of fun as he is infuriated by my criminally casual approach to the sacred game, I sicken him further by quoting my favorite lines from W. B. Yeats's "The Second Coming":

> The best lack all conviction, while the worst
> Are full of passionate intensity.

Rent-a-
TONGUE

Basic English is the name of the 20th century's unique attempt to invent a new English language.

There have been other invented languages based on English—Lewis Carroll's jabberwocky in *Through the Looking-Glass*, George Orwell's Newspeak in *Nineteen Eighty-Four*, J. R. R. Tolkien's language in *The Hobbit*, Anthony Burgess's goon lingo in *A Clockwork Orange*—but they have no life beyond the novels for which they were created.

Other, universal languages have been invented to sweep the world—L. L. Zamenhof's Esperanto has been the most successful; others include Novial, Volapük, Interlingual, and Interglossa—but their basis has not been English.

Basic English was devised in 1929 by C. K. Ogden and I. A. Richards. The "Basic" is an acronym for British, American, Scientific, International, and Commercial. The language has a vocabulary of just 850 English words, namely 600 things (nouns), 150 qualities (adjectives), and 100 operators (verbs and structural words, prepositions and conjunctions).

The inventors of Basic English maintained that with their easy-to-learn language every kind of communication was possible; Franklin D. Roosevelt and Winston Churchill were just two of the world leaders who believed them. But despite public support from FDR, Churchill, and others, the unique language has never attracted a major following.

To see why—and to realize why no "instant" language will ever live—take a look at the Lord's Prayer translated into Basic English:

> Father of all up in the sky
> You get our deepest respect
> We hope your nation with you
> asking for ruler will come
> down to us
> We hope you have your own way
> in the place we live as on high
> Give us food for now, and
> overlook wrongdoing as we
> overlook wrongdoing by persons to us
> Please guide us from courses of
> desire, and keep us from badness.

PIDGIN PIE

Here's the same prayer in a *real* language based on English: Pidgin, a language developed in the 16th century in South America and Africa, but still widely spoken in parts of West Africa and New Guinea:

> Papa belong me-fella, you stop long heaven
> All 'e sanctu 'im name belong you.
> Kingdom belong you 'e come.
> All 'e hear 'im talk belong you long ground
> all same long heaven.

Today givem kaikai belong day long me-fella.
Forgive 'im wrong belong me-fella
all-same me-fella forgive 'im wrong all
'e makem long me-fella.
You no bring-em me-fella long try 'im.
Take 'way some t'ing nogood long me-fella.

BASIC QUESTION

A recent statistical study of U.S. telephone speech revealed that only x different words were used in 96 percent of all conversations.

Bearing in mind that Shakespeare used 30,000 different words in his plays and that James Joyce used 30,000 in *Ulysses*, what do you think was the value of x?

(See Answers.)

QUIZ OF THE CENTURY

The same language that produced this (Robert Frost, 1914)—

> Home is the place where, when you have to go there,
> They have to take you in.
> I should have called it
> Something you somehow haven't to deserve.

—produced this (*Super Spiderman*, 1978)—

Back at Police HQ, Joe Macone thinks FAST ... "Can't BE COINCIDENCE! All those crimes empty OUT the precinct house ... and NOW someone is breaking IN!" ... "It HAS to have been PLANNED that way ..." ... "Somebody with power AND influence wants SOMETHING we've got." ... "And the only 'somethings' of VALUE we've got are in HERE! The stuff we hold as EVIDENCE!" ... "Sound I heard was a WALL

breaking! Anyone STRONG enough to do that can TAKE me . . .
Unless he can't FIND me!" . . . WHA-KOM . . . Clearly, this
hulking, lumbering mass of ARMOR and ENERGY knows where
he's heading . . . And MACONE doesn't have to be VERY quiet
not to be heard over the beetle's thunderous STEPS . . . "What's
he want? JEWELS . . . DRUGS . . . WEAPONS?" . . .

But the insidious invader tosses aside such treasure . . . until
he reaches a harmless-looking ATTACHÉ CASE . . . . . . "AT
LAST! All the effort . . . all the expense . . . PAYS OFF!"

—and this (Cyra McFadden, *The Serial,* 1977)—

"Fellow beings," Thurston said resonantly, "we've come together
at this point in time to lend Kate and Harry, here, peer group
support while they reaffirm their marriage vows.

"Although Kate and Harry here are already married, in the
legalistic sense, they've chosen to share with us food and wine
and nurturing and community while they celebrate their mutual
willingness to give each other space to grow. Their organic
union under the cosmos."

"Harvey," Kate hissed at Thurston. "It's *Harvey.*"

Thurston turned to her. "Kate," he said, "will you tell us all
just where you're coming from?"

Kate was now awash in tears and worried about her contact
lenses. "Well," she choked out, somewhat rattled, "I just want to
tell Harvey *openly,* I still think he's *numero uno.* Commit-
mentwise. In the human journey."

"Will you tell us what's in *your* heart, Harry?" Thurston
socked Harvey on the shoulder in a dynamic but unstructured
way and almost knocked him off the steps, so that Harvey
clutched unsteadily at Kate. He heard his own voice through
a Valium haze.

"Kate," he said, "who loves ya, baby?"

"I can't *stand* it," Martha cried, sobbing loudly on Brian's
shoulder. "God, it's just so *nostalgic,* you know."

"Kate and Harry," Thurston intoned, smiling at them beatifi-
cally, "I now pronounce you cojoined persons." He signaled that
they could break the chain and led the guests in a round of
applause, during which Jerry from the car pool whistled pierc-
ingly through his teeth.

Shortly afterward Kate and Harvey ran down the steps of

Falkirk in a shower of brown rice, headed for a weekend at Sea Ranch. Kate paused at the end of the walk and looked back at the old Victorian mansion. Lights were blazing in the windows, Martha's friend was cooking on the Moog again, and on the porch a knot of people had gathered around Spenser and Spenser's briefcase.

"I kind of blew it," she said to Harvey. "I meant to recite this quote, you know? That Lorca number that Martha did when she got married up on Tam."

"It's not the goal, it's the human journey." Harvey wondered serenely where he'd left the Volvo. "Listen, you're gonna have to drive. I think I took my six-o'clock twice."

"Great. That *tears* it," Kate said, exasperated. "I *can't* drive. I lost a contact lens. We can't go back to the wedding, that's tacky. I mean, wow, what are we gonna *do*?"

Harvey rocked gently back and forth in his Earth Shoes. "Hang loose?" he suggested vaguely.

That's the fascination of words. Harold Robbins and Harold Pinter, Isaac Asimov and Frances Parkinson Keyes, Saul Bellow and the adman who tells you that there's nothing in the cardboard pack of plastic food that doesn't "spring from the goodness of Mother Nature's own earth"—all share a common vocabulary yet use it in such varied ways. As Bertrand Russell said, "The similarity of language to explosives lies in the fact that a very small additional stimulus can produce a tremendous effect."

QUIZZICAL WORDS

Here are 25 examples of 20th-century English. What you have to decide is who wrote—or said—what. To do it the easy way, look at the two names that follow each quote and pick the likely one. (If you want to make it tough, cover the page with a sheet of paper and go down one line at a time.)

1 "I prefer to forget both pairs of glasses and pass my declining years saluting strange women and grandfather clocks."　　　　(OGDEN NASH . . . OR ART BUCHWALD?)

2 "Sex is something I really don't understand too hot. You never know *where* the hell you are. I keep making up these sex rules for myself, and then I break them right away."

(ANN LANDERS . . . OR J. D. SALINGER?)

3 "In other countries, art and literature are left to a lot of shabby bums living in attics and feeding on booze and spaghetti, but in America the successful writer or picture painter is indistinguishable from any other decent businessman." (SINCLAIR LEWIS . . . OR TOM WOLFE?)

4 "The morning this black brother was scheduled to leave I went back to his cell with a couple of sheets and asked him if he would aid me in an escape attempt. He dismissed me with one of those looks and a wave of the hand. I started tearing the sheets in strips. He watched. When I was finished he asked me: 'What are you doin' with that sheet?'
I replied, 'I'm tearing it into these strips.'
'Why you doin' that?'
'I'm making a rope.'
'What-chew gonna do with a rope?'
'Oh—I'm going to tie you up with it.'
"When they called him to be released that morning, I went out in his place. I've learned one very significant thing for our struggle here in the U.S.: all blacks do look alike to certain types of white people."

(GEORGE JACKSON . . . OR JOE MARTINEZ?)

5 "When I was a boy I was told that anybody could become president: I'm beginning to believe it."

(CLARENCE DARROW . . . OR LYNDON B. JOHNSON?)

6 "The atomic age is here to stay—but are we?"

(DR. BENJAMIN SPOCK . . . OR BENNETT CERF?)

7 "Venice is like eating an entire box of chocolate liqueurs at one go." (NEIL SIMON . . . OR TRUMAN CAPOTE?)

8 "Okie use' to mean you was from Oklahoma. Now it means you're scum. Don't mean nothing itself, it's the way they say it." (WILLIAM FAULKNER . . . OR JOHN STEINBECK?)

9 "I once told Fordie [Ford Madox Ford] that if he were placed naked and alone in a room without furniture, I would come back in an hour and find total confusion."

(F. SCOTT FITZGERALD . . . OR EZRA POUND?)

10 "The capacity of human beings to bore one another seems to be vastly greater than that of any other animals. Some of their most esteemed inventions have no other apparent purpose, for example, the dinner party of more than two, the epic poem, and the science of metaphysics."
(GORE VIDAL . . . OR H. L. MENCKEN?)

11 "It is a great shock at the age of five or six to find that in a world of Gary Coopers you are the Indian."
(LANGSTON HUGHES . . . OR JAMES BALDWIN?)

12 "He disapproved of Adolf Hitler, who had done such a great job of combating un-American activities in Germany."
(JOSEPH HELLER . . . OR KURT VONNEGUT?)

13 "Until you start plowing pertinent wives, you really aren't working. The way to a man's heart is through his wife's belly and don't you forget it."
(EDWARD ALBEE . . . OR RALPH ELLISON?)

14 "Competence, like truth, beauty, and contact lenses, is in the eye of the beholder."
(CYRUS VANCE . . . OR LAURENCE J. PETER?)

15 "The black man in this country has been sitting on the hot stove for nearly 400 years. And no matter how fast the brainwashers and the brainwashed think they are helping him advance, it's still too slow for the man whose behind is burning on that hot stove!"
(COUNTEE CULLEN . . . OR MALCOLM X?)

16 "I'm as pure as the driven slush."
(TALLULAH BANKHEAD . . . OR MAE WEST?)

17 "You cannot be absolutely dumb when you live with a person unless you are an inhabitant of the north of England or the state of Maine."
(FORD MADOX FORD . . . OR RICHARD BRAUTIGAN?)

18 "Wealth is not without its advantages, and the case to the contrary, although it has often been made, has never proved widely persuasive."
(J. K. GALBRAITH . . . OR HUBERT HUMPHREY?)

19 "I started out very quiet and I beat Mr. Turgenev. Then I trained hard and I beat Mr. de Maupassant. I've fought two

draws with Mr. Stendhal, and I think I had an edge in the last one. But nobody's going to get me in any ring with Mr. Tolstoy unless I'm crazy or I keep getting better."

(NORMAN MAILER . . . OR ERNEST HEMINGWAY?)

20 "Sex is one of the nine reasons for reincarnation . . . The other eight are unimportant."

(HENRY MILLER . . . OR BARBARA CARTLAND?)

21 "Let's talk sense to the American people. Let's tell them the truth, that there are no gains without pains."

(ADLAI STEVENSON . . . OR JERRY BROWN?)

22 "Business underlies everything in our national life, including our spiritual life. Witness the fact that in the Lord's Prayer the first petition is for daily bread. No one can worship God or love his neighbor on an empty stomach."

(GEORGE MEANY . . . OR WOODROW WILSON?)

23 "She had once been a Catholic, but discovering that priests were infinitely more attentive when she was in process of losing or regaining faith in Mother Church, she maintained an enchantingly wavering attitude."

(ARTHUR MILLER . . . OR F. SCOTT FITZGERALD?)

24 "The physician can bury his mistakes, but the architect can only advise his client to plant vines."

(RALPH NADER . . . OR FRANK LLOYD WRIGHT?)

25 "A typical quimmty old hag who spread these vile ruperts was Mrs. Weatherby—a widow by her first husbands."

(SAMUEL BECKETT . . . OR JOHN LENNON?)

(See Answers.)

POETIC PICTURES

As Picasso used to say, "It's the look of the thing that counts."
Apply the principle to poetry instead of painting and you end up
with verses like these:

                miniskirtminiskirt
               miniskirtminiskirtmi
              niskirtminiskirtminisk
             irtminiskirtminiskirtmin

legleglegleglegleglegleg   legleglegleglegleglegleg

        shoe   shoe

ON THE STREET

He bought a little block of stock
  The day he went to town;
And in the nature of such things,

> That
> *Stock*
> Went
> Right
> Straight
> Down!

☆   ☆   ☆   ☆

He sold a little block of stock:
  Now sorrow fills his cup,
For from the moment that he did,

> Up,
> Right
> Went
> Thing
> Blamed
> The

☆   ☆   ☆   ☆

He bought a little block of stock,
  Expecting he would taste of bliss;
He can't let go and can't hold on,

The blamed thing wriggles round like this.

SOMETIMES I'M HAPPY
sometimes i'm sad
SoMeTiMeS i'M HsAaPdPY.

THE MOUSE'S TALE

by LEWIS CARROLL

'Mine is a long and a sad tale!' said the Mouse, turning to Alice, and sighing.

'It *is* a long tail, certainly,' said Alice, looking down with wonder at the Mouse's tail; 'but why do you call it sad?' And she kept on puzzling about it while the Mouse was speaking, so that her idea of the tale was something like this:——

```
          'Fury  said  to
             a mouse, That
                he  met  in  the
                   house,  "Let
                       us  both  go
                          to  law:  I
                             will  prose-
                             cute you. —
                          Come,  I'll
                       take no de-
                   nial:   We
                must  have
             the  trial;
          For  really
       this  morn-
      ing  I've
     nothing
     to  do."
     Said  the
        mouse  to
           the  cur,
              "Such     a
                 trial, dear
                    sir,  With
                       no  jury
                       or  judge,
                       would
                     be wast-
                   ing  our
                 breath."
              "I'll  be
            judge,
         I'll be
        jury,"
      said
       cun-
          ning
            old
              Fury:
                 "I'll
                    try
                     the
                    whole
                  cause,
                and
              con-
          demn
         you to
      death".'
```

GEO-METRIC VERSES

by GERALD LYNTON KAUFMAN

AMOEBA-VERSE

Micro-picto-graphic rhymes
Enlarged 100,000,000 times

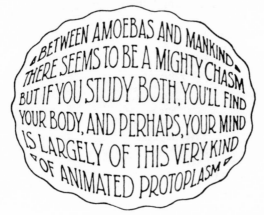

BETWEEN AMOEBAS AND MANKIND
THERE SEEMS TO BE A MIGHTY CHASM
BUT IF YOU STUDY BOTH, YOU'LL FIND
YOUR BODY, AND PERHAPS, YOUR MIND
IS LARGELY OF THIS VERY KIND
OF ANIMATED PROTOPLASM

CHRONO-LOGIC

HERE IS VERSI-FORM DESIGNED
IN A SHAPE WHICH BRINGS
TO MIND, THAT WHEN PUT-
TING THOUGHTS IN
RHYME, YOU'RE
SUPPOSED TO
MEASURE
TIME
BUT THE
MEASURE OF
YOUR OWN, YOU
SHOULD GLADLY LEAVE
UNKNOWN; FOR THERE'S
SCARCELY ANY DOUBT, THAT
YOUR SAND IS RUNNING OUT.

CUBICOUPLETS

A CUBE HAS SIX FACES A CUBE HAS SIX PLANES
RECTANGULAR SPACES FOR METRIC REFRAINS
FOR COUPLETS LIKE THESE WITH A RHYTHM, OF COURSE
TO BE READ AS YOU PLEASE EITHER DOWN OR ACROSS
EVERY FACE IS A SQUARE EVERY EDGE IS A LINE
TO HELP YOU COMPARE TO UNITE AND COMBINE
TWO PLANES AT A TIME FROM BEHIND OR BETWEEN
IN THIS CUBICAL RHYME WITH THE VERSES UNSEEN

A CUBE HAS SIX PLANES A CUBE HAS SIX FACES
FOR METRIC REFRAINS RECTANGULAR SPACES
WITH A RHYTHM, OF COURSE FOR COUPLETS LIKE THESE
EITHER DOWN OR ACROSS TO BE READ AS YOU PLEASE
EVERY EDGE IS A LINE EVERY FACE IS A SQUARE
TO UNITE AND COMBINE TO HELP YOU COMPARE
FROM BEHIND OR BETWEEN TWO PLANES AT A TIME
WITH THE VERSES UNSEEN IN THIS CUBICAL RHYME

CELLARITHMETIC

THIS SKETCH HAS
BEEN COMPOSED TO TELL
A PARADOX ABOUT A CELL
RELATING TO A SUBTLE TRICK
IT USES IN ARITHMETIC:
SO GAZE UPON ITS TINY SIZE
AND THINK HOW WHEN
IT MULTIPLIES
IT SOLVES WITH
EFFORTLESS
PRECISION, A
MAJOR PROBLEM
IN DIVISION

A VISIT FROM ST. NICHOLAS

words by CLEMENT C. MOORE

```
                              T
                             WAS
                            THENI
                           GHTBEFO
                          RECHRISTM
                         A SWHENAL L
                        THR OUGHT HEH
                       OUSEN OTA CREAT
                      UREWASS T IRRINGN
                     OTEVENAMO USETHESTO
                    C KINGSWE R EHUNGBY T
                   HEC HIMNE YWI THCAR EIN
                  HOPES THA TSAIN TNI CHOLA
                 SSOONWO U LDBETHE R ETHECHI
                LDRENWERE NESTLEDAL LSNUGINTH
               E IRBEDSW H ILEVISI O NSOFSUG A
              RPL UMSDA NCE DINTH EIR HEADS AND
             MAMMA INH ERKER CHI EFAND IIN MYCAP
            HADJUST S ETTLEDD O WNFORAL O NGWINTE
           RSNAPWHEN OUTONTHEL AWNTHEREA ROSESUCHA
          C LATTERI S PRANGFR O MMYBEDT O SEEWHAT W
         HAT WASTH EMA TTERA WAY TOTHE WIN DOWIF LEW
        LIKEA FLA SHTOR EOP ENTHE SHU TTERS AND THREW
       UPTHESA S HTHEMOO N THEBREA S TOPTHEN E WFALLEN
      SNOWGAVEA LUSTEROFM IDDAYTOOB JECTSBELO WWHENWHAT
     T ONYWOND E RINGEYE S SHOULDA P PEARBUT A MINIATU R
    ESL EIGHA NDE IGHTT INY REIND EER WITHA LIT TLEOL DDR
   IVERS OLI VELYA NDQ UICKI KNE WINAM OME NTITIM UST BESTN
  ICKMORE R APIDTHA N EAGLESH I SCOURSE R STHEYCA M EANDHEW
 HISTLEDAN DSHOUTEDA NDCALLEDT HEMBYNAME NOWDASHER NOWDANCER
N OWPRANC E RANDVIX E NONCOME T ONCUPID O NDONNER A NDBLITZ E
NTO THETO POF THEPO RCH TOTHE TOP OFTHE WAL LNOWD ASH AWAYD ASH
AWAYD ASH AWAYA LLA SDRYL EAV ESTHA TBE FORET HEW ILDHU RRI CANEF
LYWHENT H EYMEETW I THANOBS T ACLEMOU N TTOTHES K YSOUPTO T HEHOUSE
TOPTHECOU RSERSTHEY FLEWWITHA SLEIGHFUL LOFTOYSAN DSTNICHOL ASTOOANDT
H ENINATW I NKLEIHE A RDONTHE R OOFTHEP R ANCINGA N DPAWING O FEACHLI T
TLE HOOFA SID REWIN MYH EADAN DWA STURN ING AROUN DDO WNTHE CHI MNEYS TNI
CHOLA SCA MEWIT HAB OUNDH EWA SDRES SED ALLIN FUR FROMH ISH EADTO HIS FOOTA
NDHISCL O THESWER E ALLTARN I SHEDWIT H ASHESAN D SOOTABU N DLEOPTO Y SHEHADF
LUNGONHIS BACKANDHE LOOKEDLIK EAPEDDLER JUSTOPENI NGHISPACK HISEYESHO WTHEYTWIN
K LEDHISD I MPLESHO W MERRYHI S CHEEKSW E RELIKER O SESHISN O SELIKEA C HERRYHI S
DRO LLLIT TLE MOUTH WAS DRAWN UPL IKEAB OWA NDTHE BEA RDONH ISC HINWA SAS WHITE AST
HESNO WTH ESTUM POF APIPE HEH ELDTI GHT INHIS TEE THAND THE SMOKE ITE NCIRC LED HISHE
ADLIKEA W REATHHE H ADABROA D FACEAND A LITTLER O UNDBELL Y THATSHO O KWHENHE L AUGHEDL
IKEABOWLF ULLOFJELL YHEWASCHU BBYANDPLU MPARIGHTJ OLLYOLDEL FANDILAUG HEDWHENIS AWHIMINSP
I TEOFMYS E LFAWINK O FHISEYE A NDATWIS T OFHISHE A DSOONGA V EMETOKN O WIHADNO T HINGTOD R
EAD HESPO KEN OTAWO RDB UTWEN TST RAIGH TTO HISWO RKA NDFIL LED ALLTH EST OCKIN GST HENTU RNE
DWITH AJE RKAND LAY INGHI SFI NGERA SID EOFHI SNO SEAND GIV INGAN ODU PTHEC HIM NEYHE ROS EHESP
RANGTOH I SSLEIGH T OHISTEA M GAVEAWH I STLEAND A WAYTHEY A LLFLEWL I KETHEDO W NONATHI S TLEBUTI
HEARDHIME XCLAIMASH EDROVEOUT OFSIGHTHA PPYCHRIST MASTOALLA NDTOALLAG OODNIGHTP OEMBYCLEM ENTCMOORE
                          1822    1972
                           THIS MOST
                            FAM OUS
                             YU LE
                             PO EM
                           OBSE RVES
                           THIS XMAS
                       ITS 150TH ANNIVERSARY
```

ODE TO A TYPEFACE

by CHRISTOPHER REED

A Spartan Bookman in his Cloister
Thought the Antique world his oyster.
Times Roman were his great delight.
Italian Old Style girls the height
Of Radiant beauty. What a shame
No Wedding Text will he declaim.
Instead he's Stymied in his Tower
SHADOW like and wondering how or
When he'll find a Lydian pal.
A *Cursive Legend* of a gal.
He yearns to be befriended
By Venus Bold Extended

FOUR NOT POEMS

BY ADELE ALDRIDGE

DOGS
DO
DO
DO

TEACH
TEACH
TAEHC
CEHTA
CHETA
CHEAT
CHEAT

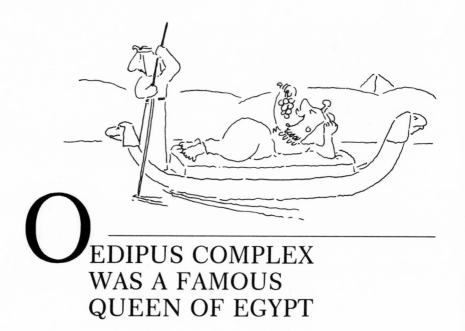

OEDIPUS COMPLEX WAS A FAMOUS QUEEN OF EGYPT

In the world of words anyone can make a mistake, and plenty of us do. Over the years—as child, then teacher and parent—I have collected schoolboy howlers. Here are the best.

NINETY-EIGHT HOWLERS

Oedipus Complex was a famous queen of Egypt.

Marseillaise is a French salad dressing.

Sodium Sulphate is the shah of Persia.

A Fjord is a Swedish automobile.

Robinson Crusoe was a great operatic singer.

Henry VIII found walking difficult because he had an abbess on his knee.

Furbelow means a vacation for soldiers.

Telepathy is a code invented by Morse.

"After me, the deluge" was said by Noah when he raised the gangplank of the ark.

Napoleon had three children, not one of whom lived to maternity.

Livid was a famous Latin poet.

An Indian baby is called a caboose.

A gulf is a piece broken off a peninsula.

People living on the equator are called equestrians.

Samuel Pepys worked in the admiralty and was always going to bed.

Abstinence is a good thing if practiced in moderation.

The plural of spouce is spice.

The inhabitants of Paris are called Parisites.

In France even the phesants drink wine.

Siena is a place in Italy famous for being burnt.

The pope lives in a Vacuum.

Jacob had a brother called Seesaw.

The first commandment was when Eve told Adam to eat the apple.

Abraham is in the Bible and is noted for his bosom.

A hostage is a nice lady on an airplane.

An optimist is a man who looks after your eyes and a pessimist looks after your feet.

Fidel Castro invented Castro oil.

Waltz time is sometimes called cripple time.

Ladies who sing a low kind of songs are called contraltos.

A trombone is an instrument you play by pulling it in and out.

Blood consists of red corkscrews and white corkscrews.

Psychology is a fairly modern disease discovered by a man called Floyd.

An oxygen has eight sides.

The Gorgons had long snakes in their hair. They looked like women only more horrible.

-Ster is a female suffix. Example, *spinster, monster,* and *sterile.*

A magnet is something to be found in a bad apple or other fruit.

There are eligible fish in the sea.

When a dog has puppies it's called a liter.

A blizzard is the inside of a chicken.

A convoy is a collection of some birds like cartridges.

Herrings go about the sea in shawls.

A ruminating animal chews its cubs.

Mushrooms look like umbrellas because they grow where it's wet.

A centimeter is an insect with a hundred legs.

The future of "I give" is "you take."

The bowels are *a, e, i, o, u,* and sometimes *w* and *y.*

Poetry is when every line starts with a capital letter.

A simile is a picturesque way of saying what you really mean, such as saying your father is a square.

A passive verb is when the subject is the sufferer, as "I am loved."

A metaphor is a suppressed smile.

Water is composed of oxygin and hydrogin. Oxygin is pure but hydrogin is gin and water.

An emolument is a sort of medicine.

There are four elements, mustard, salt, pepper, and vinegar although I think vinegar is reely an acid.

A good cosmetic is salt and water. Cosmetics make you sick.

Handel was a little boy in a tale with his sister called Handel and Grettel.

Homer wrote the *Oddity.*

Tom Sawyer was a smart boy. His character was always good sometimes.

Polonius was a sort of sausage.

The appendix is a part of the book for which nobody has found much use.

"The child is father to the man." This was written by Shakespeare. He didn't often make that kind of mistake.

Marshal Goering was a fat man because he was one of Hitler's stoutest supporters.

Washington was a great general who always began a battle with the fixed determination to win or lose.

Socrates died from an overdose of wedlock.

Dusk is little bits of fluff you find under the bed.

Reefs are what you put on coffins.

Necessity is the mother of convention.

A graven image is a nice gravestone.

A trade union is a place you go when you get fired.

Austerity is an old religion but today even politicians preach it.

Income is a yearly tax.

A surname is the name of somebody you say "Sir" to.

Faith is believing what you know is untrue.

Ambiguity is telling the truth when you don't mean to.

An epitaph is a short sarcastic poem.

Autobiography is the history of motorcars.

Pasteur found a cure for rabbis.

Pate de foie gras is an outdoor circus held in New Orleans every year.

Cosmic rays are electric treatments to make women beautiful.

Having only one wife is called monotony.

Today every Tom, Dick, and Harry is named Bill.

Asperity is the drug from which aspirin is made.

Conservation means table talk.

All strong men have good physics.

Kosher is Jewish pork.

The mother of Abraham Lincoln died in infancy.

It was the painter Donatello's interest in the female nude that made him the father of the Renaissance.

The crusaders were little chidren sent on a cruise to Jerusalem in Shakespeare's time.

A mummy is the dead mother of a gypsy.

Soviet is another name for a table napkin.

A polygon is another name for a Mormon.

A mosquito is the child of black and white parents.

A troubadour is a Spanish bullfighter.

A virgin forest is a place where the hand of man has never set foot.

When a man has more than one wife he is a pigamist.

Laissez-faire are lazy French women.

Pegasus is a hobbyhorse used by carpenters.

A commonplace is a busy corner of a city or village.

In *Mrs. Warren's Profession*, her profession is the oldest profession, but she is not really a lost woman. She is just mislaid.

In *A Streetcar Named Desire* the climax is when Blanche goes to bed with Stella's husband.

Of course, it's not only the young who make innocent slips. My father swears that when he was in the British army during the Second World War he heard this exchange between a medical officer and a new recruit:

MEDICAL OFFICER: How are your bowels working?
RECRUIT: Haven't been issued with any, sir.
M.O. I mean, are you constipated?
RECRUIT: No, sir, I volunteered.
M.O. Heavens, man, don't you know the King's English?
RECRUIT: No, sir, is he?

And many is the writer—whose business is words, after all—who has let a delicious dangler find its way into print. These are my 15 favorites from newspapers and magazines:

The bride wore a long white lace dress which fell to the floor.

Mrs. Johnson can prepare mashed potatoes as fluffy and delicious as any of my acquaintance.

The women included their husbands and children in their potluck suppers.

In Germany a person cannot slaughter any animal unless rendered unconscious first.

There was a tea party for the children, and after they were tucked in bed a banquet for the parents.

The summary of information contains totals of the number of students broken down by sex, marital status, and age.

Even more astonishing was our saving the lives of little babies who formerly died from sheer ignorance.

I can't blame you for wanting to go outside and sit on your ten-minute break.

At the age of 11 my father took me south.

For those of you who have small children and don't know it we have a nursery downstairs.

He spent his early life on the back of a horse with a pipe in his mouth.

We had Mr. Colso for dinner.

A boy scout can cook himself.

Wash your face in the morning and neck at night.

A gentleman never crumbles his bread or rolls in his soup.

NINETEEN-EIGHTY-FOUR

NEWSPEAK

In George Orwell's prophetic novel *Nineteen Eighty-Four*—which was published in 1949 and which Orwell had wanted to call *Nineteen Forty-Eight*—the country is controlled by four ministries whose very names bely their roles: Minipax, the Ministry of Peace, deals with war; Minitrue, the Ministry of Truth, deals with propaganda; Miniluv, the Ministry of Love, deals with law and order, including torture; and the Ministry of Plenty deals with scarcities. Newspeak, a language discussed at length in *Nineteen Eighty-Four,* contains a special vocabulary of words constructed for political purposes, words intended not only to deceive the user but "to impose a desirable mental attitude upon the person using them."

DOUBLESPEAK

1984 is almost upon us, but instead of Newspeak we have Double-speak. Here are ten words and phrases that win the Brandreth Doublespeak Award:

WHAT IS SAID	WHAT IS MEANT
money-motivated	greedy
relocate	move
low-cost	cheap
has an alcohol problem	drinks
manipulative methods	bribery
correctional therapeutic communities	prison
clinic for the emotionally disadvantaged	mental hospital
socially disadvantaged underachiever	backward kid from a poor background
word-processing unit	typing pool
negative deficit	profit

SOCIAL CLIMBERS

If you're looking for a job, let Doublespeak describe it for you:

ENGLISH	DOUBLESPEAK
elevator operator	member of the Vertical Transportation Corps
window cleaner	glass maintenance engineer
chimney sweep	scandiscopist
gardener	landscape technician
tax collector	revenue agent
film projectionist	multimedia systems technician
dogcatcher	canine control officer
filing clerk	information retrieval administrator

janitor	sanitation maintenance superintendent
dirty old man	sexy senior citizen

Educanto

A recent National Educational Association study states that in many classrooms half of the words used by the teachers are not understood by the students. With more and more teachers calling themselves educators and talking about "multimode curricula and empirically validated learning systems," I'm not surprised.

Other teachers, happily, are aware of the dangers of lapsing into incomprehensible Pedaguese, among them members of the National Council of Teachers of English who for years have been pointing a sharp, accusing finger at deceptive language. Since 1974 the council has been giving out annual Public Doublespeak Awards; the honored recipients have ranged from the State Department and the CIA to Yasir Arafat and the Hahnemann Hospital in Philadelphia.

The first-ever award "in the category of misuse of euphemisms" went to Colonel Opfer, USAF, a press officer in Cambodia, who after a U.S. bombing raid told reporters: "You always write it's bombing, bombing, bombing. It's not bombing. It's air support."

The council's second award "in the category of gobbledygook" went to former president Nixon's press secretary, Ronald Ziegler, for a 99-word response to a question from reporters about whether a batch of Watergate tapes were all still intact. The question would seem to require a yes or no answer, but this is what it got:

> I would feel that most of the conversations that took place in those areas of the White House that did have the recording system would in almost their entirety be in existence but the special prosecutor, the court, and, I think, the American people are sufficiently familiar with the recording system to know where the recording devices existed and to know the situation in terms of the recording process but I feel, although

the process has not been undertaken yet in preparation of the material to abide by the court decision, really, what the answer to that question is.

Of the many Doublespeak Award winners I feel these have been the worthiest:

TO THE ILLINOIS BOARD OF HIGHER EDUCATION for approving a $168,000 project with this statement: "The purpose of this project is to develop the capability for institutions of higher learning and community agencies and organizations to coalesce for the development of community services and create a model for the coordination of such services that would maximize the available resources from a number of institutions and provide communication and priority needs and the response of the educational needs of a given community."

TO HARRY VOLWEIDER, PRESIDENT OF THE SPRINGDALE GOLF CLUB, PRINCETON, N.J., who was quoted in the *New York Times* as saying when he was asked why a black was rejected for membership in his golf club: "We didn't turn him down. We didn't accept him."

TO A HOUSTON HIGH SCHOOL PRINCIPAL who sent the following message to parents about a new educational program: "Our school's cross-graded, multiethnic, individualized learning program is designed to enhance the concept of an open-ended learning program with emphasis on a continuum of multiethnic academically enriched learning using the identified intellectually gifted child as the agent or director of his own learning. Major emphasis is on cross-graded multiethnic learning with the main objective being to learn respect for the uniqueness of a person."

TO A PANEL OF PRIVATE CITIZENS HIRED BY THE DEPARTMENT OF THE INTERIOR to investigate the collapse of the Teton Dam in Idaho which caused the deaths of 14 people. The panel concluded that the collapse was due to "an unfortunate choice of design measures together with less than conventional precautions."

TO HEALTH, EDUCATION AND WELFARE SECRETARY JOSEPH CALIFANO for creativity. He wrote a 402-word definition of his "extremely confidential personal assistant," who is "responsible for managing, supervising, and performing work related to the operation of the secretary's kitchen and eating area."

TO *CURRENTS*, the house organ of the University of California Lawrence Laboratory: "Any employee whose current salary rate exceeds the new top of the salary range for his or her classification will not be eligible for the general increase unless the new top of the salary range for his or her classification exceeds the employee's current salary rate."

TO THE OCCUPATIONAL SAFETY AND HEALTH ADMINISTRATION RULE-BOOK for defining an exit as "that portion of a means of egress which is separated from all other spaces of the building or structure by construction or equipment as required in this subpart to provide a protected way of travel to the exit discharge." By way of clarification, the rulebook defines means of egress as "a continuous and unobstructed way of exit travel from any point in a building or structure to a public way and consists of three separate and distinct parts: the way of exit access, the exit, and the way of exit discharge."

READING BETWEEN THE LIES

Nowadays even when plain English is spoken it is hard to know if what is said is what is meant. Often—especially in the business world—understanding is a matter of reading between the lies. In ten typical situations:

BACKGROUND

"What did you study at college?"
   —I am immature enough to want you to ask about my studies; they were at a very smart place.

BEING MET

"I'll meet you at the airport."
   —You are very important.

"I'll send a car to meet you at the airport."
   —You are moderately important.

"I'll meet you at the bus station.
>*—Business is terrible and I cannot afford a taxi.*

"I'll expect you at our office in the morning."
>*—I suppose I'll have to face seeing you eventually.*

BRIBES

"It must be great to be able to afford vacations like that."
>*—I can be bribed.*

"Would you like to join us on our yacht?"
>*—Can you be bribed?*

BUSINESS EXCUSES

"I'm afraid your work doesn't quite suit our present professional needs."
>*—Why bother us with your crazy rubbish?*

"Our position is slightly strained."
>*—We're broke.*

CIVILITIES

"How do you spell your name?"
>*—I've forgotten your name.*

ENTERTAINING

"You must come and have dinner sometime."
>*—Thank goodness you are going; as soon as you have gone I shall tear up your address.*

"Would you and your wife like to come to dinner and a show?"
>*—I have an expense account and it's about time I gave my wife a free evening out.*

"Do have a cup of coffee."
>*—That's all you'll get.*

"I'll just phone my wife to tell her I'm bringing you for dinner; she will be delighted."
>*—I'll just phone my wife and hope she won't murder me.*

NEGOTIATIONS

"I'll think about it."
—*No.*

"We'll let you know."
—*You haven't got a hope in hell.*

PERSONAL REFERENCES

"His attitude leaves room for improvement."
—*He is bone idle.*

"He has always handled tasks given him to within the limits of which he is capable."
—*He is very stupid.*

"I have never heard anything bad of him."
—*I have never heard anything good of him.*

"He is sober, honest, and trustworthy."
—*He has not yet been found out.*

PROMOTION

"These items will be heavily promoted worldwide."
—*Some modest advertising is possible if you insist.*

SECRETARIAL EXCUSES

"Mr. Brown has just gone to lunch."
—*He won't be back until three thirty.*

"We tried several times to ring you back."
—*I hope you believe this twaddle.*

"Mr. Brown is so sorry to keep missing you."
—*He is not trying very hard.*

"I'm sorry, I told him you were waiting."
—*He's trying to face up to seeing you eventually.*

"Mr. Brown is away with a cold."
—*It's a nice day for golf.*

"Mr. Brown is busy dictating."

—*Mr. Brown has a lovely new secretary with big boobs and does not wish to be disturbed.*

"Yes, I did tell him you called and he said he would contact you the minute he could."

—*Get lost.*

MIX ME A METAPHOR

We all mix metaphors. And I mean *all*. The most famous passage in world literature contains a beauty of a mixed metaphor in the fourth line:

> To be, or not to be: that is the question:
> Whether 'tis nobler in the mind to suffer
> The slings and arrows of outrageous fortune,
> Or to take arms against a sea of troubles,
> And by opposing end them?

A mixed metaphor combines two or more inconsistent metaphors, and if Shakespeare can use one in Hamlet's great soliloquy, why shouldn't the rest of us join the fun?

The most notorious mixed metaphor is probably one attributed to Boyle Roche (1743–1807), an Irish politician who seems to have French-kissed the Blarney stone:

Mr. Speaker, I smell a rat; I see him forming in the air and darkening the sky: but I'll nip him in the bud.

(On another occasion Roche thundered: "Half the lies our opponents tell about us are not true.")

Bureaucrats have a special gift for mixing metaphors. Here are some recent examples destined to become classics:

The recovery of the house-building program will require action in a number of fields.

We now have 137½ pairs of surgical boots on our hands.

Men and women want to know the future shape of their environment and expect candid guidelines to help them mold it.

Instead of supersonic aircraft standing on their own feet by charging slightly increased fares, subsonic aircraft are required to cross-subsidize.

Flexibility is one of the cornerstones of program budgeting.

Ian Fleming is responsible for my favorite:

"Bond's knees, the Achilles' heel of all skiers, were beginning to ache."

Some of the others I like are, sadly, nonattributable, but each one is a pearl worth its weight in gold:

The sacred cows have come home to roost with a vengeance.

There is no head of steam to which one can harness oneself.

All these whited sepulchers are tarred with the same brush.

We're not out of the wood yet by a long chalk.

The skeleton at the feast was a mare's nest.

MALAPHORS

Malaphors aren't quite malapropisms and aren't quite mixed metaphors—but the best are as memorable as either. Here are four recently reported from Capitol Hill:

The problem started small, but it is baseballing.

He threw a cold shoulder on that idea.

I'm not going to bail out his chestnuts.

I support Mr. Arbuzov and the other Soviet diffidents.

PHONEYPHORS

To get an award—or even a Pullet Surprise—a verbal goof has to be unintended, not contrived. About the only exception to this rule is Goldwynisms, the brilliant boners of movie magnate Sam Goldwyn. One or two of his early gaffes may have been spontaneous, but most of them owe as much to the devotion and imagination of the publicity department as to Goldwyn's natural turn of phrase. Whoever conceived them, they're great—and here are the greatest:

"Anybody who goes to see a psychiatrist ought to have his head examined."

"Every director bites the hand that lays the golden egg."

"If Roosevelt were alive he'd turn over in his grave."

"I'll give you a definite maybe."

"It's more than magnificent—it's mediocre."

"A verbal contract isn't worth the paper it's written on."

When told a story was rather caustic:

"I don't care what it costs. If it's good, we'll make it."

Of a book: "I read part of it all the way through."

Of a piece of dialogue: "Let's have some new clichés."

"Include me out."

THE LUNCHPACK
OF NOTRE DAME

No book about the wonders of the world of words can be complete without a list of the world's most significant works of literature.

I have chosen 16 literary masterpieces and dictated the titles to my secretary—and that's where the trouble started. My diction is poor and her hearing's no better.

As you'll see when you study the list, she didn't major in world literature (she didn't major in *anything*), so I decided to make the best of a bad job and supply appropriate blurbs for her titles.

SIXTEEN MASTERPIECES OF WORLD LITERATURE

LE MALLARD IMAGINAIRE
Molière's classic play about a man who thinks he is a duck.
He makes futile attempts to get out of his predicament, but
his family is running a thriving eiderdown business and won't
let him.

OF MICE AND ME
The autobiography of Walt Disney.

THE NAMING OF THE SHREW
Shakespeare's charming story of how the shrew got its name.
Illustrated by Kate Greenaway. (Not to be confused with
Evelyn Waugh's satire, *Vole Bodies*.)

THE FORESIGHT SAGA
A remarkable story of precognition by a man who is able to
predict not only the invention of television and paperbacks, but
that he will clean up on the royalties he earns from both.
Ironically, he dies before his prophecies are fulfilled (26
volumes).

GONE WITH THE WING
The true story of a World War II air force amputee. A
companion volume to *Reach for the Sty*, the autobiography of
a pig breeder who becomes a Battle of Britain pilot, but yearns
for his old life. "A rattling yarn of muck and bullets" *(The
Pig Breeder's Gazette).*

GRIME AND PUNISHMENT
The prison memoirs of a chimney sweep.

THE TALE OF PETER RABBI
The most delightful of Beatrix Potter's stories, loved by
children of all lands, especially Israel.

ENEMA
Arguably Jane Austen's finest novel. "Purgative" *(New York
Times).*

MADAME OVARY
The powerful story of a French woman's struggle to become
the first female gynecologist. She fails, and becomes the first
female steeplejack instead.

OF HUMAN BANDAGE
The life of Florence Nightingale. "Had me in stitches" *(New
Yorker).*

LORD OF THE RUNGS
The ultimate handbook for social climbers.

OUR MUTUAL FIEND
A schizophrenic vampire terrorizes Dickens's London.
Contains conclusive evidence that Jack the Ripper was Dr.
Jekyll *and* Mr. Hyde, or possibly Victoria and Albert.

AROUND THE WORLD IN EIGHTY WAYS
Eighty novel methods of circumnavigating the globe. "Some,
such as 'skateboard across the Sahara' and 'hang-glide over
the Himalayas' are a bit far-fetched, but on the whole I
enjoyed this book immensely" *(Thor Heyerdahl)*.

SWISH FAMILY ROBINSON
The biography of the effete family which dominated an artistic
community in the 1930s.

EIGHTEEN NINETY-FOUR
Orwell's famous utopian novel, unique in being set in the
past.

THE LUNCHPACK OF NOTRE DAME
Victor Hugo's startling tale of a group of insane gourmets who
decide to eat themselves to death within the sacred precinct
of Notre Dame. With recipes.

WHAT RECIPES?

These recipes!

Plum Loco Pudding	World's Fear Special
Stuffed UN Conches	Poultry Geist
Inn Bread	Milk of Amnesia
Kooky Saint-Jacques	Traumatic Ketchup
Lemon Derange Pie	Powdread Milk
Apple Jitters	Addle Pâté
Fruit Conflict	Raw Schacktoast
Sib Ling Chow Mein	Group Therapea Soup
Dream of Celery Soup	Egg Foo Jung
Shocked Liver	Oddballed Eggs
Shuddered Wheat	Menthol Blocks

Oafmeal Cookies
Freud Oysters
Inferiority Cornflakes
Accident Prune Pie
Schizo Farina
Filet of Timid Sole
Depressed Duck
Moronated Herring

Confused Manna
Lobster Claws, Trophobia
Withdrawn Butter Cookies
I Qcumber Salad
Padded Celery Soup
Senilla Tea
Mixed Nut Cake
Oedipus Compote

KNAPSACK STRAP

"Knapsack strap" is not something I say too often. In fact, it's something I try not to say at all. I have nothing against knapsack straps, which are so valuable to knapsack owners—it's just that I can't get my tongue around the words without getting it into a terrible twist.

"Knapsack strap" is just one of the world's 50 worst tongue twisters. Try repeating one of them ten times, quickly.

THE WORLD'S 50 WORST TONGUE TWISTERS

Knapsack strap.
Cuthbert's custard.
The rat ran by the river with a lump of raw liver.
Three free thugs set three thugs free.

Freddy Thrush flies through thick fog.
Tuesday is stew day. Stew day is Tuesday.
Gig whip.
Bubble-bowls.
That bloke's back brake-block broke.
A big blue bucket of blue blueberries.
Black bugs' blood.
Crime cuts cut crime.
A crow flew over the river with a lump of raw liver.
She sells seashells by the seashore.
Dressed in drip-dry drawers.
Do drop in at the Dewdrop Inn.
Double bubble gum bubbles double.
Diligence dismisseth despondency.
There are thirty thousand feathers on that thrush's throat.
Ted threw Fred three free throws.
Freckled-faced Florence.
Pure food for four pure mules.
The gum glue grew glum.
Groovy gravy, baby!
He is literally literary.
Lame Lambs limp.
Mumbling bumblings. Bumbling mumblings.
The new nuns knew the true nuns knew the new nuns too.
Tiny orangutang tongues.
Is there a pleasant peasant present?
A regal rural ruler.
Six thick thistle sticks.
Three thrice-freed thieves.
The sixth sheik's sixth sheep's sick.
Greek grapes.
Which wristwatches are Swiss wristwatches?
Truly plural.

The big black-backed bumblebee.

A lump of red leather, a red leather lump.

Critical cricket critics.

Thin sticks, thick bricks.

Toy boat.

He ran from the Indies to the Andes in his undies.

Unique New York.

The Leith police dismisseth us.

Cheap ship trips.

Peggy Babcock.

Sister Suzie says she shall shortly sew a sheet.

This thistle seems like that thistle.

Lemon liniment.

For a tongue twister that just won't give up, try this story. Read it faultlessly, out loud, and fast.

THE TALE OF TWO BOOTBLACKS

Two bootblacks, a white bootblack and a black bootblack, stood together doing nothing.

The white bootblack proposed that he should black the boots of the black bootblack.

The black bootblack was perfectly willing to have his boots blacked by the white bootblack.

So the white bootblack began to black the boots of the black bootblack.

But when the white bootblack had blacked one boot of the black bootblack, he declined to black the other boot of the black bootblack until the black bootblack had blacked both boots of the white bootblack.

However, the black bootblack refused point-blank to black the boots of the white bootblack, and said he didn't care whether the white bootblack blacked the other boot black or not. He considered that one boot blacked was enough for a black bootblack, and that a black bootblack with one boot blacked was better than a white bootblack with no boots blacked.

Then the white bootblack called the black bootblack a black blackguard.

Of course, when the white bootblack began blacking the character of the black bootblack, the black bootblack began blacking the face of the white bootblack all black with the blacking on the boot the white bootblack had blacked, and the white bootblack blacked the black bootblack back.

When the Society of Black and White Bootblacks considered the matter, they characterized the conduct of both bootblacks as the blackest affair that had ever blackened the pages of boot-black history.

If you flunked the challenge, don't worry—you're in good company. In the early days of radio, when all the programs had to be broadcast live, one of America's most confident and accomplished actors turned down the role of a detective in a play when he saw this tongue twister in the script: "Show me the chair Schmidt sat in when he was shot."

J.Q. SCHWARTZ AND FRIENDS

J. Q. Schwartz flung D. V. Pike my box.

That's a pangram: a sentence that includes every letter of the alphabet.

PANGRAMS FROM THE BIBLE

Here is a near-pangram, from Ezra 7:21:

> And I, even I Artaxerxes the king, do make a decree to all the treasurers which are beyond the river, that whatsoever Ezra the priest, the scribe of the law of the God of heaven, shall require of you, it be done speedily.

The verse includes every letter except *j*. Another biblical near-miss, taken from 1 Chronicles 12:40 lacks only a *q*:

Moreover they that were nigh them, even unto Issachar and Zebulun and Naphtali, brought bread on asses, and on camels, and on mules, and on oxen, and meat, meal, cakes of figs, and bunches of raisins, and wine, and oil, and oxen, and sheep abundantly: for there was joy in Israel.

THE SHORTEST PANGRAMS

The best-known pangram has 33 letters, including every letter in the alphabet at least once. It is often used to check out a typewriter:

The quick brown fox jumps over a lazy dog.

This one has 32 letters:

Pack my box with five dozen liquor jugs.

And this one is down to 31:

The five boxing wizards jump quickly.

To get below 30 you have to introduce proper names. Here is one with 29:

Quick wafting zephyrs vex bold Jim.

And here is one with just 28:

Waltz, nymph, for quick jigs vex Bud.

No one has devised a 26-letter pangram that doesn't use names and initials (like J. Q. Schwartz and D. V. Pike) or archaic words. Here is a 26-letter gem which roughly translated into everyday English means, "Carved figures on the bank of a fjord in a rounded valley irritated an eccentric person."

Cwm, fjord-bank glyphs vext quiz.

If you can devise a 26-letter pangram in modern English without resorting to names and initials, rush it to *The Guinness Book of World Records*. The editors are anxious to hear from you.

ALPHABETICS

Pangrammarians are closely related to alphabeticians. While pangrammarians try to include every letter of the alphabet in a single sentence, alphabeticians try to begin each word in the sentence with a successive letter of the alphabet. For example, in 1842 the *London Times* carried this unusual advertisement:

TO WIDOWERS AND SINGLE GENTLEMEN—WANTED by a lady, a SITUATION to superintend the household and preside at table. She is Agreeable, Becoming, Careful, Desirable, English, Facetious, Generous, Honest, Industrious, Keen, Lively, Merry, Natty, Obedient, Philosophic, Quiet, Regular, Sociable, Tasteful, Useful, Vivacious, Womanish, Xantippish, Youthful, Zealous, &c.

The lady in question was obviously a prize worth winning, for as well as possessing the stated virtues she was a mistress of the art of alphabetics. (In those days *j* was considered an optional letter.) Try to devise an essay, a poem, story, or advertisement of this kind.

Here is the most famous alphabetic verse, an alliterative epic called "The Siege of Belgrade" and it doesn't feature any j's either.

An Austrian army, awfully arrayed,
Boldly, by battery, besieged Belgrade;
Cossack commanders cannonading come—
Dealing destruction's devastating doom;
Every endeavor, engineers essay,
For fame, for fortune—fighting furious fray:—
Generals 'gainst generals grapple—gracious God!
How honors Heaven, heroic hardihood!
Infuriate,—indiscriminate in ill,
Kindred kill kinsmen,—kinsmen kindred kill!
Labor low levels loftiest longest lines—
Men march 'mid mounds, 'mid moles, 'mid
    murderous mines:
Now noisy, noxious, noticed nought
Of outward obstacles opposing ought:
Poor patriots, partly purchased, partly pressed:
Quite quaking, quickly quarter, quarter quest,
Reason returns, relivious right redounds.
Suwarrow [Suvorov] stops such sanguinary sounds.
Truce to thee, Turkey—triumph to thy train!
Unjust, unwise, unmerciful Ukraine!
Vanish vain victory, vanish victory vain!
Why wish we warfare? Wherefore welcome were

Xerxes, Ximenes, Xanthus, Xaviere?
Yield! ye youths! ye yeomen, yield your yell!
Zeno's, Zapater's, Zoroaster's zeal,
And all attracting—arms against acts appeal.

It is uncertain who wrote the poem, but I suspect it was Adolph Blaine Charles David Earl Frederick Gerald Hubert Irvin John Kenneth Lloyd Martin Nero Oliver Paul Quincy Randolph Sherman Thomas Uncas Victor William Xerxes Yancy Zeus Wolfeschlegelsteinhausenbergerdorff, Senior, who, believe it or not, is alive and well and living in Philadelphia.

Is GOD A WOMAN?

"Dear God," wrote a little girl named Sylvia, "are boys better than we are? I know you are one, but try to be fair."

God is not only a man, he's called Harold Wishart. At least that's what another little girl thinks: "Our father Wishart in Heaven, Harold be thy name."

I have to admit, even as a confirmed feminist—or should it be personist?—that when I was a child the possibility that God mightn't be a man never occurred to me. Like millions of others I was brought up to be an unwitting sexist—but times are changing and feminists are waging war not only on attitudes but on the vocabulary of sexism. The chairperson is here to stay—and so are a number of other words designed to replace outmoded male-oriented words. *Woman* may have to go because it derives from an Old English word meaning *wife-man*. And *history*'s days are numbered too. The celebrated Ms. Ellen Cooperperson (formerly Mrs. Cooperman) has pioneered the use of the word *herstory*. I think she needn't have bothered—the feminine possessive pronoun *her* is from Middle English; the masculine possessive pronoun *his* is from Old English; *history* is from Latin and Greek (*historia*), further derived from *histor* or *istor* "knowing or learning"; the personal pronoun *his*, which was never present in *history*, further disappears in the form *istor*—but I still support the cause.

The cause may be just, but it's an uphill struggle. Over the years, for example, there have been attempts to coin a new common gender pronoun to replace the awkward "he or she" in a platonic, nonsexist way. They have all failed.

The longest-lived coinage was proposed by the American composer Charles Converse in 1859. *Thon*, which he derived as a contraction of *that one*, was listed in Funk & Wagnalls New Standard Dictionary of 1913 with the examples "If Harry or his wife comes, I will be on hand to greet thon," and "Each pupil must learn thon's lesson"; and the term was alive enough in 1959 to rate inclusion in the last printing of Webster's Second International. Another proposal included in the 1913 Funk & Wagnalls was *he'er*—with *his'er* and *him'er* as the possessive and objective forms—but the suggestion has had even less success than *thon*. Recent proposals, including *E, hesh, po, tey, ve, xe,* and *jhe*, have also been ephemeral.

FEMGLISH SPOKEN HERE

If you want to try your hand at creating nonsexist vocabulary, here are ten words. You may not regard any of them as particularly sexist, but some ardent feminists do and they have proposed appropriate modifications.

MANGLISH	FEMGLISH
1 *hedonism*	
2 *ottoman*	
3 *hysteria*	

4 *mankind*

5 *mandolin*

6 *manikin*

7 *womanizer*

8 *humanism*

9 *mango*

10 *manhandle*

(See Answers.)

NEVER THE TWAIN SHALL MEET

If trying to be nonsexist is too much for you, at least thank God you're not German. (Having just said that it occurs to me, *She* probably is.) The problems of sorting out genders in English are trivial compared with the corresponding German traumas. Let Mark Twain explain:

> In German, a young lady has no sex, while a turnip has. Think what overwrought reverence that shows for the turnip, and what callous disrespect for the girl. See how it looks in print— I translate this from a conversation in one of the best of the German Sunday-school books:
> "*Gretchen.*—Wilhelm, where is the turnip?
> "*Wilhelm.*—She has gone to the kitchen.
> "*Gretchen.*—Where is the accomplished and beautiful English maiden?
> "*Wilhelm.*—It has gone to the opera."
> A tree is male, its buds are female, its leaves are neuter; horses are sexless, dogs are male, cats are female—tomcats included, of course; a person's mouth, neck, bosom, elbows, fingers, nails, feet, and body are of the male sex, and his head is male or neuter according to the word selected to signify it, and *not* according to the sex of the individual who wears it—for in Germany all the women wear either male heads or sexless ones; a person's nose, lips, shoulders, breast, hands, and toes are of the female sex; and his hair, ears, eyes, chin, legs, knees, heart, and conscience haven't any sex at all. The inventor of the language probably got what he knew about a conscience from hearsay . . .

HERE LIE I

DEATHLESS PROSE

There is much to be said against being dead. For one thing, the dead cannot read their own epitaphs—unless they return as ghosts or take the precaution of penning their epitaphs before dying, as John Gay (1685–1732) did:

> Life is a jest; and all things show it.
> I thought so once; but now I know it.

Call mine a grave sense of humor, but I've been a lifelong collector of epitaphs. In case, like Gay, you're planning to word your own—and it's a pastime that positively induces insomnia— the cream of my collection will inspire you.

EPITAPH ON A DRUNKARD

> He had his beer
> From year to year,
> And then his bier had him.

244

MARTHA SNELL

Poor Martha Snell, she's gone away,
She would if she could but she could not stay;
She'd two bad legs and baddish cough,
But her legs it was that carried her off.

ANN MANN

Here lies the body of Ann Mann,
Who lived an old woman
And died an old Mann.

THE TIRED WOMAN'S EPITAPH

Here lies a poor woman who always was tired,
She lived in a house where help was not hired;
Her last words on earth were: "Dear friends, I am going
Where washing ain't done, nor sweeping, nor sewing;
But everything there is exact to my wishes;
For where they don't eat there's no washing of dishes.
I'll be where loud anthems will always be ringing,
But, having no voice, I'll be clear of the singing.
Don't mourn for me now; don't mourn for me never—
I'm going to do nothing for ever and ever."

EPITAPH FROM ABERDEEN, SCOTLAND

Here lie the bones of Elizabeth Charlotte,
Born a virgin, died a harlot;
She was aye a virgin at 17,
A remarkable thing in Aberdeen.

EPITAPH AT GREAT TORRINGTON, DEVON, ENGLAND

Here lies a man who was killed by lightning;
He died when his prospects seemed to be brightening.
He might have cut a flash in this world of trouble,
But the flash cut him, and he lies in the stubble.

EPITAPH FROM AUSTRALIA

God took our flower—our little Nell:
He thought He too would like a smell.

ARABELLA YOUNG

Beneath this stone
  A lump of clay
Lies Arabella Young
Who on the 21st of May
      1771
Began to hold her tongue.

JOHN DRYDEN'S EPITAPH FOR HIS WIFE

Here lies my wife.
Here let her lie!
Now she's at rest
And so am I.

JOHN WOOD

Here lies John Bun,
He was killed by a gun;
His name was not Bun, but Wood;
But Wood would not rhyme with Gun,
  but Bun would.

EPITAPH ON A DENTIST

Stranger! Approach this spot with gravity!
John Brown is filling his last cavity.

EPITAPH ON A CHILD OF SEVEN MONTHS

If I am so quickly done for,
What on earth was I begun for?

EPITAPH ON A WIFE

The children of Israel wanted bread
The Lord he sent them manna;
But this good man he wanted a wife
And the devil sent him Anna.

EPITAPH ON A MAN CALLED LONGBOTTAM
WHO DIED YOUNG

Ars longa, vita brevis.

EPITAPH ON A PIONEER AVIATOR

There was an old man who averred
He had learned how to fly like a bird.
    Cheered by thousands of people
    He leapt from the steeple—
This tomb states the date it occurred.

EPITAPH ON GYLES BRANDRETH

Who?

P.S.

Have you ever thought when a hearse goes by
That one fine day you were doomed to die?
They wrap you up in a big white sheet
And drop you down about 13 feet.
The worms crawl in, and the worms crawl out,
The bugs play pinochle on your snout.
Your coffin rots and you turn to dust,
And that's the end of your life of lust.
               R.I.P.

THE GREATS

I've been collecting word games and puzzles for over a quarter of a century—yes, I started *very* young—and of the thousands I've enjoyed I think I enjoyed the following ten the most. They are the work of wordsters of genius: the first five by a true prince of puzzledom, Jerome Meyer.

HEAR HERE!

Homonyms, in case you've forgotten, are pairs of words that are pronounced the same but spelled differently. *Right* and *write* are homonyms and so are *feet* and *feat*, and *meat* and *meet*. Below, fill in both words: the first fits the definition, the second is the homonymous name of an animal. The answer to No. 1 is *hoarse, horse*. What are the others? Par is 14 right in ten minutes.

1 husky: h_____ and h_____
2 long thin candle: t_____ and t_____
3 exist: b_____ and b_____
4 make a hole: b_____ and b_____
5 did know: k_____ and g_____
6 second person: y_____ and e_____
7 slang for money: d_____ and d_____
8 fly away: f_____ and f_____
9 rotate slowly: t_____ and t_____
10 barren: b_____ and b_____
11 part of the head: h_____ and h_____
12 cover the top: c_____ and s_____
13 child's cry: m_____ and m_____
14 parts of a chain: l_____ and l_____
15 furrow: r_____ and r_____
16 female relative: a_____ and a_____
17 god of the fields: f_____ and f_____
18 expensive: d_____ and d_____
19 gain by work: e_____ and e_____
20 rougher: c_____ and c_____

Now try another set from the plant kingdom. Par is 14 right in 15 minutes.

1 remove vegetation from: p_____ and p_____
2 grant, give up: c_____ and s_____
3 unit of gem, weight: c_____ and c_____
4 punish by blows: b_____ and b_____
5 escaping of water: l_____ and l_____
6 put under ground: b_____ and b_____
7 groups of birds: f_____ and p_____
8 dressed pelt: f_____ and f_____
9 existed: b_____ and b_____
10 vertical: p_____ and p_____
11 flowing onward motion: c_____ and c_____

12 shore of the sea: b_____ and b_____
13 objects placed in straight lines: r_____ and r_____
14 duration: t_____ and t_____
15 officer: c_____ and k_____
16 burned: c_____ and c_____
17 course to be traveled: r_____ and r_____
18 object used in golf: t_____ and t_____
19 gladly, willingly: l_____ and l_____
20 quick descent in a river: c_____ and s_____
(See Answers.)

YOU DON'T SAY!

Wherever you go, you can't get away from clichés. This test is no exception. Here are 20 worn-out sayings waiting to be paired off and thrown away in record time. Par is three minutes.

1 *tempt*	(a) the beans
2 *run*	(b) the works
3 *take up*	(c) the climax
4 *gild*	(d) the gauntlet
5 *cap*	(e) the fates
6 *toe*	(f) the coop
7 *throw*	(g) the growler
8 *shoot*	(h) the bucket
9 *dish*	(i) the rag
10 *bury*	(j) the lily
11 *beard*	(k) the cudgels
12 *beat about*	(l) the bull
13 *fly*	(m) the mark
14 *turn*	(n) the bill
15 *spill*	(o) the comedy
16 *kick*	(p) the tables

17 *chew*   (q) the dirt

18 *fill*   (r) the hatchet

19 *rush*   (s) the lion

20 *cut*   (t) the bush

(See Answers.)

DUO-WORDS

Thousands of words are made up of shorter words, just by coincidence. For example, *anthem* is composed of *ant* and *hem*, neither of which has any connection with an anthem.

Below are 20 six-letter words made up of two three-letter words each. The three-letter words are defined, but not the six-letter word. Par is 14 correct in four minutes.

  1 Male adults + highest card in pack

  2 Large body of water + male child

  3 Opposite of *on* + frozen water

  4 Terminal + organ of hearing

  5 Mischievous child + atmosphere

  6 Army bed + heavy weight

  7 Headgear + color

  8 Decay + past tense of *eat*

  9 Ask for charity + unity

10 Spanish nobleman + locking device

11 Chum + aviation hero

12 Deface + alcoholic drink

13 By reason of + self

14 Water barrier + writing instrument

15 Nearest star + devoid of moisture

16 Distant + noisy quarrel

17 Succeed in competition + endeavor

18 Kind of tree + rock containing iron

19 Dog + not many

20 Venomous snake + anger

Here are 20 more, a little harder. Par is 12 correct in five minutes.

1 Automobile + house dog

2 Stitch a garment + your time of life

3 Vehicle + decay

4 Meat of pig + allow

5 Large + girl's name

6 Part of a dog + man's name

7 Pretend + electrified particle

8 Join + past tense of *lead*

9 Move in fixed direction + golf term

10 Feminine pronoun + German for "with"

11 Part of a fish + kind of beer

12 Number of two digits + put on

13 Armed conflict + lion's home

14 Place + free

15 Legal profession + bottom of river

16 Amusement + man's name

17 Kitchen utensil + burned residue

18 Part of the body + purpose

19 Perceive + definite article

20 Fool + sicken
(See Answers.)

THE MEYER THE MERRIER

There is a filled-in example below. Six pairs of words are read across. On each line there is a five-letter word (e.g., *state*); on adding or inserting the boxed letter a new six-letter word is produced (e.g., *estate*). The letters in the boxes spell a seventh six-letter word, *elated*.

To solve the puzzles, fill in as many five-letter words as you can by answering the definitions. Pick letters for the boxes that will turn your five-letter words into six-letter words. See if you can guess the remaining boxed letters to make the six-letter diagonal (boxed) word. If you don't get a six-letter diagonal word right away, see if you can change any boxed letters. In the filled-in example, e.g., *slaves* could be *shaves* or *staves*.

```
E S T A T E
S L A V E S
G R A I N S
M I S T E R
G R I P E S
C L O S E D
```

In the first two puzzles, the letters in the boxes spell the names of American cities. Remember, the definitions refer to *five*-letter words, across.

1 □ — — — — —   1 Radiant energy which produces sight

2 — □ — — — —   2 Metric liquid measure

3 — — □ — — —   3 Mother

4 — — — □ — —   4 Puzzling problem

5 — — — — □ —   5 Metric measurement of length

6 — — — — — □   6 Bury

1 □ — — — — —   1 Wrath

2 — □ — — — —   2 Refuge; shelter

3 — — □ — — —   3 Hinged barriers

4 — — — □ — —   4 Restored to health again

5 — — — — □ —   5 Males of the red deer

6 — — — — — □   6 Appetizing dressing for food

In the last two puzzles, the letters in the boxes spell the names of common flowers.

1 □—————		1 Female relatives
2 —□————		2 Lays plans; conspires
3 ——□———		3 Propelled a boat with a long stick
4 ———□——		4 Clearing in an English moor
5 ————□—		5 Bony fish
6 —————□		6 Flat surface

1 □—————		1 Inclines toward
2 —□————		2 Plunges head foremost
3 ——□———		3 Lowlands
4 ———□——		4 Removed ore
5 ————□—		5 Condition of being
6 —————□		6 Depart

(See Answers.)

ROBINSON CLOUSEAUS

The Robinsons played charades the other evening. The guests were told the number of syllables in a word and its initial letter, and they had to guess the word from the actions of the host or hostess. The host, for example, sighed loudly and then started to kick vigorously. He had told everyone it was a word beginning with *p* with two syllables. The answer, of course, is *psychic*, or *sigh kick*. I think you will have a lot of fun with these charades, and you can use them at your next party:

1 The host held an ice cube in each hand and then started to press them together. (Two syllables beginning with *p.*)

2 The hostess appeared with a hairnet in her hand. She threw the net as far as she could. (Three syllables beginning with *c.*)

3 The host showed a bottle of chili sauce and placed it close to the edge of a card table. (Two syllables beginning with *s.*)

4 The hostess held up a can of soup, rouged her lips, powdered her nose, pretended to make up her eyebrows, and then made a face for an imaginary photographer. (Four syllables beginning with *s.*)

5 A startling charade followed. The host held a piece of paper with a large 8 written on it above his head and set it on fire. (Three syllables beginning with *h.*)

6 The hostess showed everyone a sign with this message: XwvutsrqponmlkjihgfedC (Three syllables beginning with *e.*)

7 The host held up a package and said, "This is a more recent brand of tea." (Four syllables beginning with *a.*)

8 The hostess entered the room, knocked on a door, then turned around and went right out again. (Two syllables beginning with *n.*)

9 The host and hostess did this one together. She pretended to faint and he brought her to. She said, "My dear nephew, I am so grateful to you for reviving me." (Three syllables beginning with *r.*)

10 The host entered with a block of wood with a large nail in it. He pulled at it for a while and said, "I guess that nail is in there so it won't come out." (Two syllables beginning with *i.*)

11 The hostess showed everyone two frail-looking letters, *s* and *n*, which she had cut from tissue. She handled them carefully and announced that they were easily torn. (Five syllables beginning with *d.*)

12 The host held up a ball-point pen and then held up the ten of spades. Finally he showed everyone a bottle of sherry. (Five syllables beginning with *p.*)

13 The hostess showed a huge letter *s* which she had printed on a big sheet of cardboard. (Two syllables beginning with *l.*)

14 The hostess shook hands with the host and said, "How do you do, doctor, I'm certainly glad I met you." (Five syllables beginning with *m.*)

15 For the last charade the host held up a penny and shouted ten times. (Three syllables beginning with *c*.)

(See Answers.)

H. E. DUDENEY'S ALPHABET

The point of this little crossword is that each of the 26 letters of the alphabet is used once and only once. We give the definitions—a few are rather old-fashioned—but do not indicate the locations of the words or their direction, horizontal or vertical. (See Answers.)

DEFINITIONS

A metal. Parts of trees. To annoy.
Whim or imagination. A sign,
example. What person or persons.
A man's shortened Christian name.
To puzzle or, make sport of.

NICHOLAS SCRIPTURE'S HOLY WRIT

In the square below, the letters form the titles of 11 famous Shakespeare plays. Letters which are next to each other in a title are adjacent horizontally or vertically in the square, and the last letter of one title is adjacent to the first letter of the next. All the words have been given the privilege of commencing with a capital letter. To make the puzzle work, Mr. Scripture had to cheat a little and spell Antony with an h. This isn't how Shakespeare did it, but then he didn't have to devise word squares.

```
A  M  i  r  e  a  t  h  e  l  l  o
e  s  d  D  s  m  O  o  Y  e  b  M
r  u  m  m  t  h  g  u  s  t  c  a
u  e  M  e  r  N  i  L  A  h  t  A
s  a  r  s  e  d  i  i  k  e  I  n
e  F  o  t  p  a  s  s  l  C  h  t
r  a  e  R  m  T  h  e  e  d  o  n
u  s  M  o  e  T  e  r  o  n  A  y
l  e  s  m  e  l  u  C  p  r  a  J
c  t  e  A  o  i  s  d  a  t  l  u
i  P  i  n  d  o  A  n  s  e  i  u
r  e  l  u  J  r  T  r  a  a  C  s
```

(See Answers.)

NICHOLAS SCRIPTURE'S TETRAHEDRON

The illustration below shows the "net" of a tetrahedron, or triangular pyramid. Erect the tetrahedron by photocopying the diagram and folding up the corners. Then you can trace out a famous definition of *news*, as given by John B. Bogart in the *New York Sun*. (See Answers.)

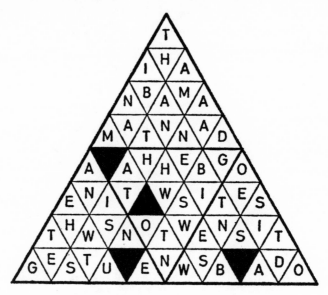

J. NEWTON FRIEND'S "IN THE MIDDLE"

J. Newton Friend invites you to make words by putting three letters on each side of the combinations below:

1 *ural*	7 *ment*	12 *epho*
2 *ocia*	8 *idel*	13 *ctro*
3 *upul*	9 *redi*	14 *hani*
4 *cina*	10 *dpec*	15 *ustr*
5 *caut*	11 *olut*	16 *gerh*
6 *hest*		

(See Answers.)

ELIZABETH KINGSLEY'S DOUBLE-CROSTIC

And lastly a first—the first of the 975 Double-Crostics created by Elizabeth Kingsley for the *Saturday Review of Literature*. It appeared in 1934—and the puzzles haven't got any easier since. (See Answers.)

DIRECTIONS—To solve this puzzle, you must guess twenty-five words, the definitions of which are given in the column headed DEFINITIONS. The letters in each word to be guessed are numbered (these numbers appear at the beginning of each definition) and you are thereby able to tell how many letters are in the required word. When you have guessed a word each letter is to be written in the correspondingly numbered square on the puzzle diagram. When the squares are all filled in you will find (by reading from left to right) a quotation from a famous author. Reading up and down, the letters mean nothing! The black squares indicate ends of words; therefore words do not necessarily end at the right side of the diagram.

Either before (preferably) or after placing the letters in their squares you should write the words you have guessed on the blank lines which appear to the right in the column headed WORDS. The initial letters of this list of words spell the name of the author and the title of the piece from which the quotation has been taken.

DEFINITIONS

WORDS

I. 1-14-23-50-95. A perfume of roses.

I. _ _ _ _ _

II. 145-6-28-90-137. Child's game played with cards and numbers.

II. _ _ _ _ _

III. 97-8-79-146-98-61-75-77-76-32-27-19-133. Light as a feather.

III. _ _ _ _ _ _ _
_ _ _ _ _ _

IV. 80-85-60-113-51-58-48. Held in high esteem; worshipped.

IV. _ _ _ _ _ _ _

V. 81-172-31-84-24-176-65-89. Insubstantial.

V. _ _ _ _ _ _ _ _

VI.   112-45-114-164-149-173-   VI.   _ _ _ _ _ _ _ _
      142-36. The business
      section of a city.

VII. 144-102-2-63. Material   VII. _ _ _ _ _
      for bandages.

VIII. 37-4-66-82-110-116-62.   VIII. _ _ _ _ _ _ _
      Upholstered backless seat.

IX.   100-106-33-5-122-41-138- IX.   _ _ _ _ _ _ _
      69-83-13-162-127. A   _ _ _ _ _ _
      Russian pianist.

X.   40-59-52-25. A drupe   X.   _ _ _ _
      with a single seed.

XI.   135-175-3-73. Movement   XI.   _ _ _ _
      of the ocean.

XII. 130-43-129-107-111-55-   XII. _ _ _ _ _ _ _ _
      139-47. To alienate.

XIII. 15-121-92-136-101-39. A   XIII. _ _ _ _ _ _
      mighty hunter.

XIV. 167-9-140-46-105. Artless; XIV. _ _ _ _ _
      simple.

XV.   119-54-104-17-153-34.   XV.   _ _ _ _ _ _
      Hebrew God.

XVI. 134-63-128-168-16-30.   XVI. _ _ _ _ _ _
      Flat, dark image.

XVII. 155-125-78-148-143-165-   XVII. _ _ _ _ _ _ _ _
      158-56. Prejudiced
      (compound).

XVIII. 12-96-120-11-7-170-150- XVIII. _ _ _ _ _ _ _
      21-68-174. Significant,   _ _ _ _
      unusual.

XIX. 87-141-171-161-67-20-10- XIX. _ _ _ _ _ _ _ _
      126. Not propitious.

XX.   177-99-152-163-108-115.   XX.   _ _ _ _ _ _
      Member of the tribe of
      Levi.

XXI. 42-88-26-159-49-91.   XXI. _ _ _ _ _ _
      Doodle dandy.

XXII. 22-71-151-118-131-147-38-94-160-29. Watchword (Bibl.).

XXII. _ _ _ _ _ _ _ _ _ _

XXIII. 109-86-132-124-72-117-123-178. Uttered a harsh sound.

XXIII. _ _ _ _ _ _ _ _

XXIV. 157-44-93-53-166-18-35-103. Forceful.

XXIV. _ _ _ _ _ _ _ _

XXV. 156-154-74-169-70-57. To stop the flow.

XXV. _ _ _ _ _ _

F
IVE BY FIVE

Five by five is a word game for two players. Draw two grids on pieces of paper, with each grid like this:

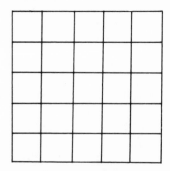

The first player calls out a letter of the alphabet, and marks it in one of the 25 squares on his grid. The opponent marks the same letter wherever he chooses on *his* grid. Then the second player calls out a letter, and they continue until the first player has called out 13 letters and his opponent has called out 12. Now the two grids are full. The same letter can be called out by one or both players as many times as they like. Each player should take care not to let his opponent see his grid until the game is over.

Your aim is to fill your grid with three-, four-, and five-letter words going horizontally and vertically. At the end of the game you get 3 points for each three-letter word, 4 points for each four-letter word, and 5 points for each five-letter word. (If you have the word *beast* you get 5 points, but you can't get 4 points for the *east* in the *beast*.) Choose letters to call out that will help you form words in your grid. When your opponent calls out a letter, incorporate it as best you can.

Here is how the grids looked at the end of a game between two pioneers of Five by Five. George called out *l, e, r, o, a, t, c, a, h, n, d, v,* and *r,* and Martha called out *e, r, a, s, r, e, s, t, d, u, t,* and *n.*

GEORGE'S GRID

L O V E R
E R R S A
A D D N N
S E A T C
T R U T H

MARTHA'S GRID

L U N C H
O T R D A
R A T E S
D R A N T
S E R V E

George scored 36 points—

Across	*lover*	5
	errs	4
	add	3
	seat	4
	truth	5

Down	*least*	5
	order	5
	ranch	5

—and Martha, 39 points:

Across	*lunch*	5
	rates	5
	rant	4
	serve	5

Down	*lords*	5
	tare	4
	tar	3
	den	3
	haste	5

Martha won the game with an impressive 39 points. If she had entered the maximum (five five-letter words across and the same down) she would have scored 50 for the words plus a bonus of 50. She would also have created what is known to wordsmiths as a word square.

A *perfect* word square has the same words going down as across:

G R A N T
R O D E O
A D D E R
N E E D S
T O R S O

Here are two, three, and four-letter word squares:

A M   C A P   L O V E
M E   A R E   O V E R
           P E T   V E E R
                    E R R S

Word squares date back thousands of years. Socrates and Aristotle loved them, and the ancient Romans are believed to have enjoyed them too. A century ago, when a Roman site was being excavated at Cirencester in Gloucestershire, England, this Latin perfect word square was unearthed on a piece of wall plaster:

R O T A S
O P E R A
T E N E T
A R E P O
S A T O R

This word square is extra special: you can read the five words backward or upward and it is still a perfect word square—the same words in another arrangement. Arepo is a proper name (a rural Roman Marx brother); the other words are legitimate Latin and actually form a sentence, which translated gives us an impression of the state of agricultural techniques 2,000 years ago: "The sower Arepo controls the wheels with an effort."

I find the effort of composing a five-letter perfect word square (in English, not Latin) peculiarly satisfying. Six- and seven-letter perfect word squares are very difficult to produce, but it has been done:

```
P R E P A R E
R E M O D E L
E M U L A T E
P O L E M I C
A D A M A N T
R E T I N U E
E L E C T E D
```

Producing eight-, nine, and ten-letter perfect word squares can also be done, but not by me. Here is a brilliant eight-letter perfect word square composed by Margaretta Strohm, a latter-day Socrates from Pennsylvania. Don't ask me what half the words mean, but most or all of them are in your unabridged dictionary:

```
A G A R I C U S
G E N E R A N T
A N A C O N D A
R E C A N T E R
I R O N W O R T
C A N T O N A L
U N D E R A G E
S T A R T L E D
```

The most remarkable of the handful of existing ten-letter perfect word squares follows. My friend Darryl Francis, one of the world's most brilliant verbivores, introduced me to it some years ago and I'm still gasping. To make sense of it you need a library of dictionaries. You also need to be indulgent and forgive the fact that lines and columns 8, 9, and 10 repeat the words in lines and columns 3, 4, and 5.

```
O R A N G U T A N G
R A N G A R A N G A
A N D O L A N D O L
N G O T A N G O T A
G A L A N G A L A N
U R A N G U T A N G
T A N G A T A N G A
A N D O L A N D O L
N G O T A N G O T A
G A L A N G A L A N
```

DEFINITIONS

Orangutang: orangutan. A spelling given by Funk and Wagnalls New Standard Dictionary (1946).

Rangaranga: In the Caroline Islands, a name for parsley fern growing in the cracks of old walls. Taken from Frederick Christian, *The Caroline Islands* (London, 1899).

Andolandol: A Chinese fly, a tincture of which is used as a blistering agent. Taken from Frank Foster, *An Illustrated Encyclopedic Medical Dictionary* (New York, between 1888 and 1894).

Ngotongota: Town on the western shore of Lake Nyasa, now spelled Kota Kota. Taken from George Chisholm, *Longman's Gazetteer of the World* (London and New York, 1902).

Galangalan: A mountain in Sorsogon Province, Luzon Island, the Philippines. Taken from U.S. War Department, *A Pronouncing Gazetteer and Geographical Dictionary of the Philippine Islands* (Washington, D.C., 1902).

Urangutang: The orangutan again. Oxford English Dictionary (1933).

Tangatanga: A name for the trinity of ancient Peruvian divinites, Pachama, Virakotcha, and Mamakotcha. Taken from E. Cobham Brewer, *The Reader's Handbook of Allusions, References, Plots, and Stories* (Philadelphia, 1880).

If you are not familiar with word squares and don't have a partner to give you a game of Five by Five, try these three puzzles. Solving them isn't as challenging as creating word squares of your own, but gives you good training. If you can solve them with ease, you are obviously a word-square creator in the making.

1. Complete the seven-letter perfect word square. I give you the first and seventh words, plus straightforward clues to the other five.

```
M E R G E R S
E — — — — — L
R — — — — — A
G — — — — — Y
E — — — — — E
R — — — — — R
S L A Y E R S
```

Row and column 2.	There's no end to this
Row and column 3.	You couldn't have one of these without water
Row and column 4.	This was known to a *serious* Isaac Newton
Row and column 5.	What would you call this?
Row and column 6.	Snake's alive!

2. There are no clues to help you complete the next seven-letter perfect word square, but three of the words are already in position.

```
— E — T — E —
E N T R A N T
— T — A — G —
T R A I T O R
— A — T — R —
E N G O R G E
— T — R — E —
```

3. Along with gangsters, the Chicago of 1928 gave us a nine-letter perfect word square by Wayne M. Goodwin. To complete it you will need a rich vocabulary, so I give you the eighth word, *Eavestone,* (the name of a town in the

West Riding of Yorkshire in England) and provide clues
for the other eight words.

```
———————— E —
———————— A —
———————— V —
———————— E —
———————— S —
———————— T —
———————— O —
E A V E S T O N E
———————— E —
```

Row and column 1.   Monastic refectories
Row and column 2.   Pertaining to a health plan
Row and column 3.   Inclined to make trouble
Row and column 4.   Minerals containing titanium
Row and column 5.   Someone who believes in
                     creation by emanation
Row and column 6.   To titrate again (and don't tell
                     me you didn't know that to
                     titrate was to determine the
                     quantity of a given constituent
                     in a compound by observing
                     the quantity of a standard
                     solution necessary to convert
                     this constituent into another
                     form)
Line and column 7.   A person who begins
                     something
Line and column 9.   Bedaubed and smeared

(See Answers.)

ELLIPTICAL KISS

Who was it who first defined the word *elliptical* as "a kiss" (*a lip tickle*)? I don't know, but he was some kind of a genius. It has to be the greatest daffynition of all time.

Daffynitions appear in fictionaries, not dictionaries, and they add hidden dimensions to the words they describe. I've culled the fictionaries for a list of the 99 best daffynitions in the English language.

acorn	An oak in a nutshell.
afford	A car some people drive.
announce	One-sixteenth of a pound.
appear	Something you fish off.
area code	A sinus condition.
arrest	What to take when you're tired.
ashtray	A place where people put ashes when the room doesn't have a rug.

attack	A small nail.
auctioneer	A man who looks forbidding.
autograph	A chart showing the sales of cars.
ax	Chopstick.
bacteria	The rear of a cafeteria.
barber shop	A clip joint.
bathing beauty	A girl worth wading for.
bee	A hum-bug.
beet	A potato with high blood pressure.
buccaneer	Too much to pay for corn.
camelot	A parking lot for camels.
cannibal	One who is fed up with people.
carbuncle	An auto collision.
cartoon	A song you hear on the car radio.
caterpillar	An upholstered worm.
chair	Headquarters for hindquarters.
chicken farm	A large egg plant.
conceit	I-strain.
crowbar	A bird's drinking place.
cube root	Diced carrots.
denial	Where Cleopatra lived.
dentist	Someone who looks down in the mouth.
drill sergeant	An army dentist.
egg	A fowl ball.
egomania	a passion for omelettes.
eraser	What the artist's wife said when he drew a beautiful girl.
extinct	Dead skunk.
flood	A river that's too big for its bridges.
foul ball	A dance for chickens.
gallows	Where no noose is good noose.
goblet	A small turkey.
gossip	Letting the chat out of the bag.

hay	Grass a la mode.
hogwash	Pig's laundry.
home run	A thing you do in a ball game when the ball goes through a window.
ice	Skid stuff.
igloo	An icicle built for two.
illegal	A sick bird.
incongruous	Where the laws are made.
information	How air force planes fly.
jaywalking	An exercise that brings that rubdown feeling.
kidney	Knee of a baby goat.
kindred	A fear of relatives coming.
knob	A thing to adore.
leopard	A dotted lion.
license number	The best thing to take when you're run down.
melancholy	A dog that likes watermelons.
mistletoe	Astronaut's athlete's foot.
motel	William Tell's sister.
mummy	An Egyptian pressed for time.
mushroom	The place where they make the school lunch.
nail	A long, round object with a flat head which you aim at before you hit your thumb.
nursery	A bawl park.
operetta	A girl who works for the phone company.
ottoman	A car mechanic.
out-of-bounds	A tired kangaroo.
panhandler	Dishwasher.
paradox	Two doctors.
paratrooper	An army dropout.
parole	A cell-out.

pea	A vegeta-pill.
pickle	A cucumber in a sour mood.
pigeon-toed	Half-pigeon, half toad.
pillow	Headquarters.
pink elephant	A beast of bourbon.
pretzel	A double-jointed doughnut.
printer	A man of letters.
propaganda	A socially correct goose.
quadruplets	Four crying out loud.
racetrack	The only place where windows clean people.
raisin	A worried grape.
rebate	Putting another worm on the hook.
rhubarb	Bloodshot celery.
ringleader	First one in the bathtub.
romance	Ants in Rome.
rug	Something that is sold by the yard and worn by the feet.
shotgun	A worn-out gun.
sleeping bag	A nap sack.
snoring	Sheet music.
southpaw	A daddy from Dixie.
tears	Glum drops.
unabridged	A river you have to swim to cross.
undercover agent	Spy in bed.
vitamin	What you do when someone comes to the house.
walkie-talkie	A grounded parrot.
washable	To bathe a bull.
water cooler	Thirst-aid kit.
wind	Air in a hurry.
woe	Opposite of giddap.
X *ray*	Bellyvision.
yellow	What you do when you stub your toe.

zinc	Where you wash the zaucepans.
zookeeper	A critter-sitter.

Here are 26 words that didn't quite make the first list. Attempt a daffynition for each one, then compare yours with the ones in the Answers.

WORD	DAFFYNITION
autograph	
blubber	
conference	
disconsolate	
extinct	
fastidious	
generally	
hatchet	
idolize	
jugular	
khakis	
lyre	
monolog	
nudist	
obesity	
prickly pear	
Quaker	
razor	
sage	
television	
unison	
volcano	
waiter	
x	
yes-men	
zebra	

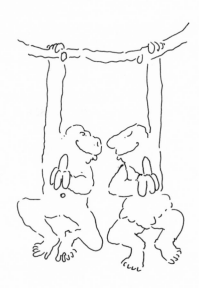

D OUBLETS

Doublets and hose were clothes to an Elizabethan gentleman. Doublets all alone is the name of my favorite word puzzle. It was devised by the Reverend Charles Lutwidge Dodgson—dodo-fancying don, mathematician, and author of *Alice's Adventures in Wonderland*—known to the world under his *nom de guerre* of Lewis Carroll. (Yes, I do mean *nom de guerre*. That's what the French call a pen name. They never, *never* call it a *nom de plume*.) Lewis Carroll, incidentally, was one of five *noms de guerre* Dodgson suggested when he began writing verses for a magazine called *The Train* in 1856. The others were Louis Carroll (like Lewis Carroll, arrived at by reversing and anglicizing the Latin for Charles Lutwidge), Edgar Cuthwellis and Edgar U. C. Westhill (anagrams of Charles Lutwidge), and Dares (an abbreviation of Daresbury, of Dodgson's birthplace). *The Train*'s editor chose Lewis Carroll, which is fortunate because *Alice's Adventures in Wonderland* by Edgar U. C. Westhill doesn't sound so good.

The rules of Doublets are simple: transform one word into another in a given number of steps, changing one letter at a time. Each link of the chain must be a word. For example, if you had to evolve MAN from APE with four links, here's how you might do it:

APE
apt
opt
oat
mat
MAN

Here are the best of Lewis Carroll's own Doublets. You may be able to manage the transformations with fewer links than he asks for but don't be a smarty: he's immortal and you're not.

1 Drive PIG into STY with four links.

2 Raise FOUR to FIVE with six links.

3 Make WHEAT into BREAD with six links.

4 Touch NOSE with CHIN with five links.

5 Change TEARS into SMILE with five links.

6 Make HARE into SOUP with six links.

7 PITCH TENTS with five links.

8 Cover EYE with LID with three links.

9 Prove PITY to be GOOD with six links.

10 Turn POOR into RICH with five links.

11 Get WOOD from TREE with seven links.

12 Prove GRASS to be GREEN with seven links.

13 Evolve MAN from APE with five links.

14 Make FLOUR into BREAD with five links.

15 Change ELM into OAK with seven links.

16 Make TEA HOT with three links.

17 Get COAL from MINE with five links.

18 Change BLACK to WHITE with six links.

19 Turn WITCH into FAIRY with 12 links.

20 Make WINTER SUMMER with 13 links.
(See Answers.)

Lewis Carroll isn't the only literary master to have enjoyed Doublets. Vladimir Nabokov—whose Lolita would surely have been one of the Reverend Dodgson's most engaging "child-friends"—has the narrator in his novel *Pale Fire* recall how he once played "word golf" and changed HATE to LOVE with two links, LASS to MALE with three, and LIVE to DEAD with four, one of which was the word *lend* and another a variant of a common tree name. Nabokov doesn't tell us how the narrator managed it, so why not fill in the blanks for him?

H A T E	L A S S	L I V E
— — — —	— — — —	— — — —
— — — —	— — — —	— — — —
L O V E	— — — —	— — — —
	M A L E	— — — —
		D E A D

(See Answers.)

If you have read *Pale Fire*, you know that the narrator is dangerously deranged. This has nothing whatever to do with Doublets.

COLLECTING COLLECTIVES

If I spoke of a jam of tarts, a pride of loins, a flourish of strumpets, an essay of Trollopes, or an anthology of pros, would you guess that I was describing a crowd of prostitutes?

There is no official collective noun for a group of women of easy virtue, but there are many official collective nouns for feathered birds, as well as for fish and other animals. Here is a list of the 50 most evocative, original, and attractive collective nouns. Can you match the collective nouns to the creatures? (See Answers.)

1 a smack of . . .	(a)	ants
2 a descent of . . .	(b)	apes
3 a kindle of . . .	(c)	badgers
4 a route of . . .	(d)	bears

5	an unkindness of . . .	(e)	caterpillars
6	a building of . . .	(f)	cats
7	a cete of . . .	(g)	cattle
8	a shrewdness of . . .	(h)	chickens
9	an exaltation of . . .	(i)	crows
10	a deceit of . . .	(j)	doves
11	a pride of . . .	(k)	ducks
12	a plague of . . .	(l)	fish
13	a dray of . . .	(m)	foxes
14	a knot of . . .	(n)	geese
15	a mummuration of . . .	(o)	hares
16	a hover of . . .	(p)	hawks
17	a flight of . . .	(q)	hens
18	a rafter of . . .	(r)	herons
19	a mustering of . . .	(s)	horses
20	a pitying of . . .	(t)	jellyfish
21	a watch of . . .	(u)	kittens
22	a host of . . .	(v)	lapwings
23	a covey of . . .	(w)	larks
24	a bale of . . .	(x)	leopards
25	a parliament of . . .	(y)	lions
26	a gam of . . .	(z)	locusts
27	a colony of . . .	(aa)	nightingales
28	an army of . . .	(bb)	owls
29	a peep of . . .	(cc)	partridges
30	a murder of . . .	(dd)	peacocks
31	a sloth of . . .	(ee)	plovers
32	a drove of . . .	(ff)	ponies
33	a nest of . . .	(gg)	rabbits
34	a dule of . . .	(hh)	ravens
35	a balding of . . .	(ii)	rhinoceroses
36	a congregation of . . .	(jj)	rooks
37	a school of . . .	(kk)	seals

38	a skulk of . . .	(ll)	sparrows
39	a leap of . . .	(mm)	squirrels
40	a harras of . . .	(nn)	starlings
41	a siege of . . .	(oo)	storks
42	a brood of . . .	(pp)	swallows
43	a clowder of . . .	(qq)	toads
44	a cast of . . .	(rr)	trout
45	a gaggle of . . .	(ss)	turkeys
46	a husk of . . .	(tt)	turtledoves
47	a string of . . .	(uu)	turtles
48	a crash of . . .	(vv)	whales
49	a pod of . . .	(ww)	wolves
50	an ostentation of . . .	(xx)	woodpeckers

Now and then I try to add to the established list of collective nouns: a gulp of swallows, a picnic of bears, a gobble of turkeys, a coat of doves, a jonah of whales, or a can of sardines. It's even better when you extend the collectives to plants, people, and things. From the ones I've come across, here are 50 of the best:

a mine of egoists

a guzzle of gourmets

a dampness of babies

a wobble of bicycles

a want of whiskey

a wagon of teetotalers

a riot of students

a condescension of know-it-alls

an I-told-you-so of pessimists

an elongation of anglers

an anticipation of aunts

a jaundice of Chinese

an envy of socialists

a corps of apples

an expanse of broads

a dependence of daughters

a Reno of divorcees

an Ali Baba of tax collectors

an evasion of virgins

a depression of neurotics

a fraud of Freudians

a column of journalists

a wince of dentists

a mammon of millionaires

a godiva of peeping toms

a promise of Democrats

a lot of realtors

a nun of your business

a peck of kisses

a complement of sycophants

a quiver of beans

a lack of principals

an unction of undertakers

a host of parasites

a dilation of pupils

an excess of pornographers

a postmortem of Republicans

an emulsion of painters

a caste of actors

a delivery of postmen

a dearth of servants

a strike of workers

a range of ovens

a wind of politicians

a delight of Turks

a furrow of brows

a habit of nuns

a knot of Windsors

a lie of Nixons

a plain of Carters

Be Brief

If brevity is the soul of wit, this must be a witty chapter. It's the briefest in the book.

THE BRIEFEST PRESIDENT

Calvin Coolidge said little . . . because he had little to say. At a dinner party at the White House an attractive young lady turned to him and said, "Mr. President, I've got a bet that I can get at least three words out of you tonight."

Replied Coolidge, "You lose."

THE BRIEFEST POETRY

This concise verse is by an unknown poet. It is called "On the Condition of the United States After Several Years of Prohibition."

Wet
Yet.

Briefer still is this poem by Eli Siegel. Called "One Question," it manages to capture in four letters the essence of mankind's quest for self-understanding:

I
Why?

Briefest of all is this gem from the early 1960s, entitled "Reactions to a Statement by Khrushchev That the Soviet Union Has No Desire to Meddle in the Internal Affairs of Other Nations."

O,
So?

BRIEFEST CORRESPONDENCE

There can have been few briefer (or more charming) exchanges than one between the Prince de Joinville and the actress Rachel Felix about 1840. Having seen her act one evening the prince sent her his card with the words: "Where? When? How much?" Rachel replied: "Your place. Tonight. Free."

Less delightful perhaps, but even briefer unbeatably so—was correspondence that took place in 1862 between Victor Hugo and his publisher. The author was on holiday and, anxious to know how his new novel *Les Misérables* was selling, wrote to the publisher: "?"

The reply came: "!"

FINALLY, A BRIEF QUESTION

What is the shortest sentence in the Bible? (See Answers.)

ALL'S WELL THAT ENDS WELL

ENDGAME

Zynder, meaning *cinder*, is the last word in the last volume of the world's largest dictionary. The compilers could hardly have thought of a more appropriate last word. Ashes to ashes, dust to dust, zynders to zynders: even those who protest that they never go to funerals have to in the end.

Even if we don't want to, we all die. And even if we don't mean to, we all utter last words. If we are famous or infamous someone may be on hand to record our last words—or to improve on them if they don't seem up to scratch. The last words of England's King George V were reported to be "How is the empire?" In fact, assured by his doctor that he would soon be well enough to visit his favorite seaside resort of Bognor, the old king muttered "Bugger Bognor!" and died.

Deciding your last words is a great game to play when you're young. At any age you can enjoy inventing apt last words for others:

THE ATHEIST: "I was kidding all along."
THE ELEVATOR OPERATOR: "Going up?"
THE JUDGE: "I have no precedent for this."
THE BRIDGE PLAYER: "I pass."
THE CHILDLESS RAILROAD CONDUCTOR: "End of the line."
THE GOSSIP: "I'm just dying to tell someone."
THE FATTED CALF IN THE PARABLE OF THE PRODIGAL SON: "I hear the young master has returned."

FAMOUS LAST WORDS

"On the whole," W. C. Fields is said to have said when saying his last, "I'd rather be in Philadelphia." Not as celebrated, but just as likable, are the last words of the playwright Henry Arthur Jones. Asked whether he would prefer to have his niece or his nurse by his deathbed, he replied, "The prettier. Now fight for it."
Here are my final favorites:

DYLAN THOMAS (poet): "I've had eighteen straight whiskeys. I think that is the record."

WILHELM HEGEL (philosopher): "Only one man understood me and he didn't understand me."

DR. ALBRECHT (Swiss physician): (After taking his own pulse) "Now I am dying; the artery ceases to beat."

DOMINIQUE BONHOURS (grammarian): "I am about to—or I am going to—die; either expression is used."

LORD PALMERSTON (British prime minister): "Die, my dear doctor, that's the last thing I'll do!"

HEINRICH HEINE (poet): "God will forgive me. It's his profession."

CECIL RHODES (empire builder): "So little done, so much to do."

WILLIAM HAZLITT (essayist): "Well, I've had a happy life."

MATTHEW PRIOR (poet): "The end."

ANSWERS

C

PAGE 13

PAGES 14–15

PAGES 16–17

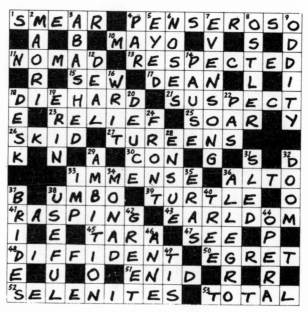

PAGES 18–19

When this puzzle was set as part of a British national crossword championship, it was solved within 30 minutes by 54 percent of the contestants.

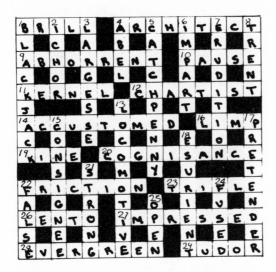

PAGES 20–23

PAGES 24–25

You didn't manage to complete Max Beerbohm's crossword puzzle? You *do* surprise me!

Actually, you don't. It looks impossible because it is. As the impish Sir Max explained when he submitted the crossword to the *London Times*:

> No doubt you, like most people, have sometimes thought of some utterly awful thing that you *could* do if you chose to, some disastrous and devastating thing the very thought of which has brought cold sweat to your brow? And you may have at some time thought: "Suppose I released into the columns of *The Times*, one of these fine days, a crossword puzzle with clues signifying nothing whatsoever," and may have hideously pictured to yourself the effect on all educated parts of Great Britain? You may incidentally have seen yourself going into your club shortly before luncheon time and observing in the armchairs men with blank, set, fixed, pale, just-not-despairing faces, poring over the current issue?—one of them perhaps rising unsteadily and lumbering out of the library and asking the librarian, "Have we a Wordsworth concordance?"—or some question of that sort. You may have figured this man going home at tea-time, and his wife saying, "Oh, Stephen, is anything the matter?" He: "No, dear, nothing." She: "But you look so pale. You . . ." He: "I've had a rather hard day, dear. But I'm quite all right."
>
> And you may further have wondered just how the apology in next day's issue should be worded—just what excuse should be offered, before the shutters in Printing House Square were briskly and slammingly put up for ever?
>
> Perhaps I oughtn't to remind you of this nightmare of yours. Forgive me.
>
> P.S.—The nightmare wouldn't be loathsomely complete unless a few of the clues were quite genuine—*and very simple*, so as to put the solvers in good heart, and make them confident of success, and keep their shoulders to the wheel. I have provided six such clues, with my usual forethought.

D

PAGE 30

1. The art of saying "Nice doggie" until you can find a rock. 2. One of the few things that a fellow is willing to pay for and not get. 3. One hundred

men imposing their prejudices on 100 million. 4. The kind of person who looks at a sausage and thinks of Picasso. 5. An appeal to the emotions by an attack on the nerves. 6. The kind of person who looks at Picasso and thinks of baloney. (From Leonard L. Levinson's *The Left-Handed Dictionary*.)

E

PAGES 31–32

1. Alternating current. 2. *Ad libitum*. At pleasure. 3. *Ante meridiem*. Before noon. 4. Absent without leave. 5. Bachelor of arts. 6. British Broadcasting Corporation. 7. Central Treaty Organization. 8. Cash on delivery. 9. Hundredweight. 10. Dichlorodiphenyltrichloroethane (insecticide). 11. *Dei gratia*. By the grace of God. 12. *Exempli gratia*. For example. 13. Greenwich Mean Time. 14. Highest Common Factor. 15. Her (His) Royal Highness. 16. *Id est*. That is. 17. Intelligence quotient. 18. Monsieur. 19. Monsignor. 20. Manuscript. 21. Ounce. 22. *Post meridiem*. Afternoon. 23. *Requiescat in pace*. May he (she) rest in peace. 24. Revolutions per minute. 25. *Répondez s'il vous plaît*. Answer, please. 26. Society of Jesus. 27. Ships' distress signal, popularly believed to stand for "Save our ship." 28. *Senatus Populusque Romanus*. The Senate and people of Rome. 29. Trinitrotoluene (explosive). 30. Union of Soviet Socialist Republics.

F

PAGES 36–37

1 (s). 2 (b). 3 (d). 4 (f). 5 (g). 6 (i). 7 (r). 8 (t). 9 (a). 10 (c). 11 (j). 12 (l). 13 (h). 14 (n). 15 (k). 16 (m). 17 (q). 18 (p). 19 (o). 20 (e).

G

PAGE 45

1. And quite obviously in great seclusion.
2. Darwin Survives!
3. But only Buddha pays dividends.
4. When do we attack?
5. And Moby Dick for king!
6. I knew you were going to say that.
7. It can't be Donne.
8. Only it doesn't leave you much time to think about anything else.
9. He just couldn't find a parking space. *Or*, He is just very, very sick.
10. Yes, but I'm only visiting.

H

PAGE 48

1. Radio Detecting And Ranging
2. Light Amplification by Stimulated Emission of Radiation
3. Zone Improvement Program
4. Situation Normal—All Fouled Up
5. Self-Contained Underwater Breathing Apparatus
6. Punjab, Afghan border states, KashmIr, Sind and BaluchisTAN
7. Women Accepted for Volunteer Emergency Service
8. To Insure Promptness (popular attribution)
9. Sealed With A Kiss
10. Sealed With A Lick Because A Kiss Wouldn't Stick!

I

PAGES 52–53

remuneration; steamer; hearthstone; indomitableness; misrepresentation; measured; supernaturalisms; waitress; upholsterers; hustlers.

legislation; untied; fluster; gonfalons; revelations; desecration; funeral; adversaries; causal; desecration.

California; Delaware; Illinois; New York; Wyoming.

organ; spinet; tabour; triangle; bandore; timpani; serpent; sittar; harmonicas.

J

PAGE 55

André Ampère (1775–1836). The ampere (amp) was named after him because of his pioneering work in electricity.

Amelia Bloomer (1818–94). She made bloomers (a form of women's dress) fashionable.

Thomas Bowdler (1754–1825). He prudishly expurgated (bowdlerized) the plays of Shakespeare.

James Bowie (1799–1836). He invented the bowie knife.

Captain Charles Boycott (1832–97). A group of Irish farmers and tenants refused to deal with (boycotted) this land agent.

Robert Wilhelm Bunsen (1811–99). He invented the bunsen burner, which every high-school chemistry student is familiar with.

Nicholas Chauvin (18th-19th century). He was the first chauvinist, because he worshiped France and Napoleon uncritically.

Thomas Derrick (17th century). A framework with a long pivoted beam for hoisting heavy objects, as on an oil derrick, looks like a gallows. Derrick was a hangman.

Rudolf Diesel (1858–1913). He invented the diesel engine, used in most trucks and some automobiles.

Johannes Duns Scotus (1265–?1308). The opponents of this theologian called his followers "dunsmen."

Luigi Galvani (1737–98). He made frogs' legs twitch by "galvanizing" them with electric current. Today the word is more often used figuratively ("to stimulate strongly").

Admiral Edward Vernon (1684–1757). He got the nickname "Old Grog" from his cloak of grogram material. He believed that serving neat spirits to sailors was causing too much drunkenness, so he ordered that their daily rum ration be diluted with water. The diluted drink got its nickname from his nickname.

Dr. Joseph Guillotin (1738–1814). He suggested the use of the guillotine during the French Revolution.

The Houlihan Family (19th-century London family). Hooligans— because that's what they were.

John Loudon McAdam (1756–1836). He pioneered the use of this kind of road.

Jean Martinet (17th century). This French general was called a martinet because he was an excessively strict disciplinarian.

Samuel Maverick (1803–70). Some of Maverick's cattle were unbranded and stood apart from the herd. Later the word was used figuratively.

Franz Mesmer (1734–1815). The doctor used hypnotism (mesmerism) as a treatment.

Ambrose Philips (1675–1749). "Namby-Pamby" was a nickname given Philips because of the sickly, sentimental poetry he wrote.

Louis Pasteur (1822–95). Among many other things he developed the pasteurization process for milk, which heats the milk enough to kill germs but not enough to ruin the taste.

George Mortimer Pullman (1831–97). He designed the first pullman (sleeping) car.

Vidkun Quisling (1887–1945). By heading the Norwegian "government" during the Nazi occupation of his country he gave treason a new subclassification.

César Ritz (1850–1918). His Ritz hotels were swanky.

The Fourth Earl of Sandwich (1718–92). The first sandwich is said to have been made for him, so that he could eat without having to leave the gaming table.

Antoine-Joseph Sax (1814–94). He invented the saxophone, and finger-keyed wind instrument.

General Henry Shrapnel (1761–1842). He devised an exploding shell. Today *shrapnel* usually means fast-flying fragments of any shell, mine, or bomb.

Ambrose Everett Burnside (1824–81). The Civil War general's side-whiskers were called *burnsides*, then *sideburns*.

Étienne de Silhouette (1709–67). He was a French minister of finance unpopular for his economics; drawing an outline is the most economical way of drawing a portrait!

Theodore Roosevelt (1858–1919). The teddy bear was named after his sparing the life of a bear cub when hunting in Mississippi.

Count Ferdinand von Zeppelin (1838–1917). He invented the zeppelin, a rigid, lighter-than-air airship.

L

PAGES 61–62

Without *h*'s:

Mary owned a little lamb,
　Its fleece was pale as snow,
And every place its mistress went
　It certainly would go;
It followed Mary to class one day,
　It broke a rigid law;
It made some students giggle aloud,
　A lamb in class all saw.

Without *t*'s:

Mary had a pygmy lamb,
　His fleece was pale as snow,
And every place where Mary walked
　Her lamb did also go;
He came inside her classroom once,
　Which broke a rigid rule;
How children all did laugh and play
　On seeing a lamb in school.

Without *e*'s:

Mary had a tiny lamb,
　Its wool was pallid as snow,
And any spot that Mary did walk
　This lamb would always go;
This lamb did follow Mary to school,
　Although against a law;
How girls and boys did laugh and play,
　That lamb in class all saw.

Without half the letters of the alphabet:

Maria had a little sheep,
  As pale as rime its hair,
And all the places Maria came
  ·The sheep did tail her there;
In Maria's class it came at last,
  A sheep can't enter there;
It made the children clap their hands,
  A sheep in class, that's rare.

M

PAGE 68

Killing a bird; a cat; liberty; minds; sheep; the old; a wife; a prophet; a mother; a race.

N

PAGES 74–75

1 (b). 2 (d). 3 (a). 4 (c). 5 (d). 6 (a). 7 (a). 8 (d). 9 (b). 10 (a). 11 (c). 12 (a). 13 (d). 14 (c). 15 (a). 16 (b). 17 (a) and (d). 18 (b). 19 (b). 20 (d). 21 (a). 22 (b). 23 (c). 24 (d). 25 (d).

O

PAGE 80

1. vesper. 2. lying. 3. chants. 4. flare. 5. lettuce. 6. raven. 7. rocks. 8. foiled. 9. breezes. 10. yarn . . . wooly- . . . nitwit.

P

PAGES 84–85

Group 1:	*fride*	*free + ride*
	gawkward	*gawky + awkward*
	grandy	*grand + dandy*
	happenident	*happen + accident*
	heartistic	*heart + artistic*
Group 2:	*identicate*	*identify + indicate*
	jummix	*jumble + mix*
	limpsy	*limp + flimsy*
	numberal	*number + numeral*
	obliviation	*oblivion + obliteration*
Group 3:	*prevusical*	*preview + musical*
	promptual	*prompt + punctual*
	prounce	*prance + flounce*
	ritzycratic	*ritzy + aristocratic*
	scrumple	*squeeze + crumple*
Group 4:	*scrush*	*squash + crush*
	shamateur	*sham + amateur*
	sizzard	*sizzle + blizzard*
	screaky	*screechy + creaky*
	slickery	*slick + slippery*
Group 5:	*slish*	*slice + slash*
	squnch	*squeeze + crunch*
	strivation	*starve/starvation + privation*
	stuffocation	*stuffy + suffocation*
	superplace	*supersede + replace*

Q

PAGES 86–87

1. *flat.*
2. *reversing lights.*
3. *elastoplast.*
4. *dressing gown.*
5. *bank note.*
6. *draughts.*
7. *cupboard.*
8. *semolina.*
9. *lift.*
10. *tap.*
11. *torch.*
12. *mince.*

13. *broad bean.*
14. *black treacle.*
15. *truncheon.*
16. *mileometer.*
17. *tights.*
18. *public school.*
19. *sultana.*

20. *pavement/footpath.*
21. *cotton reel.*
22. *drawing pin.*
23. *noughts and crosses.*
24. *waistcoat.*
25. *courgettes.*

R

PAGES 100–101

1. "Do you think so, dear? I think yours suits you perfectly. It always has."
2. "In perfect silence."
3. "I don't know. I've never tried."
4. "If you were my wife, I'd drink it."
5. "Chanel No. 5."
6. "I ought to. I married one."
7. "Join it."
8. "Thank you."
9. "It depends on the liver."
10. "Yes. And then we die and forget it all."

S

PAGE 103

1. Do very well on a test. 2. Take drugs in order to study all night. 3. Sorority dormitory. 4. Do very poorly on a test. 5. Introductory course in entomology. 6. Fraternity dormitory. 7. Introductory course in film. 8. Become enthusiastic about a game, course, weekend, etc. 9. Large pimple. 10. "If he were the last male on earth you'd be reluctant to date him." 11. Course in southern literature. 12. Pet. 13. Handsome, well-built male. 14. Preengaged. 15. Bathroom, because in the dorm it is the only quiet place to study. 16. Voracious lip. 17. Snacks. 18. Suspicious

cold cuts. 19. Conceited gorp. 20. Course in literature written for ado-
lescents. 21. Affectionate term for the post office. 22. What a lunch lip
does best. 23. Test. 24. Female chest; a bed. 25. One inordinately fond
of his bed. 26. To look over at a classmate's exam paper. 27. To play an
informal game of basketball. 28. Wigged, freaked, or otherwise slightly
removed from reality. 29. In danger of failing.

PAGES 104–105

1. Lose control. 2. Money. 3. Cadge. 4. Swindle or cheat. 5. Mild intoxicating effect from something ordinary, e.g., music, pepper, nature.
6. School. 7. Obtain a bed/floor in someone else's home. 8. Understand.
9. Don't leave me out. 10. Lose control, break down. 11. Lose control,
lose inhibitions. 12. Angry, very annoyed. 13. Apathetic, uninvolved;
relaxed. 14. In a nomadic way of life. 15. Honest, candid. 16. Incapable
of rational thought. 17. Talk. 18. Place of action, where it all happens.
19. Buy (anything). 20. Leave for a specific place. 21. Leave. 22. Find
out about. 23. Lose interest in. 24. Sexual or pharmaceutical arousal.
25. Humble, full of humility. 26. Transportation (usually a car). 27. How
are you? 28. Nervous, tense.

PAGE 107

1. Binoculars. 2. Soft-soaper. 3. Tramp. 4. Gambling house. 5. Lookout
man. 6. Drown. 7. Two-year prison term. 8. Convict profiting in prison.
9. Safecracker. 10. Safe that's easy to open. 11. Loafer. 12. Shut up.
(Pig Latin for "nark it.") 13. Wealthy man. 14. Hobo. 15. In solitary.
16. Informer. 17. Gun.

PAGE 107

1. WEB BOFFS FEMCEE

2. EXEX NOX CRIX

3. STICKS NIX HICK PIX

4. A STAR IS PORN

PAGES 108–109

1. Expert CB operator. 2. Boat trailer. 3. Police helicopter or airplane.
4. Road behind. 5. Beer. 6. Police. 7. School bus. 8. Teenage CB'er.
9. Booze. 10. Cigarettes. 11. Telephone. 12. Big mouth, gossip. 13. Best
regards (73's) and love and kisses (88's). 14. Reckless driver. 15. Smoke

or fire. 16. Talking. 17. Money. 18. Coffee. 19. FCC monitoring CB violations in the area. 20. Radar setup for catching speeders. 21. Mile markers along the highway. 22. Signing off. 23. A policeman or police-men, in a police car. 24. Many policemen. 25. Single woman. 26. Spouse. 27. Daughter. 28. Ex-young lady, wife. 29. Husband. 30. Young lady. 31. Yes.

PAGES 109–111

1 (a). 2 (e). 3 (c). 4 (a). 5 (c). 6 (c). 7 (c). 8 (c). 9 (d). 10 (d). 11 (b). 12 (c). 13 (c). 14 (c). 15 (a). 16 (b). 17 (c). 18 (c). 19 (c). 20 (b). 21 (d).

U

PAGES 115–117

1. *abstemious, facetious.* 2. *uncomplimentary, unnoticeably, subconti-nental.* 3. *misrepresentation, representationism.* 4. *strengths.* 5. *un-copyrightable; misconjugatedly* is less often used but equally acceptable. 6. *pti.* Put an *o* before and after each of the other groups of letters and it makes sense: *Ohio, Oslo, Orlando, octavo, oratorio, Otto.* 7. *rhythms.* 8. *defenselessness.* 9. *strengthlessness.* 10. *boldface, feedback.* 11. *push-chair.* 12. *bookkeeper.* 13. *bebedded, bedeafed, cabbaged, debagged,* and *debadged* are five eight-letter possibilities. 14. *underground.* 15. *in-divisibilities.* 16. All the words in the list can be reduced by one letter at a time (from front or back) and form complete words all the way to a one-letter word, e.g., *brandy, brand, bran, ran, an, a; chastens, chasten, chaste, haste, hast, has, as, a; craters, crater, crate, rate, rat, at, a.* 17. *overnervousness.* 18. *verisimilitudes.* 19. *incomprehensibility.* 20. *revolutionary!*

V

PAGE 126

1. The lamb went too, of course.

2. And only got corned beef.

3. You saw her bear behind.

4. The little car turned left.

5. And look at the damn thing now!

6. The doctors were surprised!

PAGES 126–127

It's "Twinkle, twinkle, little star"—of course.

Y

PAGES 139–140

caprine means *goatlike*. Others: 1. *hawklike*. 2. *snakelike*. 3. *gooselike*. 4. *eaglelike*. 5. *asslike*. 6. *cowlike*. 7. *doglike*. 8. *deerlike*. 9. *kingsnakelike* or *gartersnakelike*. 10. *elephantlike*. 11. *horselike*. 12. *catlike*. 13. *mongooselike*. 14. *goatlike*, especially in strong odor or lustfulness. 15. *lizardlike*. 16. *lemurlike*. 17. *lionlike*. 18. *wolflike*. 19. *otterlike*. 20. *mouselike*. 21. *songbirdlike*. 22. *sheeplike*. 23. *perching-songbirdlike*. 24. *peacocklike*. 25. *fishlike*. 26. *piglike*. 27. *froglike*. 28. *serpentlike*. 29. *hoglike*. 30. *swinelike*. 31. *bull-like*. 32. *bearlike*. 33. *viperlike*. 34. *foxlike*.

PAGES 148–151

1. *bone* (*b* on *e*).

2. Six of one, half a dozen of the other.

3. *spinach* (*sp* in *ach*).

4. Mary Overton.

5. You understand you are under oath.

6. *Much Ado About Nothing*.

7. a bad spell of weather.

8. *continue* (*c* on *t* in *u*).

9. I understand you undertake to overthrow my undertaking.

10. All in one.

11. Oh, I see you are empty.

12. a square meal.

13. a little misunderstanding between friends (a little *m* is under *stand* in *g* between *friends*).

14. Too wise you are,

 Too wise you be,

 I see you are

 Too wise for me.

15. Think twice before you speak (*th* in *k* twice before *u*'s pea *k*.

16. *frame-up*.

17. Turn the page 90°clockwise and see the words *onion, no, zoo, noon,* and *Zion*.

18. *Be independent but not too independent* (*b* in *d* pendant, butt, knot, 2 in *d* pendant).

19. doctor in the house; nothing to it; underneath the arches (underneath *the* are *che*'s), *nominal* (no *m* in *al*); *espionage* (*s*, pi on *age*).

20. World without end, amen.

W

PAGES 172–173

1. a bog dog. 2. a mad lad. 3. a crass ass. 4. a fervent servant. 5. a static attic. 6. a phony pony. 7. a truculent succulent. 8. a spectator testator; a spectatrix testatrix. 9. a prosaic mosaic. 10. a cesarean Bavarian.

V

PAGE 176

1. It is raining.

2. You must plan ahead.

3. We're trying to keep the schedules up-to-date.

4. When we arrived we found it wouldn't take long to convert the equipment.

5. Dad isn't home much.

6. Experiments show that a normal person can taste sugar in water in quantities not strong enough to interfere with his sense of smell or take away his appetite.

7. A nod's as good as a wink to a blind horse.

8. Such is life.

T

PAGE 190

Laval, Lou Nol, U Nu.

S

PAGE 192

1. *each.* 2. *raid.* 3. *ideas.* 4. *claret.* 5. *sauce.* 6. *edict.* 7. *adze.* 8. *indeed.* 9. *fringe.* 10. *right.* 11. *when.* 12. *neigh.* 13. *junta.* 14. *lake.* 15. *scale.* 16. *still.* 17. *remote.* 18. *thing.* 19. *tough.* 20. *quite.* 21. *toque.* 22. *these.* 23. *persist.* 24. *untie.* 25. *sue.* 26. *save.* 27. *vale.* 28. *newt.* 29. *weird.* 30. *town.*

PAGE 193

1. *dais, said.* 2. *sale, seal.* 3. *angle, glean.* 4. *bared, bread.* 5. *bowel, elbow.* 6. *stable, tables.* 7. *cheats, scathe.* 8. *dear, read.* 9. *leader, redeal.* 10. *dilate, tailed.* 11. *hater, heart.* 12. *there, three.* 13. *fears, safer.* 14. *field, flied.* 15. *filets, stifle.* 16. *male, meal.* 17. *swap, wasp.* 18. *pets, step.* 19. *snipe, spine.* 20. *satin, stain.* 21. *rites, tries.* 22. *draws, sward.*

PAGE 193

1. *mane, mean, name.* 2. *icons, scion, sonic.* 3. *deal, lade, lead.* 4. *edit, tide, tied.* 5. *item, mite, time.* 6. *lager, large, regal.* 7. *hears, share, shear.* 8. *kins, sink, skin.* 9. *meat, tame, team.* 10. *sprat, strap, traps.* 11. *pates, spate, tapes.*

PAGE 193

1. *baste, bates, beast, beats.* 2. *rates, stare, tares, tears.* 3. *parsed, spader, spared, spread.* 4. *onset, seton (suture), stone, tones.* 5. *pears, rapes, reaps, spare.* 6. *stake, steak, takes, teaks.*

PAGE 193

capers, crapes, pacers, recaps, spacer.

R

PAGE 196

$x = 737.$

Q

PAGES 200–202

1. Ogden Nash. 2. J. D. Salinger. 3. Sinclair Lewis. 4. George Jackson. 5. Clarence Darrow. 6. Bennett Cerf. 7. Truman Capote. 8. John Steinbeck. 9. Ezra Pound. 10. H. L. Mencken. 11. James Baldwin. 12. Joseph Heller. 13. Edward Albee. 14. Laurence J. Peter. 15. Malcolm X. 16. Tallulah Bankhead. 17. Ford Madox Ford. 18. J. K. Galbraith. 19. Ernest Hemingway. 20. Henry Miller. 21. Adlai Stevenson. 22. Woodrow Wilson. 23. F. Scott Fitzgerald. 24. Frank Lloyd Wright. 25. John Lennon.

I

PAGES 242–243

1. *shedonism*. 2. *ottoit*. 3. *testeria*. 4. *allkind*. 5. *lutolin*. 6. *humanikin*. 7. *lecher*. 8. *personism*. 9. *fruitgo*. 10. *manhandle*.

G

PAGE 249

2. *taper, tapir*. 3. *be, bee*. 4. *bore, boar*. 5. *knew, gnu*. 6. *you, ewe*. 7. *dough, doe*. 8. *flee, flea*. 9. *turn, tern*. 10. *bare, bear*. 11. *hair, hare*. 12. *ceil, seal*. 13. *mewl, mule*. 14. *links, lynx*. 15. *row, roe*. 16. *aunt, ant*. 17. *faun, fawn*. 18. *dear, deer*. 19. *earn, erne*. 20. *coarser, courser*.

PAGES 249–250

1. *pare, pear*. 2. *cede, seed*. 3. *carat, carrot*. 4. *beat, beet*. 5. *leak, leek*. 6. *bury, berry*. 7. *Flocks, phlox*. 8. *fur, fir*. 9. *been, bean*. 10. *plumb, plum*. 11. *current, currant*. 12. *beach, beech*. 13. *rows, rose*. 14. *time, thyme*. 15. *colonel, kernel*. 16. *charred, chard*. 17. *route, root*. 18. *tee, tea*. 19. *lief, leaf*. 20. *chute, shoot*.

PAGES 250–251

1 (e). 2 (d). 3 (k). 4 (j). 5 (c). 6 (m). 7 (l). 8 (b). 9 (q). 10 (r). 11 (s). 12 (t). 13 (f). 14 (p). 15 (a). 16 (h). 17 (i). 18 (n). 19 (g). 20 (o).

PAGES 251–252

1. *menace.* 2. *season.* 3. *office.* 4. *endear.* 5. *impair.* 6. *cotton.* 7. *hatred.* 8. *rotate.* 9. *begone.* 10. *donkey.* 11. *palace.* 12. *margin.* 13. *forego.* 14. *dampen.* 15. *sundry.* 16. *farrow.* 17. *wintry.* 18. *ashore.* 19. *curfew.* 20. *aspire.*

1. *carpet.* 2. *sewage.* 3. *carrot.* 4. *hamlet.* 5. *bigamy.* 6. *pawned.* 7. *action.* 8. *addled.* 9. *settee.* 10. *hermit.* 11. *finale.* 12. *tendon.* 13. *warden.* 14. *putrid.* 15. *barbed.* 16. *fungus.* 17. *potash.* 18. *legend.* 19. *seethe.* 20. *assail.*

PAGES 253–254

B L I G H T		**V** A U N T S
L **O** I T E R		P **I** L O T S
M A **S** T E R		P O **O** L E D
P O S **T** E R		H E A **L** T H
M E T E **O** R		S H A D **E** S
I N T E R **N**		P L A N E **T**
D A N G E R		**C** L E A N S
H **E** A V E N		D **R** I V E S
D O **N** O R S		F L **O** A T S
C U R **V** E D		M I N **C** E D
S T A G **E** S		S T A T **U** E
S A U C E **R**		L E A V E **S**

PAGES 255–256

1. *precise* (press ice). 2. *castanet* (cast a net). 3. *sausage* (sauce edge). 4. *superimpose* (soup primp pose). 5. *hibernate* (high burn eight). 6. *ecstasy* (x to c). 7. *annuity* (a newer tea). 8. *nocturne* (knock turn). 9. *restaurant* (restore aunt). 10. *infirm* (in firm). 11. *delicatessen* (delicate sn). 12. *penitentiary* (pen a ten sherry). 13. *largess* (large s). 14. *metaphysician* (met a physician). 15. *centennials* (cent ten yells).

PAGE 256

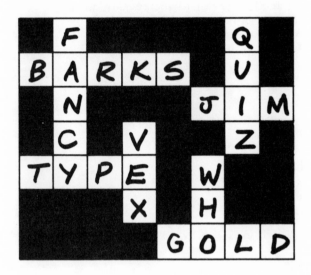

PAGE 257

A Midsummer Night's Dream; Othello; Macbeth; As You Like It; Antony And Cleopatra; Julius Caesar; Troilus And Cressida; The Tempest; Romeo And Juliet; Pericles; Measure For Measure.

PAGE 258

When a dog bites a man that is not news,
but when a man bites a dog that is news.

PAGE 258

1. *naturalist.* 2. *associated.* 3. *scrupulous.* 4. *fascinated.* 5. *precaution.* 6. *orchestral.* 7. *commentary.* 8. *infidelity.* 9. *ingredient.* 10. *woodpecker.* 11. *revolution.* 12. *telephones.* 13. *electronic.* 14. *mechanical.* 15. *illustrate.* 16. *loggerhead.*

PAGES 259–261

Alfred Lord Tennyson, "Ulysses":

and tho'
We are not now that strength which in old days
Moved earth and heaven; that which we are, we are;
One equal temper of heroic hearts,
Made weak by time and fate, but strong in will
To strive, to seek, to find, and not to yield.

F

PAGES 267-268

MERGERS	NESTLES	FRATERIES
ETERNAL	ENTRANT	REGIMENAL
REGATTA	STRANGE	AGITATIVE
GRAVITY	TRAITOR	TITANITES
ENTITLE	LANTERN	EMANATIST
RATTLER	ENGORGE	RETITRATE
SLAYERS	STERNER	INITIATOR
		EAVESTONE
		SLESTERED

E

PAGE 273

autograph: chart showing the sales of cars.
blubber: weeping and whaling.
conference: meeting of the bored.
disconsolate: record played after midnight.

extinct: dead skunk.

fastidious: someone who is quick and ugly.

generally: Arab military man.

hatchet: what a hen does to an egg.

idolize: lazy eyeballs.

jugular: shaped like a Grecian vase.

khakis: what you have to use before you can start your automobile.

lyre: dishonest harp.

monolog: unmarried piece of wood.

nudist: someone who goes around without a vest or a coat and wears pants to match.

obesity: surplus gone to waist.

prickly pear: two porcupines.

Quaker: nervous lady.

razor: alarm clock for girls.

sage: man who knows his onions.

television: radio with eyestrain.

unison: only boy.

volcano: mountain that's blown its stack.

waiter: somebody who thinks money grows on trays.

x: what hens lay.

yes-men: people around the fellow nobody noes.

zebra: horse that's excaped from jail.

D

PAGE 275

1. PIG	2. FOUR	3. WHEAT
wig	foul	cheat
wag	fool	cheap
way	foot	cheep
say	fort	creep
STY	fore	creed
	fire	breed
	FIVE	BREAD

4. NOSE
   note
   cote
   core
   corn
   coin
   CHIN
5. TEARS
   sears
   stars
   stare
   stale
   stile
   SMILE
6. HARE
   hark
   hack
   sack
   sock
   soak
   soap
   SOUP
7. PITCH
   pinch
   winch
   wench
   tench
   tenth
   TENTS
8. EYE
   dye
   die
   did
   LID
9. PITY
   pits
   pins
   fins
   find
   fond
   food
   GOOD

10. POOR
    boor
    book
    rook
    rock
    rick
    RICH
11. TREE
    free
    flee
    fled
    feed
    weed
    weld
    wold
    WOOD
12. GRASS
    crass
    cress
    tress
    trees
    frees
    freed
    greed
    GREEN
13. APE
    are
    ere
    err
    ear
    mar
    MAN
14. FLOUR
    floor
    flood
    blood
    brood
    broad
    BREAD
15. ELM
    ell
    all
    ail
    air
    fir
    far
    oar
    OAK

16. TEA
    sea
    set
    sot
    HOT
17. MINE
    mint
    mist
    most
    moat
    coat
    COAL
18. BLACK
    blank
    blink
    clink
    chink
    chine
    whine
    WHITE
19. WITCH
    winch
    wench
    tench
    tenth
    tents
    tints
    tilts
    tills
    fills
    falls
    fails
    fairs
    FAIRY
20. WINTER
    winner
    wanner
    wander
    warder
    harder
    harper
    hamper
    damper
    damped
    dammed
    dimmed
    dimmer
    simmer
    SUMMER

PAGE 276

HATE	LASS	LIVE
late	mass	line
lave	mast	lind
LOVE	malt	lend
	MALE	lead
		DEAD

C

PAGES 277-279

1 (t). 2 (xx). 3 (u). 4 (ww). 5 (hh). 6 (jj). 7 (c). 8 (b.) 9 (w). 10 (v). 11 (y). 12 (z). 13 (mm). 14 (qq). 15 (nn). 16 (rr). 17 (pp). 18 (ss). 19 (oo). 20 (tt). 21 (aa). 22 (ll). 23 (cc). 24 (uu). 25 (bb). 26 (vv). 27 (a). 28 (e). 29 (h). 30 (i). 31 (d). 32 (g). 33 (gg). 34 (j). 35 (k). 36 (ee). 37 (l). 38 (m). 39 (x). 40 (s). 41 (r). 42 (q). 43 (f). 44 (p). 45 (n). 46 (o). 47 (ff). 48 (ii). 49 (kk). 50 (dd).

B

PAGE 282

"Jesus wept" (John 11:35).

GYLES BRANDRETH

Gyles Brandreth is one of Britain's most prolific and successful authors, having sold over five million copies of his many books. A dozen of his children's titles have already been published in the U.S., but THE JOY OF LEX is his first adult book to appear in America.

Born in 1948 and educated at Oxford University (where he was a Scholar at New College and, like six British Prime Ministers before him, President of the Oxford Union), Gyles Brandreth is also a journalist who has written for most of Britain's top newspapers and magazines, a broadcaster who has made over a thousand appearances on radio and TV, the Chief Executive of a multi-million-dollar publishing company, a theatrical producer with three London hits to his credit, the founder of the British Scrabble Championships, a former European Monopoly Champion and the holder of the world record for the longest ever after dinner speech—eleven hours.

He has lived in Hollywood, Baltimore, Washington, D.C. and New York, but now lives in London with his wife who is also a writer and their three children who all have unique English names: Benet, Saethryd and Aphra.

According to the *Scottish Sunday Post*, "Gyles Brandreth is the most likeable genius I've ever met!" According to the London *Daily Mail*, "Gyles Brandreth is the sort of person that a breakfast cereal company would give their right arm for. He's bursting with vigour, fizzing with happiness, sizzling with vim and *Cosmopolitan* magazine once picked him as one of England's most eligible bachelors, though he was actually married at the time." According to the London *Sun*, "Gyles Brandreth is a writer, talker, wit and diversified character with a bowling-over effect on anyone he meets."